MW00812401

GOD
Is Calling You

Discerning the Calling of God

by

REV. NARESH K. MALHOTRA, PH.D.

President, Global Evangelistic Ministries, Inc.
https://www.globalevangelisticministries.net

ISBN 978-1-0980-1810-8 (paperback)
ISBN 978-1-0980-1812-2 (hardcover)
ISBN 978-1-0980-1811-5 (digital)

Christian Faith Publishing, Inc.
832 Park Avenue
Meadville, PA 16335
www.christianfaithpublishing.com

Printed in the United States of America

Dedication

These books are dedicated to those who have a desire to discern the calling of God and then pursue that calling with passion and obedience, relying on the Lord Jesus Christ to fulfill the calling by doing His work in them and through them. They are dedicated to all who want to take their relationship with God to a higher level.

"I press toward the mark for the prize of the high calling of God in Christ Jesus" (Philippians 3:14).

"Wherefore also we pray always for you, that our God would count you worthy of this calling, and fulfil all the good pleasure of his goodness, and the work of faith with power" (2 Thessalonians 1:11).

FOREWORD

You've probably heard the phrase "the call of God," but maybe you don't know exactly what it means. Is the Lord still calling people, or was that something He did only in Bible times? Does He speak only to a specific few or to everyone? Although He may not use an audible voice, He's still in the business of seeking followers.

In his books, Dr. Naresh Malhotra thoroughly explains the various callings of God with great insight from the Scriptures. Whether you are trying to discern and respond to the calling of God on your life, I encourage you to read both books, starting with *God Is Calling You: Discerning the Calling of God*, and following it up with his second book, *God Is Calling You: Responding to the Calling of God*.

Dr. Charles Stanley
Pastor Emeritus, First Baptist Church, Atlanta
Founder and President of In Touch Ministries
Atlanta, Georgia

Dr. Naresh Malhotra has a passion to bring the lost into the Kingdom of God, as evidenced by the 1.9 million documented professions of faith, and to disciple believers to grow in their faith. Dr. Malhotra's books, *God Is Calling You*, use Scripture and personal experience to guide readers in the discernment of, preparation for, and response to the call of God. Believers and nonbelievers, individuals and groups, no matter their learning style, will have a deeper understanding of God's perfect plan and life "more abundant." I highly recommend these books for passionate followers of Jesus Christ.

Dr. Doug Shaw
Past President/CEO, International Students, Inc.
Colorado Springs, Colorado

CONTENTS

ENDORSEMENTS

Endorsements from the United States

From the heart and pen of Dr. Naresh Malhotra come these timely and riveting volumes, *God Is Calling You: Discerning the Calling of God* and *God Is Calling You: Responding to the Calling of God*. Dr. Malhotra's life and work are the embodiment of this calling about which he writes so extensively. The first book begins by establishing the foundation of God's calling as His overwhelming love for us. Understanding God's perfect and incomparable love as the basis of His calling transforms our view of the call, often seen as rigid and obligatory, to that of a gracious privilege and opportunity. Proceeding from this foundation, Dr. Malhotra expands on the various dimensions of God's calling, basing every premise on a specific passage of Holy Scripture. I heartily recommend this resource to those who desire a deeper perspective of the all-encompassing calling of God on our lives. *God Is Calling You* books are thoroughly Biblical, immensely practical, and deeply insightful. I pray that God will use this literary fruit of Dr.

Malhotra's labor to extend and solidify His calling so that all who hear and obey it will bring honor and glory to His Name.

Dr. Anthony George
Senior Pastor
First Baptist Church, Atlanta

Rev. Naresh Malhotra is a noted scholar, a renowned educator, an accomplished author, but most of all he is a devout Christian who has surrendered his life to the Lordship of Jesus Christ. His unique and insightful understanding of God's Word and his sensitivity to God's call upon his own life have given him an amazing ability to communicate God's truth in a personal and poignant way. God has given to every believer grace gifts and a calling which are to be used to edify the Church and impact this world for His glory. These powerful and compelling volumes, *God Is Calling You: Discerning the Calling of God* and *God Is Calling You: Responding to the Calling of God,* will not only inspire and challenge you to greater Christian living, but could very well bring spiritual renewal and revival to the Christian Church.

Dr. J. Gerald Harris
Pastor for 41 years and
Retired editor of *The Christian Index*
Atlanta, Georgia

In God's economy, nothing is wasted. Everything is useful and its value awaits discovery along life's journey.

Who but God would have known to choose a university professor as His instrument to lead over 1.9 million people to salvation? God has chosen Dr. Naresh Malhotra as a yielded instrument to not only speak to the highly educated, but also in such a simple language that even children can understand. These books are manuals for those who first accept Christ as well as a challenge to all of us to know our calling and the extent of our natural abilities. God knew that you would one day be standing at the crossroads of decision.

He has guided you to select these books as a challenge and an encouragement, so that nothing stands in your way when God provides the opportunity. He walks you through the phase of being a fisher of men to becoming a hunter specific to your call. It is an invaluable lesson to understand that talent alone is insufficient, and this has crippled many from being used by God. I recommend these books to every individual, especially those who are in search of applying their lives to a larger purpose, along with those who do not know where to go or what they should do. Dr. Malhotra's life speaks louder than his words. His pursuit in missions is the continuation of his story.

Rev. Woodrow Walker, II
Senior Pastor
Cross Culture Church
Lithonia, Georgia

God Is Calling You is a unique presentation of the various stages of our calling that God has ordained for our lives. These books equip one to be able to listen, hear, and respond in a positive way to what God has called us to do as we make disciples in all the earth for His Kingdom. At the heart of this great teaching is a clear and precise understanding of our responsibility as Christians to share the Word of Christ with all we come into contact with and mentor them into becoming disciples of Christ. I highly recommend these books for personal growth and discipleship.

Dr. Jamie T. Pleasant
Senior Pastor, New Zion Christian Church, Suwanee, Georgia
Professor of Marketing & Associate Dean
of Business, Clark Atlanta University

I am delighted to write a few words of endorsement for Professor Malhotra's books on *God Is Calling You*. I know Naresh in his capacity as a world-renown excellent marketing professor. Anyone who knows him even casually also knows he is an excellent representative of the Christian faith and behaves in exemplary manners; he has a true servant's heart.

The work is tightly Scripturally-based. The exegesis is illuminating and easy to understand and not controversial. These books should appeal to the breadth of a conservative or liberal audience.

There is a lot we all struggle with, and Rev. Malhotra helps explain why things happen and how to keep faith and keep going—with more detail than either the glorious, "Thy will be done" or the colloquial, "Hang in there."

In sum, I think these books will enjoy a prized position on many believers' (and maybe struggling nonbelievers') shelves, both lay and professional.

Dr. Dawn Iacobucci
E. Bronson Ingram Professor of Management in Marketing
Vanderbilt University
Nashville, Tennessee

"One man through one God reaching millions for God"—These words aptly introduce Dr. Naresh Malhotra's incredible books titled *God Is Calling You*. I predict these will someday be ranked as one of the very best in regards to this subject.

Dr. Malhotra is not only a widely recognized scholar in the business and marketing world, but also in his soul-winning endeavors. Consider: In the past six years (2009–2015), this amazing man has seen over a million and a half souls coming to Christ through his ministry.

I am sure he will hear these words from his Master some day: Well done, good and faithful servant.*

Dr. H. L. Willmington
Founder & Dean, Willmington School of the Bible
Founder & Dean, Liberty Home Bible Institute
Professor, Rawlings School of Divinity
Liberty University, Lynchburg, Virginia

* Title from the original one-book manuscript changed to reflect the two-book series. Recommendation was received prior to Dr. Willmington's passing away.

Naresh Malhotra's books *God Is Calling You* will benefit those who want to know more about Jesus and what it can mean to follow Him in their personal lives. Naresh grounds the precepts he shares in content of the Bible. The result is an evangelism and discipleship tool that will lead readers to pursue spiritual formation in a more structured way. Naresh's own story spans continents and professional career fields. These books will be valued by those around the world and in different kinds of work who seek to share the good news of Jesus wherever they might be called.

Dr. Mark Peterson
Professor of Marketing & Sustainable Business Practices
Editor, Journal of Macromarketing
University of Wyoming College of Business
Emmaus Road Community Church, Laramie, Wyoming

With prolific careers in both academia and ministry, Dr. Malhotra is a well-published and highly respected Marketing Professor as well as a world-traveled evangelist who has led more than 1.9 million to Christ. Dr. Malhotra is uniquely positioned to speak on a topic of importance to every follower of Christ—discerning and following the call of God. Each chapter is both well-grounded in Scripture and filled with inspirational accounts from his own faith journey, which began as a Hindu-background international student coming to Christ in Buffalo. His personal experiences and Scriptural insights will surely inspire you to be all that God has called you to be.

David Larson
Northeast Regional Field Director
International Students, Inc.
Ithaca, New York

A devout Christian, an accomplished educator, and an award-winning Marketing scholar, Reverend Naresh K. Malhotra, Ph.D. combines his Christian faith and God-given talents as a Biblical student, preacher, and teacher to write a powerful and timely two-volume book series—*God Is Calling You*. In this series, Rev. Malhotra helps you understand why God is calling you: to know His unconditional love, to experience the gift of salvation, and to develop a personal relationship with Him so that you may live a joyful and meaningful life by discovering and acting on the purpose He has designed especially for you!

Practical and anchored in the Word of God, the *God Is Calling You* series is unique in its applied approach and the scope of its coverage. As a fellow Marketing educator and Christian, I personally enjoyed the applied learning techniques employed in each chapter which help to employ Biblical principles in daily life. Additionally, the scope of the series not only provides tools to understand your God-given purpose in the first volume, *Discerning the Calling of God*; but, equally important and unique, the second volume, *Responding to the Calling of God*, impels and instructs you on how to act on that discovery to lead a fulfilling life of service to God. The *God Is Calling You* series will empower you to live the fulfilling Christ-centered life that God intended for you.

Dr. Gina L. Miller
Professor of Marketing
Stetson School of Business and Economics
Mercer University
Atlanta, Georgia

It has been a blessing and privilege to know Dr. Naresh Malhotra and his family over the years. His acclaimed and fruitful career as a professor at the Georgia Institute of Technology now flows into the writing of two immensely useful books for the Christian life. *God Is Calling You: Discerning the Calling of God* and *God Is Calling You: Responding to the Calling of God* are companion volumes, which could be viewed as two parts of the whole. The structure of each chapter is Biblically based, clearly explained, and punctuated with personal application from Dr. Malhotra's life and ministry as an evangelist. These valuable resources will allow you to deepen your understanding of and living out God's call in your life.

Rev. Jerry K. Baker
Intercultural Church Planting and Mission Ministry
Specialist (retired)
Georgia Baptist Mission Board
Duluth, Georgia

The calling of God is where your deepest desires meet the world's greatest needs. But discerning the call of God and then responding to the call of God require both humility and vision. To follow the call of God is to take the path of humility to see the harder side of the Gospel. Dr. Malhotra explores the essential questions of who has God called me to be; who has He called me to follow; and who has He called me to serve with? To follow the call of God is to be a kingdom seeker, a kingdom builder, and under the cross to be the nonanxious voice of the truth of God. Dr. Malhotra's books will help you to do that.

Rev. Greg Smith, President of InStep Global
Atlanta, Georgia

Dr. Naresh Malhotra is known to me for about forty years, and what I want to say for Dr. Malhotra is that he is a true servant of the Lord Jesus Christ. He is always busy living a Godly life in obedience to Christ Jesus and His command of making disciples of all people by being the salt and the light for Jesus in this world of darkness and sin. His desire is to see every person on this earth to be saved, starting from India, his homeland, as he wants every Hindu to be converted to faith in Christ like him. He spends a lot of time for ministry in India and other places as well. I came in contact with the Malhotra family when I was serving as South Asian Church Planting Missionary for Georgia and I was planting Asian Indian churches in the greater Atlanta area. He was very supportive of my church planting ministry in Metro Atlanta. He took interest and hardly missed any ministry events of outreach, special worship services, evangelistic meetings, and other special celebrations that I planned for Asian Indians in Atlanta. He liked preaching, and he preached at times in some of our new churches. He was a great help and a blessing to me.

From the beginning, I was greatly blessed by his zeal and witness for our Lord. His deep insights into the Word of God, his great passion for proclaiming the Gospel and that he was living his life for the Lord Jesus Christ in the power of the Holy Spirit are certainly the marks of true Christian discipleship. These aspects of his life are captured in the two engrossing books *God Is Calling You: Discerning the Calling of God* and *God Is Calling You: Responding to the Calling of God*. These are excellent resources for spiritual growth and ministry, highly recommended for pastors, church leaders and lay people. Read and discover and fulfill your potential in Christ by discerning and fulfilling your calling. I highly recommend these books. Read and be blessed.

Norma S. Charles
South Asian Church Planting Missionary
(For Georgia, USA)—Retired
Georgia Baptist Convention & North American Mission Board
Atlanta, Georgia

I have the blessing of knowing Dr. Naresh Malhotra for more than twenty-five years. He is a humble man of God. He has preached in our church a few times. I have been greatly impressed by his testimony; his dedicated and committed Christ-centered life; his disciplined, close walk with the Lord; his deep knowledge of the Bible; and his Scripture memorization. He has a deep passion to win the souls to expand the Kingdom of God locally and globally, which can be seen clearly by his powerful ministry of Global Evangelism. His books, *God Is Calling You: Discerning the Calling of God* and *God Is Calling You: Responding to the Calling of God,* are valuable contributions to the Body of Christ. I wholeheartedly recommend these books. You will be greatly blessed by reading them and thankful that you did.

Rev. Avinash Raiborde
Senior Pastor, First India Baptist Church
Scottdale, Georgia

I have the blessing of knowing Dr. Naresh Malhotra for more than twenty years. He is a very devoted and zealous servant of our Lord Jesus Christ. His books, *God Is Calling You: Discerning the Calling of God* and *God Is Calling You: Responding to the Calling of God,* are the product of his deep and rich understanding of Biblical principles and his own discernment and response to the call of God in his life. These books are a *must read* by everyone. They will change your life and destiny forever.

Rev. Eddie M. Banquillo
Pastor, Filipino International Ministry
Kennesaw First Baptist Church
Kennesaw, Georgia

I first met Dr. Malhotra in Bilbao, Spain while a missionary there. Dr. Malhotra was invited as a guest lecturer on Marketing at the University of Deusto. He mentioned to his host, Dr. Dionisio Camara, that when not lecturing at the University, he wanted to be connected to an evangelical church there. I was contacted. Dr. Malhotra and I met. I became his guide in Bilbao and translator for nonmarketing speaking. When not at the University, we arranged for him to speak in churches and to share his testimony in a public school. He was very well received at every venue. His testimony to the students was "From Hinduism to Christianity." It had quite an impact. We spent considerable time together talking of God's work. He was such a bold witness I assumed that, given the opportunity, he would charge Hell with a squirt gun. We have maintained contact since then, discussing God's work in our lives and sharing prayer requests. Dr. Malhotra's passion to honor the Lord Jesus Christ and His Word, as well as his responsiveness to the Spirit's leading, have been an inspiration to me. As a professor teaching in the realm of man's pursuit of marketing, he has faithfully kept the pursuit of God's Kingdom first above all. I highly recommend both his books on *God Is Calling You*.

Rev. Gary Powell
Wyoming Pastor
Conference and Workshop Leader
Former International Mission Board Missionary

Endorsements from Foreign Countries

Argentina

One thing that impressed me of Dr. Naresh Malhotra is his love and respect for Jesus Christ. In one opportunity, he preached the Gospel in a Baptist church in La Plata City, Argentina, and when we realized it, he finished and no one presented him to the audience. After the service, I apologized to him; and his answer was: "do not worry. As long as they heard about Jesus Christ, everything is OK. He must be presented—not me!"

Listening to the voice of God is always a challenge. Responding to the call of God is also a challenge. Dr. Naresh Malhotra helps us through his knowledge of the Scripture, experience and love for Jesus Christ and the unreached to hear and answer to our Creator through his two volumes *God Is Calling You: Discerning the Calling of God* and *God Is Calling You: Responding to the Calling of God*. These two pieces of work are an inspiration for those who desire to know God more intimately, to love Him, and to serve Jesus Christ.

Dr. Carlos Hugo Braunstein
Senior Pastor, First Baptist Church, La Plata City,
Buenos Aires, Argentina

Canada

God Is Calling You: Discerning the Calling of God and *God Is Calling You: Responding to the Calling of God* beautifully capture God's unique plan for each person; His plan of salvation, sanctification, and service empowered by the Holy Spirit—all for the glory of the Lord Jesus Christ. These two books are a goldmine of precious truths from the Word of God that contain verse-by-verse exposition of key Scriptural principles and precepts. The two volumes are an excellent evangelism and discipleship tool—rolled into one. As a world-renowned scholar and Legendary Professor of Marketing, Dr. Naresh K. Malhotra has distinctively positioned these volumes in a structured way, providing his own "Author's Account" application of how God has worked, and is working, in his life. I have known Professor Malhotra for the last 30 years. He is a serious scholar, thinker, visionary, and a man of prayer and humility with deep passion to preach the Gospel of Jesus Christ—no matter what. These volumes bring together his life experiences and the priceless lessons learned from Scriptural principles and precepts. The additional supplements that come with these books provide great pedagogical learning tools as well. These books are a *must read* for every person on a quest for truth in life; for every born-again believer who has found the truth in Christ Jesus and is hungry for the "meat;" and for every mature believer who wants to fulfill the vision God has given her or him. You will be blessed, for sure.

Dr. James Agarwal
Haskayne Research Professor & Professor of Marketing
Haskayne School of Business, The University of Calgary
Canada

Colombia

It has been a blessing to work with brother Naresh for about thirty years, translating his messages in the churches, schools, cemeteries, parks, and other public places in Colombia. He is a mighty man of God, and I have witnessed God's power in his life and in his ministry. His messages have been well received in my country. His hunger for God's Word and his deep desire to know the Lord Jesus are reflected in his books *God Is Calling You: Discerning the Calling of God* and *God Is Calling You: Responding to the Calling of God.* I have translated many of the messages in these books as he has preached them in Colombia; and I know that you will be blessed by the deep, verse-by-verse, exposition. Your life will be transformed as you apply the many Bible principles given in these books. I encourage you to read these books if you are at all serious about knowing Christ and living your life for His glory.

Jannsen Duarte
Evangelist
World Wide Missionary Movement
Bogota, Colombia

I have had the great privilege to work with Dr. Naresh Malhotra for about twenty years in Bogota, Colombia. I have arranged his Marketing presentations in many universities in Bogota. His presentations are in two parts. First part is a professional presentation. In the second part, Brother Naresh shares his personal testimony that is followed by an invitation to receive Jesus Christ as personal Lord and

Saviour. We have seen thousands of professors, academic staff, students, and business professionals give their lives to Christ. Even the churches, public and private schools in Bogota have been blessed by his powerful preaching of the Gospel. The Holy Spirit moves in a mighty way to do His deep work of grace. Dr. Malhotra loves the Bible and has a very close walk with the Lord. I know that you will be greatly blessed by his books *God Is Calling You: Discerning the Calling of God* and *God Is Calling You: Responding to the Calling of God*. Please read these books prayerfully, and your life will be changed for the glory of God.

Myriam Rocha Donato
Senior Marketer and Startup Coach
World Missionary Movement Church
Bogotá, Colombia

India

I have had the pleasure and privilege of working with Dr. Naresh Malhotra, President of Global Evangelistic Ministries, for the past few years. It has been a delight to translate his messages in northern India. His preaching is anointed; and his messages are very insightful, reflecting his profound knowledge of the Bible. Many of the messages that he has preached have been from his two companion books *God Is Calling You: Discerning the Calling of God* and *God Is Calling You: Responding to the Calling of God*. These books are full of Scriptural principles that are universal and can be applied in any setting. Also, we have used these materials in our pastor's conferences with very good results. No matter where you are on your spiritual journey, you will be greatly blessed by reading these books and applying the principles they contain. I am delighted to recommend both these books.

Rev. Amit Malik
Senior Pastor, New Creation Church
New Delhi, India

Dr. Naresh is passionate about making the calling of God known to all. We have had the privilege of having him minister with us and have been struck by his untiring zeal to call people into an authentic relationship with the God of the Universe through His Son, the Lord Jesus Christ. Discharging a debt to his native land, Dr. Naresh has taken time to help people hear the call of God and then walk in that calling.

One of the greatest injustices of our time is that millions have not really heard the true Gospel of a loving Creator calling out to His crowning creation to enter into a living relationship through the Saviour, our Lord Jesus. We have so many fundamental rights enshrined in the constitutions of our modern democracies. Should we not have the 'Right to Hear the Gospel' added to them? Dr. Naresh has made it his life ambition to present the call and to give everyone a compelling opportunity to respond to it. My prayer is that many would read these books, discern the call of God in their lives, and respond to Him.

Rev. Victor A. Nazareth
Senior Pastor & Overseer, New Life Church, Delhi NCR
Founder & President, New Life Fellowship Trust

Kenya

Does God speak to His people and give them a call to His ministry today? This is a question that bothers so many people, including believers. Many Christians today, when they hear God calling them to His ministry, they start praying for God's direction and revelation—whether He is the One speaking or not. Dr. Naresh has been burdened by God to write these two books—*God Is Calling You: Discerning the Calling of God* and *God Is Calling You: Responding to the Calling of God*. They will answer and clarify God's call and how we should respond to His call. I therefore strongly encourage you to read these books so that you can understand what it means to be called by God to His ministry.

Pastor Timothy Kyuli
National Director
Source of Light Ministries International—Kenya branch
Nairobi, Kenya

I have been working with Dr. Naresh Malhotra since 2013 when he started his ministry in Kenya. From the beginning, I noticed that he operated with a deep sense of God's calling upon his life. I was also struck with the deep insights from the Bible that he shared in his messages in the churches in Kenya. I had the blessing of translating these messages. I am delighted that these deep Scriptural insights and his experiences of God's calling are shared in his books *God Is Calling You: Discerning the Calling of God* and *God Is Calling You: Responding to the Calling of God*. We, in Kenya, are waiting for these books to be published so that we can use them to train pastors and church leaders. They will be a great resource for our ministry here and, I believe, around the world. All who read these books will be greatly blessed.

Rev. Christiano Mboyi
Senior Pastor
GFE Church, Kenyenya
Global Field Evangelism Missions
Kenya

I was introduced to Dr. Naresh by my younger brother about seven years ago. He has discipled my brother for over twenty-five years, and I have had the blessing of coordinating his ministry in Kenya since 2013. Dr. Malhotra has conducted evangelism in the public schools, preached in churches and open air meetings, and ministered in pastor's conferences. He has preached the Gospel in the slums, including KIBERA SLUM (largest slum in Africa and fifth in the world), and ministered to refugees from several countries housed in Kakuma. He has covered several cities in Kenya. He has presented the Word with power, persuasion, and simplicity to those who did not know Christ. Yet, he unveiled the riches of the Word and keen insights as he taught Biblical principles in pastor's conferences and church services. I am thankful that his teachings are now available in his books *God Is Calling You: Discerning the Calling of God* and *God Is Calling You: Responding to the Calling of God*. These books will help you discover your purpose in life by knowing your calling and finding great joy and peace as you respond to your calling. I do pray and believe that God will use these books in a powerful way to glorify the Name of Jesus and bless all those who read them.

Wycliffe Ayoyi
Bible Training Center for Pastors Leader
Ag. Deputy County Commissioner Turkana West, Kenya

Mexico

Dr. Naresh Malhotra preached three services in my church during his visit to Mexico in 2017. His preaching was anointed and he proclaimed the Word of God with power, clarity, and forcefulness. In the Sunday morning service on 23 April 2017, more than 500 people prayed to receive salvation in Jesus Christ. There was such a mighty movement of the Holy Spirit. Dr. Malhotra's deep knowledge of the Bible is captured in his books *God Is Calling You: Discerning the Calling of God* and *God Is Calling You: Responding to the Calling of God.* I strongly recommend that you read these books. You will experience great spiritual growth and be blessed in your walk with Christ.

Dr. David Camela Hernandez
Senior Pastor, Salem Church, San Martin, Mexico

I have the privilege of knowing Dr. Naresh Malhotra. He has come to Mexico, and I have seen how God has used his life to touch the hearts of hundreds of students in the schools in my country. Many of them have prayed to receive Jesus in their hearts. I am a witness of his response to God in obedience to the call He made on him to bring the Gospel to different countries in the world. He is a faithful brother who has answered God's call. Through these books, you can find the purpose of God for your life to serve Him with your total lifestyle, including your spiritual life, family life, ministry, and vocation. These are great books to help you to respond to the calling God has on you to serve Him. I wholeheartedly recommend both these books.

Rev. Fernando Garcia
International Missionary and Evangelist
Former OM Mexico National Director
Mexico

It is a pleasure for me to write about Dr. Malhotra whom I had the honor of meeting in the spring of 2017. He now has written a couple of wonderful books *God Is Calling You: Discerning the Calling of God* and *God Is Calling You, Responding to the Calling of God.* I have been a personal witness of his ministry when he visited our city, Puebla, Mexico, in April of that year. He was also a special guest at our Cornerstone Puebla Church, where he preached three powerful messages. One of them—about the fact that Jesus turned water into wine—lasted for more than two hours, and yet we wanted more of the Word exposed. The other messages he preached are also contained in his books. Dr. Malhotra is a passionate man about leading people to the salvation of Christ. In his one week of ministry in our city, we documented 662 decisions for the Lord Jesus Christ. I recommend that you read his books. In his particular and simple way in which he writes them, your life will be transformed for the Glory of God.

Pastor Omar Cuateta Melo
Senior Pastor of Cornerstone Church, Puebla, Mexico

I have long been an admirer of Dr. Naresh Malhotra and used and taught from his books on Marketing Research. Dr. Malhotra is widely regarded as the number one Marketing Research Scholar in the world based on several published rankings. In April 2017, I invited him to visit UPAEP, Puebla, Mexico to give talks to our faculty, alumni, and students. He agreed to come on the condition that I would set up several Bible preaching engagements for him. He was the first non-Catholic priest to preach in the Catholic Church on our campus in its 46 years history. One of the most beautiful experiences I have ever had in my life happened at this UPAEP's Catholic Church while Dr. Naresh Malhotra asked all the attendants to close our eyes in the last part of his preaching. Suddenly, I saw an intense yellow light in front of me that looked as if someone in the audience had turned on a camera flash. No one was there. Immediately I realized that the yellow light was the presence of the Holy Spirit. I believe the Holy Spirit descended among us that evening.

I was with him in all his ministry engagements. I was struck by his deep knowledge of the Bible, his passion for Jesus Christ, and his intense desire to make Christ known. He is truly seeking first the Kingdom of God. I, my fiancé, and my parents all accepted and committed our lives to

Jesus Christ, as did several hundred others, when we heard him preach and give an invitation.

It is my great privilege and honour to very highly recommend Dr. Malhotra's two books on *God Is Calling You*. I know you will be blessed beyond measure as you read them. I hope that these two books, like his books on Marketing Research, will also be translated into Spanish so that people in Mexico and other Spanish countries are blessed to discern, follow, and fulfill the calling God has for them.

Mtro. Mauro García Domínguez
Responsable del Área de Investigación de Mercados
Universidad Popular Autónoma del Estado de Puebla
(UPAEP)
Puebla, Mexico

Peru

It is a great honor for me to highly recommend the books by Dr. Naresh Malhotra, *God Is Calling You: Discerning the Calling of God* and *God Is Calling You: Responding to the Calling of God*. These books capture his deep insights into the Scriptures in discerning and responding to the calling that God has for every person. They will be a great blessing and an encouragement to all who read them—no matter where they are in their faith.

Reading these books will help you to understand that to be called is not enough; for many are called, but few are chosen. To be counted among the few chosen, you have to give all diligence to make your calling and election sure by discerning and responding to the most holy calling of God for your life.

I first met Dr. Malhotra when he visited Peru in 2006. I had arranged for him to speak in universities, churches, and to business and professional people. I also served as his interpreter. His messages were Bible based, tailored to the audience, and delivered with power and anointing. I was impressed with his passion and commitment to Christ. During his stay in Peru, he had food poisoning. Yet, he met all his ministry engagements and kept his heavy schedule. At the end of his trip, while still unwell, he departed for Mexico to preach the Gospel there. I am certain that you will be greatly motivated, encouraged, and inspired to follow Jesus. Discern and fulfill your calling as you read these books.

Victor Carrera
Presidente
Ministerio Palabra de Vida
Trujillo, Perú

Philippines

God Is Calling You books reflect Dr. Naresh Malhotra's deep knowledge of the Bible, his heart and passion for evangelism, and his life story. These books are full of rich spiritual insights that will benefit anyone. Having the pleasure of working with Rev. Malhotra since 2011, I have seen the many Biblical concepts and principles highlighted in these books exhibited in his life. Working with him, we have been blessed to see more than one million people in the Philippines pray to receive Jesus Christ as Savior and Lord!

Rev. Jimpet John Fortich
Senior Pastor, Crossed Over Christian Church
Chairman, Pinoy Movement for Moral Excellence
Pasig, Metro Manila, Philippines

I personally know Dr. Malhotra and have been with him in campus mission in the Philippines.

God Is Calling You: Discerning the Calling of God and *God Is Calling You: Responding to the Calling of God* are two books that come from his heart and experience of doing God's calling for him in the mission fields.

These books can really be of help to those who are new and even old in the faith in knowing how or what is God's calling for you and responding to it. I know these books are God's blessing for all of us.

Rev. Arturo V. Payaoan
Senior Pastor, Fort A. Bonifacio Christian Church, SBC
Pateros, Metro Manila, Philippines

South Africa

We praise God for the ministry of Dr. Naresh Malhotra in South Africa over the past few years and for his "partnership in the Gospel." He is a humble servant and a great expositor of God's Word. His knowledge of the Word is amazing; and his preaching style is very clear, simple, and relevant in any context. He preaches Christ in the power of the Spirit, and God has used him to win many souls for Christ—from seniors to children—within our country.

It has been my privilege to personally hear him preach some of the messages/sermons in these books and witness how listeners sit in amazement, waiting to hear what he is going to say next.

I highly recommend these books. The outline and structure will prove very helpful to any reader or student of God's Word. I can assure you that you will be blessed, inspired, and spiritually challenged as you read them and study God's Word.

Rev. Angelo Scheepers
General Secretary
The Baptist Union of Southern Africa
Johannesburg, South Africa

I have had the privilege of hosting Dr. Naresh both in our church as a guest speaker and in my home as a visitor. As a Bible teacher, he has a powerful anointing on his ministry. His insight into the Word is astounding; and his ability to teach the Word—in a manner that even a child can understand—makes him a very special man of God. Having spent some time with him in Cape Town, South Africa in my home, I discovered that what makes his teaching so powerful is the close relationship he has with Jesus, Who is the Truth, and how he lives by what he teaches others. Whenever I spent time with Dr. Malhotra, I left feeling that truly I have been in the presence of a prophet of God. I endorse the man and his message without any reservation.

Rev. Salwyn A. Coetzee
Senior Pastor, Blomvlei Baptist Church
Past President, Baptist Union of Southern Africa
Chairman of the Board, Cape Town Baptist Seminary
Cape Town, South Africa

I was introduced to this man of God a few years ago. I have acted as his host and organised his preaching schedule while here in South Africa. As such, I travelled with him to the various preaching points both during the day and evening services. I was privileged to hear him preach. Each time, I sat with awe for a solid hour for the exposition of God's Word. Then at a simple invitation, hundreds of people respond, in repentance with first-time decisions for Christ, for healing, deliverance, etc. I was deeply inspired and awed by the anointing of the Holy Spirit upon this man. His preaching is Bible based, Cross centred, and Holy Spirit anointed. He is also a man of prayer, as in every short space available he will be praying. In a new country, he is not interested in sightseeing and fun-loving times. He would rather have his itinerary full of ministry. We look forward to eating out of his hands through his books *God Is Calling You: Discerning the Calling of God* and *God Is*

Calling You: Responding to the Calling of God. So should you! God bless and use him to see many more decisions made for Christ and many drawn closer to God.

Rev. Nelson Abraham
Missions Director, Baptist Union of Southern Africa
Past President, Baptist Union of Southern Africa
Johannesburg, South Africa

Uganda

We are all called to turn away from our sins and to turn toward God and His plan for our salvation. This is indeed the fundamental requirement for the performance of any Christian service. We are all called to live according to God's law; we are all called to a life of service to God and fellow man. So every person born on the face of the Earth has a calling of sort, but the ability to detect and distinguish what one's calling is—and correctly respond thus—is not an easy feat. In his books *Discerning the Calling of God* and *Responding to the Calling of God,* Dr. Naresh Malhotra clearly explains, with a strong Scriptural backing, how to discern and respond to the calling of God.

I warmly commend Dr. Naresh's two books about the call of God to anyone who is seeking to have a deeper understanding of God and His assignment to humanity.

Dickens Zziwa Ssenyonjo
National Director, Scripture Union Uganda
Kampala, Uganda

Dr. Naresh Malhotra has a great call to reach the lost and a burning passion for souls. He has preached in my church on his visits to Uganda. We have also been working in partnership with him and Scripture Union in reaching the schools in Uganda and leading many souls to Christ. I am very pleased to strongly endorse his books *God Is Calling You: Discerning the Calling of God* and *God Is Calling You: Responding to the Calling of God.* He is an anointed man of God and has a deep knowledge of the Bible and a heart for reaching the lost that is reflected in these books. I strongly encourage you to read them. You will experience life-changing transformation and be drawn closer to the Lord Jesus Christ by discerning and fulfilling your calling.

Rev. Martin Ocheing Ngollah,
Senior Pastor, Harvest Church
Harvest Vision Ministries
Kampala, Uganda

INTRODUCTION

Most people are coasting along in life. They are good people, trying to do well. They are good persons, husbands, wives, parents, children, employees, friends, and co-workers who are serious about their various responsibilities and duties. They are leading average to above-average lives. While leading good lives, they are missing out on the best. They have yet to discover their true purpose in this life—let alone pursue that with a passion. Why are they here? What are they supposed to be doing? Where should they be going? Are they making any difference in this world? Most will go through life without really grappling with these and similar questions or discovering their true purpose. As a result, they will not experience the fruitfulness, fulfillment, joy, and satisfaction God has for them. While living good lives, they will miss out on God's best. You do not have to be among them!

The secret to living a life full of meaning, fruitfulness, fulfillment, joy, and satisfaction is to discover, pursue, and fulfill God's calling. God has a unique and wonderful plan for every individual—a calling. God is calling you to be reconciled and united with Himself (Romans 5:10, 2 Corinthians 5:18, Colossians 1:21). Your calling is rooted in the call to follow Jesus Christ as your Savior and Lord (Matthew 8:22, Mark 2:14, Luke 9:23, John 10:27). In

Biblical terms, calling refers to belonging to Christ and participating in His redemptive work in the world in the special way He has called you (Romans 1:6, 8:28; 1 Timothy 2:4).[1]

Your calling encompasses all your being and doing. It defines and encompasses your total lifestyle and includes your spiritual life, family life, ministry, and vocation. It uniquely fits God's plan and purpose for your life. There are many callings on a person, for example, to be a spouse, parent, child, community member, and citizen. Yet there is one calling that uniquely defines your mission and sets you apart to serve the Lord Jesus Christ on this earth. No one else can fulfill your calling but you, as it has been designed by God just for you. Discerning, pursuing, and fulfilling your calling are what will give purpose and significance to your life. The two books in this series will help you to do just that. Instead of simply coasting along, you will live an exciting, fruitful, victorious life as you daily experience the presence and supernatural power of God. You will experience the abundant life God intends you to have (John 10:10).

The first book in this series, *God Is Calling You: Discerning the Calling of God,* will help you to recognize and determine the calling of God. The second book in this series, the sequel *God Is Calling You: Responding to the Calling of God,* will aid you in pursuing that calling with a passion, relying on God to fulfill that calling by doing His work in you and through you. In the process, you will experience miracles from God—all to the glory of the Lord Jesus Christ! You will benefit by getting to know God in a personal way, deepening your daily walk with Him, and fulfilling your calling. As a result, you will live a life full of meaning, significance, and fruitfulness. You will experience much joy, peace, and satisfaction in your heart. These two books will help fill the innermost need every person has to know God, to experience His presence and His power, and to lead a life full of significance and fruitfulness that is at the center of God's will. No matter where you are in your spiritual journey—even if you do not know Christ as your Savior, these books will help you.

Let me assure you the many principles given in these books work in real life. They are based on the Holy Bible—the Word of God. Thus, they carry God's authority and power. Jesus said, *"Heaven and earth shall pass away, but my words shall not pass away"* (Matthew 24:35). The Word of God must come to pass, that is, it must be fulfilled in your life. As a keen student of the Bible for more than forty years, I have discovered and practiced several principles from the Word and share them from my heart. God has worked and is working in my life most of these principles. Each chapter, in both books, has a major section, entitled "Author's Account," where I share how the concepts and principles discussed in that chapter have been fulfilled and are being fulfilled in my life. The material shared in these books comes straight from my heart. I pray it will touch your heart and change your life. The goal is not simply to appeal to your intellect but to transform your life for God's glory. *"As in water face answereth to face, so the heart of man to man"* (Proverbs 27:19).

I received the Lord Jesus Christ as my personal Savior and Lord on March 19, 1978, after having been a staunch

Hindu for more than twenty-seven years. In the fall of 1980, I discerned the calling of God upon my life after going through this process for about a year. I immediately embraced my calling and have tried to pursue it with passion and obedience to God. In the process, God has done many miracles in many areas of my life. As one example, in 2006, God gave me a vision to see more than one million people pray to receive Jesus Christ as Savior and Lord. In 2009, Global Evangelistic Ministries was founded to pursue this vision. Since then, God has blessed me to see more than 1.9 million people pray to receive the Lord Jesus Christ as their personal Savior and Lord. All these professions of faith are documented carefully in independent reports with each report signed by multiple local pastors and Christian leaders. These reports can be accessed at https://www.globalevangelisticministries.net. I praise God and give Him all of the glory. Truly, this outcome is the grace of God and the work of God in my life that is shared in these two books. It is a fulfillment of the vision the Lord Jesus Christ gave to me. These books will help you get a vision from God in the area of your calling and to see its fulfillment as you pursue it with passion, purpose, and obedience, depending on the Holy Spirit.

Structure of the Books

These books are about discerning and responding to the calling of God and much more. They are designed to be evangelism and discipleship tools. Each and every chapter serves as a springboard for the reader's spiritual growth and development by providing a solid grounding in the Word of God.

God Is Calling You: Discerning the Calling of God

The first book comprises five chapters and focuses on discerning the calling of God. This book will help you determine the calling of God upon your life and begins by emphasizing God loves you totally, unchangeably, and unconditionally. He has demonstrated His perfect love for you by sending His Son Jesus Christ to die on the cross for you. To live this life as God intends, it is imperative you receive God's love for you in Christ (chapter 1). The next chapter introduces the greatest miracle anyone can experience—the miracle of salvation in the Lord Jesus Christ. Chapter 2 discusses your need for salvation, God's plan for salvation, God's calling to salvation, and the miracle of salvation. Once you begin to experience the love of God (chapter 1) by receiving Jesus Christ as your Savior and Lord (chapter 2), you need to grow spiritually in your faith and in your daily walk with Him. In chapter 3, the focus is on the need for personal spiritual growth, daily surrender, prayer, Bible study, worship, fellowship, service and witness. However, you cannot grow spiritually by relying on your efforts, strengths, and abilities. None of the ingredients for spiritual growth in chapter 3 is to be performed in the flesh, that is, with self-effort or in a legalistic manner. Chapter 4 stresses the way to grow spiritually is to grow in grace. You will get a basic understanding of what grace is, grace to overcome temptation, the law, and the law versus grace. Chapter 5 explains the concept of your calling in more detail and discusses its importance. You will understand how your calling relates to ministry, your natural skills, talents, abilities, spiritual gifts, your deepest desires and burdens. You will see the difference between your calling and career. This chapter will help you discern the calling of God. Once you have determined the calling of God, you should pursue it with passion, purpose, obedience, and dependence on the Holy Spirit, as discussed in the second book in this series.

God Is Calling You: Responding to the Calling of God

The second book, or the sequel, consists of seven chapters and focuses on responding to the calling of God. While God does not want you to lean on your own preparation, He does prepare you for the call He has placed upon your life. Chapter 1 deals with preparation, and storms are an important tool used by God to prepare you for your calling. It highlights several principles that will enable you not to be fearful but be faithful in pressing onward in the storms of life. God will empower you in the midst of storms and see you through the storms to victory. As God prepares you for your calling, He will transform your life and begin conforming it more and more to the image of His Son, our Savior and Lord Jesus Christ. This conformation is the will of God for every believer (Romans 8:29). Chapter 2 brings out the many principles involved in the transformation process. God wants to transform your life and mine, conform us to His image, and use our lives mightily for His glory. Chapter 3 deals with the vision God has for you. This vision deals with what God wants to do with your life, and it has a special focus on what He wants to accomplish in your calling. Every Godly vision has certain Biblical characteristics. If you understand these character-istics, then you will be able to obtain and fulfill the vision God has for you. As you seek to fulfill God's vision, He will multiply the gifts, talents, abilities, resources, and your very life and use them mightily for His glory—as discussed in chapter 4. God is in the ministry of multiplication, as seen throughout the Bible. One such instance where God took five loaves and two fish and multiplied them to feed about five thousand men, besides women and children, is examined in detail. I draw out principles you can apply to experience the ministry of multiplication God has for each believer.

Given the reality of the spiritual warfare encompass-ing every believer, you will encounter several obstacles in fulfilling the vision and pursuing your calling. From the human perspective, many of these obstacles may seem like giants that dwarf you. How to defeat these giants is dis-cussed in chapter 5. These principles are drawn from how David defeated Goliath. Practicing them will prepare you to defeat these giants and overcome the obstacles the devil is likely to throw in your path. As you overcome the obsta-cles in the power of the Holy Spirit, God will give you the fulfillment of your vision. He will give you your mountain as a part of your inheritance in the Lord Jesus Christ. There are several principles given to us in how Caleb received Mt. Hebron as an inheritance, and these are highlighted in chapter 6. The final chapter discusses the continuing charge you have to keep on preaching the Gospel in the specific way that God has called you—even after the ful-fillment of the initial vision God gave to you. I describe this charge by using several key words—all of these begin with a C such as *charge, consistency, content, characteristics, conflict, courage, clarity, cost, consequence, continuity, correct, completion, crown,* etc. In fact, more than seventy-five such C words are used.

Style and Format

Both books are written in the same uniform style and format, and each chapter is structured in the same way based on principles of learning. Each chapter begins with a Bible verse, laying the foundation for that chapter. The first major section, "Preamble and Preview," gives an overview of the chapter. The following section, "Central Concepts," discusses the key concepts. These concepts are illustrated with a key passage from the Bible that is exposited verse-by-verse in a section called "Scripture Spotlight." Each verse is discussed using simple language and terminology to help you grasp its essentials. Then I share my personal testimony of how God the Father has worked these concepts in my life by the power of the Holy Spirit to the glory of the Lord Jesus Christ in the "Author's Account." Next "Quest Questions" challenge you to do some soul searching and answer a number of questions at a personal level. Then a section, entitled "Principles and Precepts," highlights the key Scriptural principles found in the chapter. These universal principles can be applied easily—regardless of your situation or circumstance. "Life Lesson" contains the most important lesson to be learned in the chapter. The next section in each chapter, "Prayer Power," contains an effectual, Scriptural prayer you are encouraged to pray to experience the power and the presence of God—especially as it pertains to the concepts discussed in that chapter. The final section, "Message Ministry," gives the link to an audio message of about thirty minutes you should hear. Access to these messages comes with the books, and there is no extra cost involved.

How to Use These Books

While simply reading these books will help you, to get the most benefits, you should really study them. You should focus on one book at a time, beginning with the first. The books can be used in individual as well as group study.

Individual Study

The books are systematically structured based on principles of learning I taught and practiced as a professor of marketing in the Scheller College of Business, Georgia Institute of Technology for thirty years.[2] You can read and study at your own pace. They are very rich and full of Biblical principles and precepts and deeper insights from God's Word. To get the most out of each book, you will have to read it many times, dwell upon the truths it contains, and apply them to your life. You should keep your Bible open while reading the book. You not only will have to refer to the Bible as you read the "Scripture Spotlight" section in each chapter but also as you read other parts of the chapter. There are extensive Bible quotations and references. Memorize the opening verse and other Scriptures the Holy Spirit lays on your heart. The Bible quotes are from the King James Version (KJV) unless stated otherwise. However, you should feel free to use your favorite version of the Bible. It is strongly recommended you read each book sequentially, beginning with chapter 1 since the chapters have been arranged in a logical order. It is extremely important you sincerely pray the prayer given in the "Prayer Power" section toward the end of each chapter to experience change.

Group Study

These books also are very useful for studying in small or large groups in churches, homes, and other settings. Group discussion can be centered on any, some, or all of the following major sections of each chapter: "Central Concepts," "Scripture Spotlight," "Quest Questions," and "Principles and Precepts." Participants should be encouraged to share their insights, applications, and testimonies. The group leader should moderate the discussion and offer summary comments by way of arriving at a consensus. She or he should close the session with the prayer given in the "Prayer Power" section at the end of each chapter.

The following supplements can further aid the reader in either individual or group study.

Book Supplements

As they are intended to be study books, each comes with an array of supplements, including the following:

- *Study Guide.* Given the in-depth discussion of Bible concepts and passages, this resource is particularly valuable. The Study Guide is structured with an integration of principles from Proverbs 4 and the three well-known theories of learning—classical conditioning, instrumental conditioning, and the cognitive theory—to maximize learning and retention of material in the books.

- *PowerPoint Slides.* A complete set of slides is provided for each chapter of both books. These slides are a good way of summarizing each chapter in a bullet-point format. Of course, they also can be projected on a screen and used as visual aids in a group setting.
- *Audio Messages.* Twelve audio messages, one for each chapter of both books, are available in MP3 format. Each message is about thirty minutes. You can access these messages free of cost by using CallingYou as the password.
- *Online Courses.* There are two online courses for each book. The basic course can be accessed free of cost from the website. The advanced course can be taken for a nominal price.
- *Website.* The books are supported by an informative and a useful website that can be accessed at https://www.globalevangelisticministries.net. This website is linked to a variety of social media, including a blog, Facebook, Twitter, LinkedIn, Instagram, Google+, and YouTube. While the audio messages are free, the Study Guide and PowerPoint Slides can be purchased from this website for a nominal price. In addition, the website contains several free materials such as additional audio and video messages.

God bless you as you read and study these books and as God works in your life in a powerful way for His glory! Let us all glorify the Name of the Lord Jesus Christ by discerning, pursuing, and fulfilling our calling!

CHAPTER 1

The Calling to God's Love for You:
It Is Not Your Love for God

"Herein is love, not that we loved God, but that he loved us, and sent his Son to be the propitiation for our sins."
—1 John 4:10

Preamble and Preview

A central truth that runs through the Bible, from Genesis to Revelation, is God loves you totally, unchangeably, and unconditionally. He has demonstrated His perfect love for you by sending His Son Jesus Christ to die on the cross for you. This chapter discusses the "Central Concepts" of the various aspects of God's love for you—denoted by the Greek word *agápē*. I explain how the emphasis on your love for God in the Old Testament has shifted to God's love for you in the New Testament. Experiencing God's love for you is the greatest key to living this life: gaining victory over sin and temptation, determining God's will and His calling, following the Lord Jesus Christ, overcoming fear, seeing

Jesus in the Scriptures, and experiencing God's abundance. I attempt to communicate the indescribable measure of God's love and God's calling to rest in His love for you. "Scripture Spotlight" shows how nothing, absolutely nothing, can separate us from the love of God in Christ Jesus, our Lord. This is followed by "Author's Account," where I share my personal testimony of how I began to sense the love of God. The following section, "Quest Questions," contains several questions that I hope will cause you to reflect on the reality of God's love in your life. There are several "Principles and Precepts" you can apply to experience the love of God. These principles are universal, and you can apply them easily—regardless of your situation or circumstance. "Life Lesson" contains the most important lesson you can learn with respect to God's love in Jesus Christ. "Prayer Power" contains an effectual, Scriptural prayer you are encouraged to pray to set the stage for experiencing God's love. The final section, "Message Ministry," gives a link to an audio message you are exhorted to hear.

Central Concepts

We see a manifestation of God's love for us from Genesis to Revelation in the creation, redemption, and restoration of man. All human beings have a need to experience God's love as they were so created by Him. This agápē love can be experienced only through Jesus Christ. It is the key to discerning God's will and calling. It will help you to live victoriously in this life. You will be able to fulfill your calling by following the Lord Jesus Christ and experiencing the abundant life Jesus Christ alone can give. These concepts will be discussed in more detail.

God's Love from Genesis to Revelation

God's pure, unconditional, and absolute love for humanity is evident all through the Bible from Genesis to Revelation. God's love for us can be seen in creation, redemption, and restoration of man. As seen in the very first chapter of the Bible, God created man in His image and after His likeness (Genesis 1:26–27). What is God like? *"God is love"* (1 John 4:8, 16). Thus, God created man to reflect His love. As further demonstration of His love for us, God gave man a free will and dominion *"over all the earth"* (Genesis 1:26). Unfortunately, the first man Adam surrendered that dominion to Satan by willfully disobeying God. Man was separated from God because of sin. As He loves us greatly and unconditionally, God paid the highest cost, the blood and life of His eternal Son Jesus Christ, to redeem man from the dominion of Satan. Christ reconciled man to God. The Father's motivation in sending His Son to die on the cross for our redemption is His absolute and unconditional love for us (John 3:16). The demonstration of God's love for mankind continues throughout the Bible—even to the book of Revelation. The very last chapter in the Bible, Revelation 22, describes the finished work of restoration. The earthly paradise, lost by the sin of Adam, is more than restored by the Lord Jesus Christ with *"the holy city, new Jerusalem"* (Revelation 21:2). There is *"a pure river of water of life"* (Revelation 22:1); the *"tree of life"* is restored (Revelation 22:2); all curse is removed

(Revelation 22:3); His children *"shall see his face; and his name shall be in their foreheads"* (Revelation 22:4); and God bestows eternal dominion to His children *"and they shall reign for ever and ever"* (Revelation 22:5). The complete restoration of all things conclusively demonstrates God's pure and unconditional love for man. Thus, the entire Bible, from the first chapter of Genesis to the last chapter of Revelation, is the story of God's love for mankind that is demonstrated perfectly on the cross of Calvary.

Agápē Love

The love God has for you is denoted by the Greek word agápē. This concept is unique to the Christian faith. The Bible states clearly and repeatedly—no matter who you are, no matter what you have done or not done—God loves you. He loves you with a perfect, unchanging, unchangeable, everlasting love. He loves you just as you are. God relates to you personally and knows all about you (Psalm 139:3, Isaiah 49:16, Luke 12:7). He knows you are a sinner, totally undeserving and unworthy of His love; yet He has chosen to love you. In John 4, we read about the encounter of Jesus with the Samaritan woman. Jesus told the woman all about her sinful past (John 4:39). Why? Because He wanted her to know He loved her—even though He knew what a sinful woman she was. So do not say to yourself, "If God really knew what a sinner I am and what bad things I have done, He would not love me." God knows you and what you have done. Yet He loves you. God loves you as if you were the only person on earth. In contrast, in other religions, God is represented as a distant God, above and beyond the reach of sinful man; and the emphasis is on your love for God, not on God's love for you.

Agápē is the term that defines God's unconditional, immeasurable, and incomparable love for you. God gives His love to you without any conditions and without any reservations although you are totally undeserving and inferior to Him. God does not love you because you are lovely. He loves you because you are you, and His love for you makes you lovely. If you receive it, it will transform you to the person He created you to be. His love is the highest and purest form of love; it is love at its ultimate. It involves faithfulness, commitment, and an act of the will. This form of love is totally selfless and does not change—whether the love given is returned or not. In fact, God pursues you relentlessly with His love.

Agápē love is rooted in the very nature and character of God. The Bible says *"God is love"* (1 John 4:8, 16). God does not merely love; He is love. There is a perfect, eternal love relationship among God the Father, God the Son, and God the Holy Spirit Who comprise the Holy Trinity (John 17:24). God loves you because that is His nature, the expression of His being, and an overflow of the agápē love in the Trinity. He loves you, the unlovable and the unlovely, not because of any characteristic you possess but because that is His very nature and character. God is always true to His nature and character. Everything God does flows from His love for you. His love for you is the underlying motivation for all of His actions. It should be emphasized that you are totally unworthy and undeserving of God's love. There is nothing you can do or not do to merit His love even to the slightest degree. The Bible says you are the undeserving recipients of His lavish agápē love (1 John 3:1).

Agápē also is used to describe how we ought to love God (Matthew 22:37, Luke 10:27); our neighbors (Matthew 22:39); and even our enemies (Matthew 5:43–46). In such cases, it denotes God's kind of love—love that is rooted and has, as its source, the character of God and the love of God for us.

The Old and New Testament Emphases on Love

According to the New American Standard (NAS) New Testament Greek Lexicon, agápē appears 106 times in the New Testament.[1] Apart from about twenty occurrences in the Greek version of the Old Testament, it is almost non-existent before the New Testament. In the Old Testament, under the law, the emphasis was on your love for God. *"And thou shalt love the LORD thy God with all thine heart, and with all thy soul, and with all thy might"* (Deuteronomy 6:5). No one, born of a man, has been able to keep this commandment. Abraham, the father of our faith, could not keep it. He lied about his wife twice that she was his sister (Genesis 12:18–19, 20:2). Moses, to whom the law was given, could not keep it. He disobeyed God by smiting the rock twice rather than speaking to it and could not enter the Promised Land (Numbers 20:7–12). David, a man after God's own heart, could not do it. He committed adultery and murder (2 Samuel 11:1–12:13). If you break even a single commandment of the law, you are guilty of breaking the whole law. *"For whosoever shall keep the whole law, and yet offend in one point, he is guilty of all*" (James 2:10).

Jesus did affirm, "*This is the first and great commandment*" (Matthew 22:37–38). But Jesus said that in response to a question from a lawyer who was "*tempting him*" (Matthew 22:35). The specific context was the question: "*Master, which is the great commandment in the law?*" (Matthew 22:36). Moreover, Jesus said that before He died on the cross and established the New Covenant. In the New Covenant of grace, the emphasis is not on your love for God but on God's love for you. "*Herein is love, not that we loved God, but that he loved us, and sent his Son to be the propitiation for our sins*" (1 John 4:10). God loves you totally and unconditionally. God's perfect demonstration of agápē love is in the sacrifice of His Son Jesus Christ. The positive, undeniable, irrefutable proof of God's love for you is the cross of Calvary. "*Hereby perceive we the love of God, because he laid down his life for us*" (1 John 3:16). Romans 5:8 in the International Standard Version states, "*But God demonstrates his love for us by the fact that the Messiah died for us while we were still sinners.*"

We see the cross as a demonstration of God's love also in the Old Testament. God told Israel in Malachi 1:2–3, "*I have loved you, saith the LORD. Yet ye say, Wherein hast thou loved us? Was not Esau Jacob's brother? saith the LORD: yet I loved Jacob, And I hated Esau, and laid his mountains and his heritage waste for the dragons of the wilderness.*" The word "loved" used twice by the Lord in Malachi 1:2 is the Hebrew word *'āhab* that describes the unspeakable love and tender mercies of God in the covenant relationship with His people. It has its counterpart in the Greek word agápē.[2] In these verses, Esau is a reference to Christ, Who like Esau is the firstborn (Matthew 1:25; Luke 2:7; Colossians 1:15, 18; Hebrews 12:23). Jacob here is a reference to the believers who are referred to as "*brethren*" of Christ (Romans 8:29). This picture is seen also in the reconciliation of Jacob with Esau in Genesis 33. God has, does, and always will love Jacob, that is, the believers who are Christ's brothers and sisters. When God said, "*I loved Jacob, And I hated Esau*," He is saying He loves us so much that He, so to speak, hated Christ for our sake by sending Him to shed His blood and die on the cross for our redemption (Isaiah 53:4–5). As God chose Jacob and rejected Esau, so He chose faith in Christ and rejected the works of the law as the condition of salvation. Paul has quoted Malachi 1:3 in Romans 9:13.

Even as He was taking His lasts breaths on the cross, Jesus loved the criminal next to Him and promised him salvation in response to his repentance and trust in Him (Luke 23:39–43). The suffering and sacrifice of Jesus on the cross are a perfect portrayal of the outpouring of God's love for sinners. A direct implication is that the only way you can appropriate and experience God's love for you is by coming to the cross. That is, by believing Jesus Christ is the Son of God, He loves you and died on the cross for you. God raised Him from the dead to live forevermore, indicating the sacrifice Jesus made for you is acceptable to God.

God created us from agápē love, for agápē love, and to agápē love, as He made us in His image (Genesis 1:26). However, agápē love does not come normally and naturally to us. Man is born and lives with a fallen nature and, thus, is incapable of producing such love. If we are to love as God loves, that agápē love can come only from its source: God Himself. Our ability to love God develops as we experience His love for us in Christ. "*We love him, because he first loved us*" (1 John 4:19). It should be added that our love for one another also comes only after we experience God's love for us. It stems from an overflow of God's love for us in Christ. "*Beloved, if God so loved us, we ought also to love one another*" (1 John 4:11). Jesus made this very clear when He said in John 13:34, "*A new commandment I give unto you, That ye love one another; as I have loved you, that ye also love one another.*" As you experience the love of Christ, you will be able to love others with agápē love. You cannot express love unless you first experience love, the love of God for you in Christ. The more you realize how much God loves you in Christ, the more you will be able to love God and love other people. The only way you can be capable of loving God and loving other people is to realize how much God loves you in Christ. This was difficult for people to do in the Old Testament when they were under the law. However, under grace, it is possible for you to do so under the New Testament because of the perfect, finished work of Jesus Christ on the cross.

The Bible says in Galatians 5:6, "*For in Jesus Christ neither circumcision availeth any thing, nor uncircumcision; but faith which worketh by love.*" A lot of people misinterpret this statement to mean faith works by our love for God. Actually, in the original Greek, the word that is used for love is agápē, again referring to God's love for us. Thus, faith works by God's love for us. For our faith to work, we must realize how much God loves us. The more we realize the love of God in Christ for us, the more our faith will work for us. God's love will generate faith, not fear, in you. Experiencing His love will make it effortless for you to believe His promises. God's love is the greatest key.

God's Love for You: The Greatest Key

The apostle Paul gave us the greatest key to living this life. It is also the key to discerning your calling. It is: *"And now these three remain: faith, hope and love. But the greatest of these is love"* (1 Corinthians 13:13, New International Version). The word for love appearing twice in this verse is both times the Greek word agápē, denoting God's love for us. This is true each time the word "love" appears in the entire 1 Corinthians 13. As background to this chapter in the Bible, the temple of Aphrodite, the goddess of sensual love, was in the city of Corinth. This temple had a thousand prostitutes who offered their services each night to the Corinthians. Paul contrasted this immoral expression of love with the holiness and beauty of God's love.

Agápē love is superior to faith and hope for three reasons. First, faith, hope, and God's love are the sum total of life on earth; we need all three on earth. However, faith is superior to hope since faith is the substance of things hoped for (Hebrews 11:1). Without faith, hope would be mere wishful thinking. Agápē love is superior to faith because it is this love that makes faith work (Galatians 5:6). Through hope, we expect an eternal future. By faith, we receive from God our Father. By love, we resemble God. Realization of God's love for us is the necessary condition for our dwelling in God and God in us. Love is the image of God in us, for God is love (1 John 4:8, 16). Second, God's love alone is the essence of life in Heaven. In Heaven, hope will come to fruition and faith will be changed to sight. We will see God face to face, and all of the unfulfilled promises of God will be realized. However, the love of God for us will continue in Heaven for all eternity. Third, agápe love is a part of God's character; but hope and faith are not. God does not need hope because He knows all things and is always in complete control. Hope relates to the future, and the future is present for Him. He said, I AM. God also does not need faith in the way we need it because He never has to "trust" outside of Himself.[3] God does have perfect faith in Himself, that is, in the Trinity. For example, God the Father has perfect faith in Himself, in His Son Jesus Christ, and in His Holy Spirit. But God does not need to trust in anyone or anything outside the Trinity. However, God is love and always will be love.

The love of God, agápe, is the greatest thing in this universe. It can revolutionize your life completely. But it all depends on you, on your willingness to allow God's Spirit to produce this tremendous love in your heart and life. Agápe is a supernatural fruit of the Holy Spirit (Galatians 5:22).

God's Love for You: The Key to Victory over Sin

At the root of all of Satan's temptations, beginning with the Garden of Eden, is his strategy to get you to doubt God's love for you. He does that by pointing to your difficult situations and circumstances. Satan will ask, "If God really loves you, why is this happening to you? Look at you, you are caught in such trying situations and circumstances."

You should not evaluate God's love for you by looking at your circumstances. We live in a fallen world where bad things can happen to good people and good things can happen to bad people. By and large, God's will is not being done on earth, especially by the unbelievers. That is why Jesus taught His disciples to pray, "*Thy kingdom come. Thy will be done in earth, as it is in heaven*" (Matthew 6:10). So do not let Satan deceive you by pointing to your situations and circumstances. The way to successfully defeat Satan is to point to the cross of Jesus Christ as the undeniable proof of God's love for you. Conscious awareness of God's love for you will result in victory over sin and temptation.

Always base your beliefs and convictions on the Word of God as you see it for yourself directly in the Bible—never based on what you hear from a preacher, pastor, or someone else, or on any other source. That way, it will be more difficult for Satan to cause you to doubt God's Word and His love for you. This is the reason why Satan tempted Eve and not Adam. The commandment not to eat "*of the tree of the knowledge of good and evil*" was given by God to Adam (Genesis 2:16–17). Eve was not formed at that time. She was created later (Genesis 2:21–22). There is no record that God gave this commandment directly to Eve. Therefore, it is likely Eve heard this commandment later from Adam, not directly from God. Thus, it was easier for Satan to cause Eve to doubt God's Word and His love than to tempt Adam directly. In effect, Satan told Eve, "If God really loved you, why would He ask you not to eat of the tree of the knowledge of good and evil." I urge you to check in your Bible every Scripture verse quoted or referenced in this book. It is very important you do not add to or subtract from the Word of God as given in the Bible (Revelation 22:18–19). Eve both added and subtracted. She added, *"neither shall ye touch it"* (Genesis 3:3). When God gave the commandment to Adam, He never said not to touch it. *"But of the tree of the knowledge of good and evil, thou shalt not eat of it: for in the day that thou eatest thereof thou shalt surely die"* (Genesis 2:17). Furthermore, Eve subtracted because she failed to mention *"freely"* and *"surely"* in Genesis 3:2–3. No wonder Eve fell to Satan's temptation.

We see a sharp contrast to Eve's handling of temptation in the earthly life of our Savior. Toward the end of Matthew 3 is the description of the baptism of Jesus. *"And lo a voice from heaven, saying, This is my beloved Son, in whom I am well pleased"* (Matthew 3:17). God said this about His Son even before Jesus had started His ministry, before He had performed any miracles at all. It was based on Their relationship, not on any works. In Matthew 4, we read about the temptation of Jesus by the devil. When the devil tempted Jesus, he said, *"If thou be the Son of God"* (Matthew 4:3, and again in Matthew 4:6). The devil also said that the third time he tempted Jesus. (See Luke 4:9.) Notice each of the three times the devil left out the word "beloved." Why? Because the devil knew if Jesus realized He is the beloved Son of God, there was no way He would yield to the temptations. The devil does not give up easily and tried the same trick again through those who were passing by when Jesus was dying on the cross, but he failed yet again (Matthew 27:40). Jesus knew He is the beloved Son of God, and He walked in the conscious awareness of His Father's love. The Father's love propelled Jesus into His calling. This was the key to His victory over temptation and Satan. Knowing you are loved by God is essential to discerning and fulfilling your calling and accomplishing all that God has called you to do.[4]

God the Father also reaffirmed Jesus as His beloved Son when Jesus was transfigured on a "high mountain" (Matthew 17:1–9, Mark 9:2–9. See also Luke 9:28–36). Many scholars believe this place was Mt. Hermon, the highest mountain in Palestine, a short distance to the north of Caesarea Philippi. The place where Jesus was baptized in Jordan is close to the Dead Sea, physically the lowest point on the earth. Thus, the Father affirmed Jesus as His beloved Son when He was physically at a low point and when He was at a high point. Why? To give us an understanding of who we are in Christ. In Christ, you are a beloved child of God! This is true whether you are at a low point or a high point spiritually. If you are a believer, then you were in Christ when He was baptized and when He was trans-figured. Thus, what God said about His Son Jesus, He said about you. This truth is stated many times in the New Testament. In fact, the phrase *"in Christ"* appears 78 times in 77 different verses in the King James Version of the New Testament. Of these, 75 occurrences are in the writings of Paul. Many of these references are to the believer being in Christ. See, for example, Romans 8:1, 1 Corinthians 1:30 and 2 Corinthians 5:17. Likewise, Christ is in you (John 17:23, Colossians 1:27). Believers are referred to as *"beloved of the Lord"* (2 Thessalonians 2:13). Next time when you are tempted, say this, aloud if appropriate, "I am a beloved child of God in Christ. Thank You, Abba, Father, You love me so very much that You sent Your Son, the Lord Jesus

Christ, to die on the cross for me." Then you will not yield to the temptation.

Notice, Satan questioned the identity of Jesus. "*If thou be the Son of God*" (Matthew 4:3, 6; Luke 4:9). Satan also will tempt you by questioning your identity. First and foremost, your identity should be rooted in who you are in Christ—a beloved child of God, if indeed you have received Christ as your Savior and Lord. Secondly, your identity should be rooted in what Christ has done for you. We read in Revelation 1:5–6, "*And from Jesus Christ, who is the faithful witness, and the first begotten of the dead, and the prince of the kings of the earth. Unto him that loved us, and washed us from our sins in his own blood, And hath made us kings and priests unto God and his Father; to him be glory and dominion for ever and ever. Amen.*" Christ has loved you, washed your sins by His own blood, and made you a king and a priest. A king has authority on the earth and a priest has authority in Heaven. Christ has given you that authority. These are three of the distinguishing characteristics of the Christian faith: (1) God loves us, (2) He has washed our sins by the blood of His own Son, and (3) He has made us priests with Jesus Christ as our great High Priest. Also, He has made us kings with Jesus Christ as the "*KING OF KINGS, AND LORD OF LORDS*" (Revelation 19:16). In contrast, other religions emphasize: (1) our love for God, (2) we have to pay for our sins, and (3) there are priests, there are kings, and then there are the people as three separate groups. Even in the Old Testament, under the law, a person could not be both a king and a priest. This is the reason God pronounced judgment upon Kings Saul and Uzziah because, as kings, they tried to usurp the office of a priest.

Your Love for God Versus God's Love for You

We see your love for God contrasted with God's love for you in the lives of Peter and John. Peter boasted of his love for Jesus Christ. The night when He was betrayed, *"And Jesus saith unto them, All ye shall be offended because of me this night: for it is written, I will smite the shepherd, and the sheep shall be scattered"* (Mark 14:27). *"But Peter said unto him, Although all shall be offended, yet will not I"* (Mark 14:29). Peter boasted his love for Jesus was stronger than even the Living Word (Jesus) and the Written Word (the Bible). Sadly, he ended up denying Jesus three times. (See Matthew 26:33–35.) After his third denial, *"And the Lord turned, and looked upon Peter"* (Luke 22:61). That was a look of love. Peter *"went out, and wept bitterly"* (Luke 22:62). Peter wept not so much because he had denied Jesus but because Jesus loved him even when he had denied Him thrice. You may have denied Jesus multiple times. Let me assure you, based on the Word, Jesus still loves you.

On the other hand, John boasted of the love Jesus had for him. Five times in the Bible, John is referred to as the disciple whom Jesus loved. All five occurrences are in the Gospel of John (13:23; 19:26; 20:2; 21:7, 20). In other words, John said that about himself; he was boasting about Jesus's love for him. Five is also the number of grace. John was acknowledging the love of Jesus for him as the grace of God. The result? John was standing near to Jesus at His crucifixion whereas Peter was nowhere to be found. At the cross, Jesus also carried the burden of taking care of His mother, being the eldest son in the family. He entrusted that burden to John (John 19:26–27). Why to John? Because He knew John focused on the love of Jesus for him. That would empower John to take good care of Mary as his mother. His focus on the love of Christ for him was the secret to John's long, strong, and victorious life. John outlived all the other apostles. Do you see yourself as the disciple whom Jesus loves? If you are a believer, say this aloud, "I am the disciple whom Jesus loves." This will give you victory over sin and temptation, as discussed earlier.

Determining God's Will and His Calling

Your conscious realization and acknowledgement of Jesus's love for you is also critical in your walking close to God and getting direction for His will and calling for your life. Again, this truth is evident in the lives of Peter and John as recorded in John 13:21–26. Jesus had said, "*Verily, verily, I say unto you, that one of you shall betray me*" (John 13:21). Peter, who had boasted of his love for Jesus, felt distant from God and asked John "*that he should ask who it should be of whom he spake*" (John 13:24). Peter knew John felt closer to Jesus than he did. Then John, "*lying on Jesus' breast saith unto him, Lord, who is it?*" (John 13:25). Notice John first leaned on Jesus's breast, acknowledging the love of Jesus for him before he asked Him the question. Do you want to determine God's will in a particular situation? Do you want to determine God's calling for your life? First, lean on Jesus's breast, that is, acknowledge His love for you and then make your request. This principle is also seen in the Old Testament. The Urim and the Thummim, used to determine God's will, were worn on Aaron's heart (Exodus 28:30). Aaron is a picture of the Great High Priest, the Lord Jesus Christ; and his heart represents God's love for us. Thus, Aaron, wearing the Urim and the Thummim on his heart, symbolized acknowledgement of God's love for us in Christ before getting direction from God. David illustrates this principle in 1 Samuel 30:7–8. *"And David said to Abiathar the priest, Ahimelech's son, I pray thee, bring me hither the ephod"* (1 Samuel 30:7). Abiathar means "my father is great," Ahimelech means "my brother is king," and David means "beloved." Our Father in Heaven is the Great One, our brother Jesus is King, and like David we are God's beloved.

Another instance where John was closer to Jesus than Peter is the third time Jesus appeared to His disciples after His resurrection. This incident is recorded in John 21:1–14. The disciples had gone fishing on the lake of Tiberias, also called the Sea of Galilee. They fished all night but caught nothing. *"But when the morning was now come, Jesus stood on the shore: but the disciples knew not that it was Jesus"* (John 21:4). John first recognized Jesus and made Him known to Peter. You will walk closer to the Lord if you focus on His love for you than if you focus on your love for Him. Even Peter had now learned he could not depend upon his love for Jesus but must depend upon the love of Jesus for him. This is evident from Peter's response. When Peter learned from John that it was Jesus standing on the shore, *"he girt his fisher's coat unto him, (for he was naked,) and did cast himself into the sea"* (John 21:7). Peter could not wait for the boat to reach the shore. Why? Because he knew Jesus loved him—even though he had denied Him thrice. If Peter had focused on his love for Jesus that had failed, he would have run away from Jesus—not jumped into the lake and swam toward Jesus. The love of Jesus for him drew Peter to the shore. It should be noted, after His resurrection, Jesus appeared to Peter before He appeared to the twelve (1 Corinthians 15:5; see also Luke 24:34). This fact, no doubt, convinced Peter that Jesus loved him and had forgiven him.

In contrast, when Adam and Eve sinned, they ran away from God because they believed Satan's lie and doubted God's love for them. *"And they heard the voice of the LORD God walking in the garden in the cool of the day: and Adam and his wife hid themselves from the presence of the LORD God amongst the trees of the garden"* (Genesis 3:8). Here is a lesson for all of us. When we sin, we should focus on the love of Jesus for us and that will cause us to run to Jesus rather than run away from Him.

Following Jesus

Focusing on the love of God for you in Christ will lead you to follow Him. Again, we see this truth clearly in the lives of Peter and John. At the time of his arrest, Peter, who had boasted of his love for Jesus, *"followed him afar off unto the high priest's palace"* (Matthew 26:58; see also Mark 14:54, Luke 22:54). Peter was following Jesus at a distance because he did not want to identify himself with Christ. However, another disciple, most probably John because he frequently speaks of himself without mentioning his name, *"went in with Jesus into the palace of the high priest"* (John

18:15). Thus, John was following Jesus closely—just as John later was present at the crucifixion.

In John 21:15–17, Jesus reinstated Peter to his apostolic ministry after his fall. Jesus afforded Peter a threefold public affirmation of love to overcome a threefold denial. In each of these three verses, Jesus asked Peter if he loved Him. However, in John 21:15 and John 21:16, Jesus used the Greek word agápē: love based on the love of God and on the character of God. Only in John 21:17, Jesus used the Greek word *phileo*: love that denotes reciprocal, friendly affection. Thus, Jesus emphasized the love of God for us twice as much as He emphasized our love for God and others. In each of these verses, Jesus entrusted to Peter the ministry of feeding and shepherding His flock. Peter and the other apostles were evangelists as well as pastors. As evangelists, they were to bring into the fold the sheep that had gone astray. As pastors, they had to provide food for the sheep and the lambs. Thus, in evangelizing and shepherding the sheep, the ministers of God should emphasize the love of Jesus for us far more than they stress our love for Jesus and others. By all means, tell God you love Him. It is a good thing to do. However, acknowledge and thank God for His love for you twice as much.

When you focus on the love Christ has for you, then you will, even subconsciously, follow the Lord Jesus Christ. After restoring Peter to his apostolic office, Jesus told him, *"Follow me"* (John 21:19). He had no need to tell that to John. Why? Because John already was following Jesus. *"Then Peter, turning about, seeth the disciple whom Jesus loved following"* (John 21:20). When you focus on how much God loves you in Christ, you will want to obey the

Lord Jesus Christ and keep His commandments. Jesus said in John 14:15, *"If ye love me, keep my commandments."* The only way to do that is by focusing on the love of God in Christ for you. The more you focus on God's love for you, as demonstrated on the cross, the more you will realize how much you have been forgiven. The more you realize how much you have been forgiven, the more you will love the Lord Jesus Christ. Jesus said of *"a woman who was a notorious sinner"* (Luke 7:37), *"So I'm telling you that her sins, as many as they are, have been forgiven, and that's why she has shown such great love. But the one to whom little is forgiven loves little"* (Luke 7:47, International Standard Version). The fact is, each believer was a notorious sinner who has been forgiven much. It is a matter of realizing how much you have been forgiven. The more you realize it, the more you will love Christ. The more you love Christ, the more you will obey Him and keep His commandments—not because you have to but because you will want to.

This principle is illustrated consistently in the Old Testament as well. The Old Testament saints, who followed God and lived victoriously, did so not by trying to keep the law but by walking in the conscious awareness of God's grace and love in Christ, looking forward to the cross. Abraham, the father of our faith, so walked. He told Isaac, *"My son, God will provide himself a lamb for a burnt offering"* (Genesis 22:8). Jesus affirmed that when He said in John 8:56, *"Your father Abraham rejoiced to see my day: and he saw it, and was glad."* Moses died when he was 120 years old (Deuteronomy 34:7). What was the secret of Moses's long life? The answer is given in Hebrews 11:24–27: *"For he endured, as seeing him who is invisible"* (Hebrews 11:27).

Although Moses was the one to whom the law was given, he himself walked not under the law but under grace, constantly focusing on the love of God in Christ, "*Esteeming the reproach of Christ greater riches than the treasures in Egypt*" (Hebrews 11:26). That is how he endured. Moses realized the only way to fulfill the law was by faith, focusing on the love of God in Christ. This truth applies to all the Old Testament saints as Paul has explained in Romans 9:31–32.

Overcoming Fear and Emotional Baggage

As you experience God's love for you, you will overcome fear. Love is the opposite of fear. The love of God will cast out fear in your life. "*There is no fear in love; but perfect love casteth out fear*" (1 John 4:18). Then the devil will not be able to use fear as a weapon against you. We see this truth in the life of Peter when King Herod had put him in jail. Far from being afraid, on the night before his trial, Peter was sleeping (Acts 12:6). Why was he able to sleep? Because, by then, Peter had learned to rest in the perfect love of Jesus Christ for him.

As an Old Testament illustration, when King Jehoshaphat was surrounded and outnumbered by his enemies, the Spirit of the Lord came upon Jahaziel and He said to the king, "*Don't be afraid nor dismayed because of this great multitude, for the battle is not yours, but God's. You will not need to fight in this battle. Position yourselves, stand still and see the salvation of the Lord, who is with you. Don't fear or be dismayed. Tomorrow, go out against them for the Lord is with you*" (2 Chronicles 20:14–17). What King Jehoshaphat did next was full of faith. He acted on the love of God for Israel. Instead of putting his army in front, he put worshipers in front! What did the worshipers sing? They sang of God's love for them—*"Praise the Lord for His love endures forever!"* And God utterly destroyed their enemies (2 Chronicles 20:21, New International Version; the King James Version says "mercy" but the New International Version, the New Living Translation, the English Standard Version, International Standard Version, and several other translations correctly use the word "love." The original Hebrew uses the word *Hesed* (חֶסֶד), meaning "lovingkindness," "mercy," "loyalty." Perhaps "loyal love" is the closest here.)

Likewise, God's love will help you overcome other mental, emotional, or physical baggage you may be carrying, for example, self-hatred and loneliness. Lots of people hate what they see in the mirror. Many waste tremendous amounts of money and resources trying to change their physical features and appearance. However, realizing God loves you and accepts you the way you are and, in His opinion, you are *"fearfully and wonderfully made"* (Psalm 139:14) will set you free from this stronghold. It will cause you to love and accept yourself. Lots of people feel lonely in life. They have no one to turn to, depend upon, and look to in good times and bad. Receiving the love of God in Christ will address the problem of loneliness. Jesus is *"a friend that sticketh closer than a brother"* (Proverbs 18:24). He *"will never leave you or abandon you"* (Hebrews 13:5, International Standard Version).

Seeing Jesus and Experiencing God's Abundant Power

When you focus on God's love, you will be able to see Jesus Christ in all His resurrected splendor, glory, and majesty. On resurrection Sunday, Peter went into the empty tomb before John but left *"wondering in himself at that which had come to pass"* (Luke 24:12). In contrast, John *"saw, and believed"* (John 20:8). As you experience Christ's love, you will see Him for Who He really is: *"the Lamb of God, which taketh away the sin of the world"* (John 1:29). Jesus Christ is referred to as the Lamb thirty-two times in the entire New Testament. Of these, twenty-eight times are in the book of Revelation and two are in the Gospel of John.[5] In other words, thirty of the thirty-two references to Jesus as the Lamb are in the writings of the apostle John! Thus, John saw Jesus as the Lamb of God more clearly than anyone else. Do you want to see Jesus more clearly in the Scriptures? Then focus on His love for you! On another note, Paul, under the inspiration of the Holy Spirit, authored at least thirteen books in the New Testament— more books than any other author in the Old or the New Testament.[6] Why did God choose Paul for this honor? In large part because, like the apostle John, Paul understood and experientially knew the love of God for us in Christ. This will be evident from the Scripture Spotlight section of this chapter. More of God's Word will become alive to you as you focus on His love for you in Christ.

Many Christians are familiar with Ephesians 3:20–21. God *"is able to do exceeding abundantly above all that we ask or think, according to the power that worketh in us"* (Ephesians 3:20). What will cause this power of God to be manifested in your life? The answer is found in the preceding verses, particularly in Ephesians 3:17, 19. In both these verses, the word for "love" in the Greek is agápē and means "divine love" or "the love of God for us in Christ." This is the emphasis in the book of Ephesians as seen in Ephesians 1:4. The answer then is *that ye, being rooted and grounded in love*" (Ephesians 3:17) so you may experientially *"know the love of Christ, which passeth knowledge"* (Ephesians 3:19). Then you will see a fulfilment of Ephesians 3:20 in your lives; you will experience God's abundant power. Focusing on the love of God for you in Christ is a key also to obtaining the full reward of your inheritance, as discussed in chapter 6 of *God Is Calling You: Responding to the Calling of God.*

The Indescribable Measure of God's Love for You

God's love for you is beyond description. Nevertheless, let me attempt to do so by making some statements that will shock you. Get ready! If you are a child of God, the Father loves you just as much as He loves His eternal Son, Jesus Christ. Jesus said, *"I in them, and thou in me, that they may be made perfect in one; and that the world may know that thou hast sent me, and hast loved them, as thou hast loved me"* (John 17:23). When the Father looks at you, He sees Jesus! In terms of quantity, quality and in every way, God the Father loves you just as much as He loves His Son, Jesus Christ! What an awesome truth. Think about it. Dwell on it. Meditate upon it. Get it into your spirit.

The first time the word "love" is mentioned in the Bible is in Genesis 22:2: "*And he said, Take now thy son, thine only son Isaac, whom thou lovest, and get thee into the land of Moriah; and offer him there for a burnt offering upon one of the mountains which I will tell thee of.*" This verse foreshadows the love of God the Father for His Son, the Lord Jesus Christ. It also foreshadows the Father sacrificing His Son Whom He loves. Isaac is a type of Christ in the Bible. God did not want Isaac's blood because his blood was stained with sin. God spared Abraham of this pain, a pain He Himself would and did endure when He sacrificed His Son, Jesus Christ on the cross for us. All through the Bible, we see the love of God the Father for us in Jesus Christ, His Son.

What about the Lord Jesus Christ? What about His love for you? Jesus loves you just as much as the Father loves Him. "*As the Father hath loved me, so have I loved you: continue ye in my love*" (John 15:9). The second time the word "love" is mentioned in the Bible is in Genesis 24:67: "*And Isaac brought her into his mother Sarah's tent, and took Rebekah, and she became his wife; and he loved her: and Isaac was comforted after his mother's death.*" This verse typifies the love of Jesus Christ for His Bride, the Church.

The love of God in Christ is experienced through the Holy Spirit Who also loves you so much (Romans 5:5; 2 Corinthians 6:6, 13:14). "*And hope maketh not ashamed; because the love of God is shed abroad in our hearts by the Holy Ghost which is given unto us*" (Romans 5:5). The Holy Spirit is the Spirit of love (2 Timothy 1:7). "*The grace of the Lord Jesus Christ, and the love of God, and the communion of the Holy Ghost, be with you all. Amen*" (2 Corinthians 13:14). In this verse, all three Persons of the Trinity are involved in loving us! If you are a believer, God's love for you is immutable. There is nothing you can do or not do that will cause Him to love you any more or any less! He loves you with a perfect, unchanging, unchangeable love. True love gives. The Father loves us by giving us His Son (John 3:16). Jesus loves us by giving us His blood and the gift of the Holy Spirit (John 16:7). The Holy Spirit loves us by giving us the gifts of the Spirit (1 Corinthians 12:1–12). It is all the love of God for you! Partake of it freely.

Resting in God's Love for You

The Lord Jesus Christ found His rest by expressing His love for you perfectly on the cross of Calvary. In Matthew 8:19, a scribe came to Jesus and said to Him, "*Master, I will follow thee whithersoever thou goest.*" We read in Matthew 8:20, "*And Jesus saith unto him, The foxes have holes, and the birds of the air have nests; but the Son of man hath not where to lay his head.*" The word for "lay" here in the Greek is κλίνω (*Klino*). It means "to lay," "to rest" and "to be bowed." In His life on earth, Jesus had no place to rest. However, on the cross, "*When Jesus therefore had received the vinegar, he said, It is finished: and he bowed his head, and gave up the ghost*" (John 19:30). The word "bowed" in this verse is the same Greek word κλίνω (*Klino*) used in Matthew 8:20. Finally, Jesus found a place of rest to lay His head on the cross. On the cross, Jesus rested in His love for you and me. Why on the cross? Because, on the cross, He demonstrated His perfect love for you and me (1 John 4:10). This fulfilment of prophecy was given in Zephaniah 3:17: "*The LORD thy God in the midst of thee is mighty; he will save, he will rejoice over thee with joy; he will rest in his love, he will joy over thee with singing.*" Thus, Jesus is resting in His perfect love for you; and He is calling you to rest in His love for you. Amen! Will you rest in His perfect love for you, or will you continue to struggle in your love for Him?

Walking in Love

As stated earlier, the natural man does not have the ability to love with a Godly love. However, when we respond to God's love by receiving the Lord Jesus Christ as Savior and Lord, God, in the Person of the Holy Spirit, comes and indwells us. With Him comes the love of God into our hearts (Romans 5:5). Then we have the capacity to love God and love others with a Godly or agápē love. When we so love others, we are acting just like God for that is Who He is. Our love for others must be grounded in this truth. Furthermore, our love must be surrendered to the God of love as He is the source of agápē love. Otherwise, it is difficult to love others when they do not love us in return or are not worthy of our love. Agápē is God's divine love. It is His perfect, unconditional, unreserved and unchangeable love for us. Agápē love is associated with the love of God.

Loving God involves loving people: the believers as well as those who are lost. The commandment to love other believers was given by our Lord Jesus Himself (John 13:34). Further, Jesus said in John 13:35, "*By this shall all men know that ye are my disciples, if ye have love one to another.*" Regarding loving unbelievers, this truth is demonstrated all through the ministry of the Lord Jesus Christ. Jesus loved the sinners. Likewise, Jesus loved the self-righteous. In Mark 10:17–23, we read the account of a rich ruler who came to Jesus seeking eternal life based on his self-righteousness that was embodied in keeping the law. Far from condemning him, *"Jesus beholding him loved him"* (Mark 10:21). However, this person went away grieved because he was not willing to follow Jesus and pay the cost of discipleship. The point is Jesus still loved him. So are we to love the lost because God loves them. Finally, we are to love ourselves because God loves (*agapao*) us and the Lord Jesus Christ died for us (John 3:16). Thus, on a daily basis, we should love God, love the believers, love those who are lost and love ourselves. The key to walking in love in this manner is to focus on the love of God for us in Christ, as explained earlier in this chapter.

Scripture Spotlight

Our Inseparability from God's Love

We will focus on the love of God for us in Christ as told so vividly and beautifully in Romans 8:35–39. This passage should be interpreted in the context of the preceding two verses where Paul asks two rhetorical questions. In Romans 8:33, the question is who dares to accuse us whom God has chosen as His own? God certainly will not accuse us as He has justified us and has given us right standing with Himself. The question asked in Romans 8:34 is who then will condemn us? Jesus Christ certainly will not condemn us, for He died for us and was raised to life for us. He now is sitting at the right hand of God, the place of highest honor, and interceding for us. The accusations and the condemnation we feel are from Satan to cause us to doubt the love of God. Knowing the truth of Romans 8:35–39 will cause us to reject the accusations and condemnation of the devil, experience God's love for us and walk in victory the Lord Jesus Christ already has won for us.

We live in a world full of uncertainties. There are few certainties in life. One of them is the love of the Lord Jesus Christ for a believer. A beautiful description of this truth is given in our Scripture text. In a verse-by-verse exposition of Romans 8:35–39, it will be clear that nothing, absolutely nothing, can separate us from the love of God that has been manifested perfectly on the cross of Calvary. Please look at these verses in the Bible as you read this book.

Scripture Source: Romans 8:35–39

Verse 35

1. "*The love of Christ*" does not meant the believers' love for Christ but Christ's love for them. In the original Greek, the word used for love is agápē referring, in this context, to God's love for us. Paul's objective here is to strengthen the faith of the believers and comfort them under the various adverse circumstances that are mentioned. The afflictions listed here are apt to lead to doubts and misgivings about the love of Christ and the love of God in Christ. So Paul assures the believers nothing "*shall separate us from the love of Christ*"—that is, Christ's love for the believers.[7]

2. Christ's love for the believers is evident from what He has done for them. Jesus assumed our lowly nature, died on the cross in our place, paid all of our sin debts in full and redeemed us by His shed blood. Furthermore, Christ has prepared a place for all of the believers, is constantly interceding for us, is supplying us with all grace and making us sufficient in every way to do what He has called us to do, that is, to fulfill our calling.

3. Christ's love for us also is manifested through various difficult situations we face in life. Let us look at the situations mentioned and see how we can experience Christ's love through them.

- *"Tribulation"* or "affliction" is designed to strengthen our faith by deepening our trust in God. We can experience Christ's love as we look to Him as the Author and Finisher of our faith (Hebrews 12:2).

- *"Distress"*—whether of body, soul, spirit or circumstances—can help us experience His love when we see His faithfulness as a part of His character (1 Corinthians 1:9) as demonstrated in our lives in the past and as we rely on the promises of His Word. *"If we believe not, yet he abideth faithful: he cannot deny himself"* (2 Timothy 2:13). God is faithful to His covenant and to His promises in the Bible.

- *"Persecution"* from the world is evidence of Christ's love for us. The world hates us because it hates Him and He loves us. We can experience His love by appropriating His grace, as did Paul. *"And he said unto me, My grace is sufficient for thee: for my strength is made perfect in weakness. Most gladly therefore will I rather glory in my infirmities, that the power of Christ may rest upon me"* (2 Corinthians 12:9).

- *"Famine"* denotes want of the necessities of life such as food, drink and shelter. We can experience God's love by experiencing His provision and supply as we look to Him for our needs. *"But my God shall supply all your need according to his riches in glory by Christ Jesus"* (Philippians 4:19).

- *"Nakedness"* implies want of proper clothing. Christ's love is experienced by clothing ourselves in His glory. He took our shame and gave us His glory. This was the case with Adam and Eve before their fall. *"Whom he justified, them he also glorified"* (Romans 8:30).

- *"Peril"* denotes dangers that threaten our lives and make us feel unsafe. Christ's love is manifested in our lives as we look to Him and experience His presence. Safety is not the absence of danger, but it is an awareness of God's presence. *"The beloved of the LORD shall dwell in safety by him; and the LORD shall cover him all the day long, and he shall dwell between his shoulders"* (Deuteronomy 33:12).

- *"Sword"* means death. While death may separate the soul and body, death cannot separate us from the love of Christ, which we will experience for all eternity. Moreover, for a believer, death is the gateway to Heaven; to be absent from the body is to be present with the Lord (2 Corinthians 5:8).

"O death, where is thy sting? O grave, where is thy victory?" (1 Corinthians 15:55).

In sum, neither people nor external things can separate us from the love of Christ. All of these adversities, mentioned in verse 35, separate us from the love people have for us. For instance, as we read in 2 Timothy 4:16–17, when Paul was brought before Nero, all men forsook him; only the Lord stood by him. However, none of them, nor indeed all of them combined, can separate believers from the love Christ has for them. Christ has promised every believer, *"I will never leave thee, nor forsake thee"* (Hebrews 13:5). In contrast, an unbeliever can choose to separate herself or himself from the love of Christ by rejecting Him and His perfect, finished work on the cross.

Verse 36

1. This verse refers to a passage quoted from Psalm 44:22, *"For thy sake we are killed all the day long"* as were the saints and especially the prophets in the Old Testament. *"Killed all the day long"* means they were continually exposed to and expecting death. We are accounted as sheep for the slaughter implies that, like sheep, they were made for the slaughter. Christians were killed during the days of Paul and are put to death even today. This is the way the world looks at believers, as fit only for the slaughter. The world has always been opposed to Christ and His perfect, finished work on the cross and is, therefore, opposed to believers today.

REV. NARESH K. MALHOTRA, PH.D.

In our day and age, not only are Christians facing the dangers of persecution for the sake of Jesus; but in a real sense, there are also dangers of prosperity and worldliness along with dangers of adversity. Christians face dangers of prosperity, materialism and indulgences of all kinds that draw them away from Christ. Jesus said in the parable of the sower in Matthew 13, *"He also that received seed among the thorns is he that heareth the word; and the care of this world, and the deceitfulness of riches, choke the word, and he becometh unfruitful"* (Matthew 13:22). Although believers may be drawn away by riches and worldliness, yet they can never *"separate us from the love of Christ"* that remains constant and unchanging.

Verse 37

1. *"We are more than conquerors"* through Jesus Christ our Lord because of His great love for us. The believers will triumph in all of these afflictions mentioned in verses 35 and 36. We are not only conquerors in spite of them; we conquer all the more because of them. It is all because of the perfect, finished work of our Savior. Jesus triumphed over all principalities and powers. *"And having spoiled principalities and powers, he made a shew of them openly, triumphing over them in it"* (Colossians 2:15). Through Him and in Him, we can triumph over all adverse situations and circumstances and victory is assured. *"Now thanks be unto God, which always causeth us to triumph in Christ, and maketh*

manifest the savour of his knowledge by us in every place" (2 Corinthians 2:14). We are more than conquerors not only over sin and Satan but also over the world and all of its afflictions, adversities and persecutions.

2. We are more than conquerors in other ways also. We get all the spoils of a conqueror without having to do the conquering. How come? Our Savior and Lord Jesus Christ has done the conquering on our behalf, and we inherit all the spoils of His victory.

3. Notice that verse 37 states "*through him that loved us*" and Christ is not mentioned by name. The reason is that, to be more than conquerors, we have to walk in the active realization of Christ's love for us. As we focus on Jesus's love for us, we will get the strength, the courage and the fortitude to emerge victoriously from all of the calamities mentioned in verses 35 and 36. Furthermore, His love will enable us to subdue and exercise dominion over all of these adverse situations and circumstances. The key is that we should feast and focus on the love the Lord Jesus Christ has for us—love He has demonstrated perfectly on the cross. His love for us is invincible, and nothing can stand against it—no demon, difficulty, failure or disappointment (Song of Solomon 8:6–7).

Verses 38–39

1. "*For I am persuaded*" means we can have full persuasion and complete assurance that nothing

whatever could separate us from God's love for us in Christ Jesus. We can be certain of His love because of the death, resurrection and intercession of Christ. None of the things mentioned in verses 38 and 39 is able to separate us from the love of God. These are the following:

- *"Death."* As stated earlier, death separates the soul from the body; but it is not able to separate us from the love of God in Christ.
- *"Life."* This life is mortal, and it cannot separate us from the immortal and everlasting love of God. *"Keep yourselves in the love of God, looking for the mercy of our Lord Jesus Christ unto eternal life"* (Jude 1:21). (See also Jeremiah 31:3.)
- *"Angels nor principalities nor powers."* Here the reference is to evil angels, the devils. Good angels will never attempt to separate us from God. As seen earlier, Jesus Christ has defeated Satan and all of his evil principalities and stripped him of all power on the cross. The good angels will not, the bad shall not; and neither can separate us from the love of Christ.
- *"Things present nor things to come"* whether evil or good. God permits evil or afflictions into our lives to strengthen our faith and to enable us to experience a greater measure of His love for us. On the other hand, all of the good things in the present or the future are gifts of love from Him. We read in James 1:17, *"Every good gift and every perfect gift is*

from above, and cometh down from the Father of lights, with whom is no variableness, neither shadow of turning." Also implied are things in the past that are embodied in the previous verses in Romans 8:33–35. Thus, our sins and failures of yesterday, our fears for today and our worries about tomorrow cannot separate us from the love of God in Christ Jesus, our Lord!

- *"Nor height, nor depth"* encompass Heaven, earth and hell and include any high or low place. *"Any other creature"* includes all of the created beings in Heaven, earth and the sea. None of these can separate us from the love of Christ.

Paul had the assurance that none of these things *"shall be able to separate us from the love of God, which is in Christ Jesus our Lord,"* first and foremost based on the Word of God. Secondly, he had faced all of these situations victoriously through Jesus. Thus, the love of God in Christ was an experiential reality in his life. Anyone can experience this love by coming to the Source, Jesus Christ, the Son of the living God.

Conclusion

Nothing living or dead, angelic or demonic, yesterday, today or tomorrow, high or low, thinkable or unthinkable—absolutely nothing in the whole universe shall be able to separate us from the love of God in Christ Jesus our Lord. This is a direct and positive conclusion of the whole matter: No one and nothing can take Christ from the believer. No one and nothing can take the believer from Christ. That ends the matter!

Author's Account

My first real encounter with the love of God was through Christians after I had been in the United States for about two years.

My First Encounter with the Love of God

I was born into a middle-class Hindu family in India. My parents did their best for their four children. As a middle-class family, they had limited means; but they consistently put the interest of their children above their own. I have very happy memories of my childhood. My father was an officer in the Indian government and was a hardworking and an honest man. He was an intellectual and passed on to me his many qualities. I very much appreciated the love our parents had for us but understood it as familial love. They had to love us because we were their children!

My father put great emphasis on the education of his children. We went to the best private school in the city where my father was posted. These convent schools were run by the Irish missionary brothers and sisters. I had my entire education through high school in such schools. However, I never heard about the love of God or the Gospel even once. Looking back, this is amazing as most of these Irish missionaries—called fathers, brothers and sisters—probably were not born again.

I not only had excellent education through high school but excellent post-secondary education as well. After graduating from St. Columba's High School in New Delhi in 1966, I joined the Indian Institute of Technology, Bombay (IITB) to pursue a degree in mechanical engineering (Bombay is now called Mumbai). The IITs were then, as they are now, the top engineering schools in India—among the best in the world. Graduating from IITB in 1971, I joined the Indian Institute of Management, Ahmedabad (IIMA), another world-class institute and the most prestigious business school in India then and now. I graduated from IIMA in 1973 with a post-graduate diploma in business administration (equivalent of an MBA), placing in the top 10 in my class. Upon graduation, I joined the Administrative Staff College of India as a consultant and worked for them for about two years before coming to the United States.

In all these years in India, I never heard about the love of God. As a devout Hindu, I firmly believed in the Hindu gods and had great reverence for and fear of these gods. I did believe then, if I offended them, they would inflict evil upon me. On the other hand, my obedience to them would bring blessings. The concept that God loved me was foreign to me.

At age twenty-five, I came to the United States to enroll in the doctoral program at the State University of New York at Buffalo. For the first two years, I shared an apartment with two other students from India. That was a positive experience in many ways. All three of us were serious about our studies and spent most of our time studying. Then the landlord sold our apartment. All three of us had to move out, and we went to different places. Not having a car, and given the severity of the winters in Buffalo, I looked for a place to stay close to the campus. International Students Incorporated (ISI) was starting a living center for foreign students very close to the campus. On learning ISI was a Christian organization, I said to myself I have nothing against the Christians. On checking out the place, I found it reasonable and one that would meet my needs. Thus, I moved into the ISI house in the fall of 1977 and became the first occupant of this center at 156 Winspear Avenue, Buffalo that had room for four students and a center director.

The center director, named Steve Settle, was a postdoctoral fellow and a wonderful Christian. He and I became good friends and did many things together such as shopping for groceries and going to the laundromat. Steve had a car and I did not, so it was quite convenient for me to do things with him. Steve genuinely was concerned about my welfare—beyond what I would expect from another friend.

Once a week, ISI conducted a Bible study at the house. While there was no requirement for the house occupants to attend, I attended because, before the Bible study, they served a big meal that was free for the students. Because it would look bad to eat and run, I stayed for the Bible study but seldom to the end. While not understanding much about the Bible, I was impressed by the testimonies of the guest speakers who led these studies.

Another factor that impressed me greatly was the love I received from the elderly ladies who worked with the international students. Three of them—Mrs. Gertrude Springborn, Ms. Ruth Westenfelder and Mrs. Eleanor Blackburn—later became precious to me as my American mothers. These ladies would show great acts of kindness such as baking cakes, bringing apples and giving rides to the students. This love was unselfish on their part, as we students had little, if anything, to offer them. It became obvious to me these ladies knew God and loved people in a way I did not. They had a special relationship with God, as I also could see in Steve. Although I did not realize it then, they were reflecting the love they experienced from God through Jesus Christ. Unknown to me at that time, I was seeing the love of God for me in action. As shared in the next chapter, this significant factor led me to receive Jesus Christ as my Savior and Lord and begin my own glorious journey of walking in God's love for me in Christ.

Quest Questions

Please do some soul searching, and answer the following questions. You need not share your answers with anyone. However, if you so choose, share them with your accountability partner or a person you trust.

- Do I see God's love for me in the creation, redemption and restoration of man?
- Am I consciously aware of and walking in God's perfect and unconditional love for me?
- Do I have a tendency to evaluate God's love for me by looking at my situations and circumstances?
- What is the undeniable proof God loves me?

- Am I trying my best to be worthy and deserving of God's love?
- Do I put forth my best self-effort in trying to love God?
- Do I really believe, in and of myself, I am totally incapable of loving God as the law requires?
- Do I base my beliefs and convictions directly on the Bible or based on what I hear from a preacher, pastor or other sources?
- On a daily basis, do I emphasize my love for God or God's love for me or neither?
- Do I really know, based on the Bible, I am a beloved child of God in Christ?
- Is the conscious awareness and experience of God's love for me in Christ motivating me to walk by faith?
- Do I put in a lot of self-effort to make my faith work?
- What do I believe is the greatest key to living this life?
- Do I fail to attack sin because it appears to be invincible?
- How successful am I in fighting temptation and sin?
- When I sin, do I run to Jesus or run away from Him?
- How close is my walk with God? How can I walk closer to Him?
- Do I love God and other people?
- How well am I following Jesus?

- How do I determine God's will in a particular situation?
- Do I see Jesus Christ for Who He really is: "*the Lamb of God, which taketh away the sin of the world*"?
- Am I fearful? Why? How do I deal with fear?
- Am I experiencing God's abundant power in my life?
- Do I really believe the Father loves me just as much as He loves His Son, Jesus Christ?
- Do I really believe Jesus loves me as much as the Father loves Him?
- Am I resting in Christ's love for me? How?
- Am I secure in Christ's love for me, or do I fear losing His love?
- Do I doubt the love of God when I am facing difficult situations and circumstances?
- Do I have a tendency to view myself as a conqueror, a winner or a loser?
- Am I convinced nothing, absolutely nothing, can separate me from the love of God?

You can evaluate your answers to these questions in light of the following principles and precepts.

Principles and Precepts

- A manifestation of God's love for us is seen in the creation, redemption and restoration of man (Genesis 1:26–27, John 3:16, Revelation 22:1–5).

- God's love for you is unconditional, unchanging, unchangeable, immeasurable and incomparable and is defined by the term agápē (John 3:16, 1 John 3:16).
- You are totally unworthy and undeserving of God's love. There is nothing you can do or not do to merit His love (1 John 3:1).
- God is love, and that is His nature and the expression of His being (1 John 4:8, 16).
- No one has been able to love God as the law requires (Romans 3:19–20).
- If you break even a single commandment of the law, you are guilty of breaking the whole law (James 2:10).
- In the New Covenant of grace, the emphasis is not on your love for God but on God's love for you (1 John 4:10).
- Never evaluate God's love for you by looking at your situations and circumstances (Romans 8:35–39).
- God has demonstrated perfectly His perfect love for you by sending His Son, Jesus Christ to die on the cross for you (1 John 3:16, 1 John 4:10).
- The positive, undeniable, irrefutable proof of God's love for you is the cross of Calvary (1 John 3:16).
- God created you from agápē love, for agápē love and to agápē love, as He made you in His image (Genesis 1:26).

- Agápē love does not come normally and naturally to us; it comes as we, through the Holy Spirit, experience God's love for us (Romans 5:5).
- Only as you experience God's love for you in Christ are you able to love God and love other people with agápē love. You cannot express love unless you first experience love, the love of God for you in Christ (1 John 4:11, 19).
- By love, faith is activated, is working, is producing fruit and is perfected (Galatians 5:6).
- For your faith to work, you must realize how much God loves you. The more you realize the love of God in Christ, the more your faith will work for you (Galatians 5:6).
- The greatest key to living this life is to realize God loves you and He has demonstrated perfectly that love in Jesus Christ, His Son (1 Corinthians 13:13, 1 John 3:16).
- God's love for you is the key to experiencing victory over sin and temptation (Galatians 5:6, 1 John 5:4).
- Always base your beliefs and convictions on the Word of God as you see it for yourself directly in the Bible—never based on what you hear from a preacher, pastor or someone else or on any other source. That way, it will be more difficult for Satan to cause you to doubt God's Word and His love (Genesis 2:16–17, Romans 10:17).
- If you are a believer, you are a beloved child of God in Christ (2 Thessalonians 2:13).

- Never boast of your love for God; always boast of how much Jesus Christ loves you. You are the disciple whom Jesus loves (John 13:23; 19:26; 20:2; 21:7, 20).
- To determine God's will in a particular situation, first, lean on Jesus's breast, that is, acknowledge His love for you and then make your request (Exodus 28:30, John 13:25).
- As you boast of Christ's love for you, then you will walk closer with God (John 21:20).
- When we sin, we should focus on the love of Jesus for us and that will cause us to run to Jesus rather than run away from Him (John 21:7).
- It is a good thing to tell God you love Him. However, acknowledge and thank God for His love for you twice as much (John 21:15–17).
- When you focus on the love Christ has for you, then you will follow Him even subconsciously (John 21:19–20).
- When you focus on God's love, you will be able to see Jesus Christ for Who He is, as *the Lamb of God, which taketh away the sin of the world*" (John 1:29).
- As you experience God's love for you, then you will overcome fear (2 Chronicles 20:21, Acts 12:6, 1 John 4:18).
- As you experience Christ's love, God will do exceeding abundantly above all you ask or think or dream (Ephesians 3:17–21).

- If you are a believer, God the Father loves you just as much as He loves His Son, Jesus Christ (Genesis 22:2, John 17:23).
- If you are a believer, Jesus loves you just as much as the Father loves Him (John 15:9).
- Jesus Christ is resting in His love for you. Likewise, you should rest in His love for you (Zephaniah 3:17, Matthew 8:20, John 19:30).
- We should love God, love people and love ourselves (Mark 12:30–31).
- God's love for you is unchanging and unchangeable—even when you are facing difficult situations, trials and tribulations (Romans 8:35).
- I am a winner in Christ and through the Lord Jesus Christ. I can experience victory in any situation or circumstance by focusing on Christ's love for me (Romans 8:37).
- Nothing, absolutely nothing, can separate us from the love of God for us in Christ (Romans 8:38–39).

Life Lesson

The most important thing in life is to know, experience and walk in the unconditional, unchanging, unchangeable and perfect love of God for us in Christ.

Prayer Power

Dear God, the Bible says You love us with an unconditional, unchanging, unchangeable and perfect love that You have demonstrated by sending Your Son, Jesus Christ, to die on the cross for us. God, I want to know and experience Your love. I want it to become the guiding principle in my life. I ask You to show me how I can appropriate Your love for me in Jesus Christ. In Jesus's Name, I pray. Amen!

Message Ministry

You can access the audio message for this chapter by using CallingYou as the password at

https://www.globalevangelisticministries.net/Calling1-Chapter1.

CHAPTER 2

The Calling to Salvation in the Lord
Jesus Christ: Your Greatest Miracle

"For whosoever shall call upon the name
of the Lord shall be saved."

—Romans 10:13

Preamble and Preview

Of all the miracles documented in the Holy Bible, undoubtedly the greatest is the miracle of salvation in the Lord Jesus Christ, the eternal Son of the Living God. This is the one and only way to experience God's love discussed in chapter 1. This chapter discusses the "Central Concepts" of the need for salvation, God's plan for salvation, God's calling to salvation and the miracle of salvation. In "Scripture Spotlight," we look at the salvation of blind Bartimaeus and draw several insights into the miracle of salvation and the other miracles God has for us. "Author's Account" gives personal testimony of my miracle of salvation. The following section, "Quest Questions," contains several questions that I hope will cause you to reflect on your life as it relates to your salvation experience. Then there are "Principles and Precepts" you can apply to experience the miracle of salvation God has for you. These principles are universal, and you can apply them easily—regardless of your situation or circumstance. "Life Lesson" contains the most important lesson you can learn with respect to salvation in Jesus Christ. "Prayer Power" contains an effectual, Scriptural prayer you are encouraged to pray in order to personally experience the greatest of all miracles. The final section, "Message Ministry," gives a link to an audio message you are exhorted to hear.

Central Concepts

Every person is born with a sinful nature and has the need for salvation so she or he can experience the love of God in Christ as discussed in chapter 1. The good news is God loves you and has a wonderful plan of salvation. He sent His Son, the Lord Jesus Christ, to pay fully the penalty for all of your sins—past, present and future—on the cross. God raised Jesus Christ from the dead, and He now offers salvation as a gift. God calls every person to receive this gift of salvation in Jesus Christ. This is the greatest miracle anyone can receive from God. These concepts will be discussed in more detail.

The Need for Salvation

The Bible says God created man in His image and gave man a free will. Man was and is free to worship God or to sin against Him. The first man, Adam, chose to sin against God by knowingly, willfully and deliberately disobeying Him. Thus, sin entered into the human race. Since then, every person, who has been born of a human father, is born with a sin nature. Then the sin nature manifests itself in acts of sin. The Bible says every person is a sinner. *"For all have sinned, and come short of the glory of God"* (Romans 3:23). Sin separates man from a righteous, Holy God. *"Wherefore, as by one man sin entered into the world, and death by sin; and so death passed upon all men, for that all have sinned"* (Romans 5:12).

In the book of Romans chapters 5–8 the word *sin* appears forty-one times. Of these, forty times it is used as a noun and only one time as a verb.[1] You are not a sinner because you sin; you sin because you are a sinner. You are born a sinner; you are born with a sin nature you inherited from Adam. Everyone born of a man is born with a sin nature—that is all of us. Only Jesus Christ, Who was born of a woman, was born without a sin nature. Furthermore, He did not commit even a single sin so that He could be our Savior as He was *"without blemish and without spot"* (1 Peter 1:19). Amen! Since every person is a sinner, every person has a need to be saved, to have forgiveness of sins and to be reconciled with God. Seeing yourself as a sinner is critical to seeing your need for salvation and being saved.

God's Plan of Salvation

God loves you; He loves the whole world. As emphasized in chapter 1, God is love (1 John 4:8, 16). God is also a righteous, Holy God. He cannot and will not condone sin. He must judge and punish sin (Exodus 34:7; Ezekiel 18:4, 20). Every sinner is charged with and accountable for her or his sins; they must be punished. However, we are all sinners and cannot pay for our sins. God realized that and sent His only begotten Son, the Lord Jesus Christ, in human flesh on this earth. Jesus Christ was born of Virgin Mary. He had no earthly father. Thus, Jesus Christ was born without a sin nature. Furthermore, He did not commit any sin. The Bible says Jesus Christ was *"without sin"* (Hebrews 4:15), *"knew no sin"* (2 Corinthians 5:21), *"did no sin"* (1 Peter 2:22), *"and in him is no sin"* (1 John 3:5). This reflects a picture of Jesus Christ as the Passover Lamb as described in Exodus 12. This Old Testament passage presents a shadow or a type of the perfect, sinless Lamb of God. Israel was instructed by God, *"Your lamb shall be without blemish"* (Exodus 12:5), that is, *"without sin"* (Hebrews 4:15). *"You must roast the whole lamb over a fire. The lamb must still have its head, legs, and inner parts"* (Exodus 12:9, Easy-to-Read Version). The head points to Jesus *"knew no sin"* (2 Corinthians 5:21), the legs point to *"did no sin"* (1 Peter 2:22), and the "inner parts" point to *"and in him is no sin"* (1 John 3:5).[2] This virtue uniquely qualified the Lord Jesus Christ to make atonement for our sins. One sinner cannot atone for the sins of another. Christ was sinless, the spotless Lamb of God. *"The next day John seeth Jesus coming unto him, and saith, Behold the Lamb of God, which taketh away the sin of the world"* (John 1:29).

Jesus Christ died on the cross to make full atonement for all of our sins—past, present and future. All of our sins were laid upon Him. He paid for them by His blood and by His death on the cross for us. This is the clear teaching of both the Old Testament and the New Testament. *"All we like sheep have gone astray; we have turned everyone to his own way; and the LORD hath laid on him the iniquity of us all"* (Isaiah 53:6). *"Who gave himself for us, that he might redeem us from all iniquity, and purify unto himself a peculiar people, zealous of good works"* (Titus 2:14). By making the full payment for our sins, Jesus purchased our forgiveness, our pardon and a place for us in Heaven that He now offers as a gift.

Jesus had to shed His precious, sinless blood because *"without shedding of blood is no remission"* of sins (Hebrews 9:22). But why did Jesus have to die on the cross? This question demands an answer since the capital punishment of Israel during that time was stoning and not crucifixion. (See John 8:4–7, Acts 7:58–60.) Jesus shed His blood and died on the cross because of the law, *"he that is hanged is accursed of God"* (Deuteronomy 21:23) and *"for it is written, Cursed is every one that hangeth on a tree"* (Galatians 3:13), the tree here referring to the cross. God wanted to redeem us from every curse of the law; so Jesus went to the cross, *"being made a curse for us."* On the cross, Jesus took all of our curses of the law upon Himself and gave us all of His blessings! While Christ could have shed His blood and died in other ways for the forgiveness of our sins, He had to do so on the cross to redeem us from every curse of the law. The moment you receive Jesus Christ as your Savior and Lord, every curse in your life is destroyed and all of the blessings of God will come upon you! (Galatians 3:29).

God's Call to Salvation

Salvation is freely available to all—a gift available universally. "*For whosoever shall call upon the name of the Lord shall be saved*" (Romans 10:13; also see Acts 2:21). While salvation is available to all, not all will be saved. Only those who receive this gift by faith will be saved. "*For by grace are ye saved through faith; and that not of yourselves: it is the gift of God: Not of works, lest any man should boast*" (Ephesians 2:8–9). To receive salvation, a person must confess she or he is a sinner, that Jesus Christ is the Son of God and the risen Savior, repent of personal sins and receive Jesus Christ as personal Savior and Lord.

Your only part in salvation is to come to Jesus, confessing and repenting of your sins and believing in Him in your heart. You have to do this transaction with understanding and as an act of your free will. You must choose to put your faith and trust in Jesus Christ as your Savior and Lord. It is not something that can be forced upon you. Jesus addressed this issue in John 6:28–29: "*Then said they unto him, What shall we do, that we might work the works of God? Jesus answered and said unto them, This is the work of God, that ye believe on him whom he hath sent.*"

Confessing to Christ you are a sinner is the first step. When returning to Canaan, Jacob wrestled with God, as we read in Genesis 32:22–32. Rather, it would be more accurate to say God wrestled with Jacob. The Angel Who wrestled with him was the Son of man, Who is also the Angel of the Covenant and the Son of God, the Lord Jesus Christ.[3] In Genesis 32:27, God asked Jacob, "*What is thy name? And he said, Jacob.*" Why did God ask Jacob his name when He surely knew it? He wanted Jacob to confess who he really was—a deceiver or supplanter. Earlier, Jacob had deceived his father to steal the blessing and had said, "*I am Esau thy firstborn*" (Genesis 27:19). God wanted Jacob to see himself as God saw him. Now he had to tell the truth to God. Once he did, God blessed him and changed his name to Israel (Genesis 32:28). Here is a general principle: God will not bless you until you see yourself as God sees you (Matthew 4:17, Acts 2:38). This double-edged sword works both ways. If you are not saved by the blood of Christ, to get God's blessings, you must see yourself a sinner. Jesus said in Luke 5:32, "*I came not to call the righteous, but sinners to repentance.*" "Righteous" in this verse refers to the self-righteous, to those who think of themselves as righteous when God says they are sinners; see the New Living Translation. As long as you cling to your self-righteousness, you cannot experience the blessings of salvation in Jesus Christ. On the other hand, if you are saved by His blood, you must see yourself as a beloved child of God in whom He is well pleased, as discussed in chapter 1. You must see yourself as God sees you in Christ. Only then can you receive all of God's blessings in full measure.

I should emphasize there are no good works you can do to obtain, earn, deserve or merit your salvation. Salvation is by grace alone, through faith alone, in Christ alone. Period! You cannot add anything to the perfect, finished work of the Lord Jesus Christ on the cross; and you cannot take anything away from it. In this respect, the Christian faith is very different from all of the other religions that teach essentially that salvation is earned through good works. In sharp contrast, according to the Bible, good works are use-less for salvation. No amount of good works can ever save you. Jesus Christ is the only way to salvation; He is the only way to God (Acts 4:12). *"Jesus saith unto him, I am the way, the truth, and the life: no man cometh unto the Father, but by me"* (John 14:6). As Peter put it, *"Neither is there salva-tion in any other: for there is none other name under heaven given among men, whereby we must be saved"* (Acts 4:12). To obtain salvation, pray the prayer given toward the end of this chapter in the section entitled "Prayer Power."

The Miracle of Salvation

Why is salvation the greatest miracle? According to the Bible, God exists in three persons: God the Father, God the Son and God the Holy Spirit. When a person confesses to be a sinner, repents and prays to receive the Lord Jesus Christ as Savior and Lord, God, in the Person of the Holy Spirit, comes and permanently indwells that person. That person is saved, born again, becomes a child of God; and her or his name is written in the Lamb's Book of Life. All of these terms mean the same thing, denoting the person now has been reconciled to God, is in right standing with God and has forgiveness of sins. The power and the indwelling presence of the Holy Spirit make the person a new creation in Christ. *"Therefore if any man be in Christ, he is a new crea-ture: old things are passed away; behold, all things are become new"* (2 Corinthians 5:17). That person becomes new. I have seen dramatic changes in some people the moment they become Christians. Some have been set free instanta-neously from alcohol, tobacco, drugs, abusive behavior and other forms of dysfunctional behavior. All experience great peace. *"Therefore being justified by faith, we have peace with God through our Lord Jesus Christ"* (Romans 5:1).

While some changes are immediate, others take place over time as sanctification becomes an experiential reality in our lives. Salvation is a one-time act, but the manifestation of sanctification is a lifelong process. Sanctification is the process of growing in our faith and in our walk with the Lord Jesus Christ and being conformed to His image. As we grow in our faith by reading the Bible, seeing the glory of the Lord Jesus Christ in the Scriptures, praying, serving and leading obedient and Godly lives, we become more and more like our Savior and Lord Jesus Christ. We experience the power and presence of God in our lives on a day-by-day, even moment-by-moment basis. We can talk to God, hear His voice and experience His presence much like we experience the presence of humans. We are never lonely and never alone. God is always with us. *"He hath said, I will never leave thee, nor forsake thee"* (Hebrews 13:5). This is the greatest of all miracles that a mere human can have constant fellowship with Almighty God, the Creator and Sustainer of this entire universe. Anyone can experience it by calling upon the Name of the Lord Jesus Christ and receiving Him as Savior and Lord. If you have not already done so, I urge you to do it now by praying the prayer given toward the end of this chapter.

The Past, Present and Future Tense of Salvation

The Bible teaches humans consist of three parts: spirit, soul and body. *"And the very God of peace sanctify you wholly; and I pray God your whole spirit and soul and body be preserved blameless unto the coming of our Lord Jesus Christ"* (1 Thessalonians 5:23). Salvation in Jesus Christ, the Son of God and our Savior and Lord provides redemption for the whole man. It caters to our spirit, soul and body. It provides:

Forgiveness for our spirit
Deliverance for our soul
Healing for our body

In the short passage given in Matthew 8:2–4, a leper receives all three: forgiveness, deliverance and healing. *"And, behold, there came a leper and worshipped him, saying, Lord, if thou wilt, thou canst make me clean"* (Matthew 8:2). By worshipping Him, addressing Jesus as Lord and acknowledging His ability to heal leprosy, the leper was receiving Jesus as his Savior and Lord. Until the coming of Jesus, no Israeli leper had been cleansed. Miriam's leprosy was temporary and lasted only seven days (Numbers 12:15). Naaman, who was cleansed of leprosy, was a Syrian and not an Israeli. The cleansing of an Israeli leper was prophesied as a sign of the Messiah. Jesus Himself cited this truth to the disciples of John the Baptist as a proof that He was the Messiah (Matthew 11:5, Luke 7:22). Thus, the leper clearly received Jesus as his Messiah and Lord and obtained forgiveness for his spirit. What was the response of the Messiah? *"And Jesus put forth his hand, and touched him, saying, I will; be thou clean. And immediately his leprosy was cleansed*" (Matthew 8:3). Up to that point, lepers were ostracized by the Jewish people. So why did Jesus touch him when He could have spoken the Word and healed the leper? Jesus touched Him because the leper had not been touched for a long time by anyone. In all likelihood, the leper thought of himself as an untouchable. Jesus wanted to deliver his soul from that poor self-image and self-concept. Thirdly, Jesus imparted physical healing to his body: "*And immediately his leprosy was cleansed.*" In the "Scripture Spotlight" section, we will see a blind man also receive all three miracles from Jesus.

I should emphasize the redemptive work of Christ is perfect, complete and finished. "*When Jesus therefore had received the vinegar, he said, It is finished: and he bowed his head, and gave up the ghost*" (John 19:30). Of course, Jesus arose from the dead and is seated at the right hand of God the Father. "*So then after the Lord had spoken unto them, he was received up into heaven, and sat on the right hand of God*" (Mark 16:19; see also Colossians 3:1, Hebrews 10:12). The reason Christ is sitting down is because His work of redemption is complete. Sitting signifies completion. In contrast, in the Tabernacle of the Old Testament, there was no place or provision for the priests to sit down as their work was never complete. (See Hebrews 10:10–14 for a New Testament perspective on this truth.) The price for our total redemption is paid already by the Lord Jesus Christ in full; actually, He made an overpayment for it. The price of the precious blood of Jesus is worth far more than the cost of all the sins of all mankind! However, in terms of the manifestation of Christ's finished work in our lives, there is the past, present and future tense of our salvation. Our spirits have been saved. Our souls are being saved; that is why we are admonished to renew our minds with the Word of God. *"And be not conformed to this world: but be ye transformed by the renewing of your mind, that ye may prove what is that good, and acceptable, and perfect, will of God"* (Romans 12:2). Our soul consists of our mind, will and emotions. Our bodies will be saved in the future when we receive resurrected and glorified bodies at the rapture. Christ's resurrection was a bodily resurrection so that we, who are believers, can look forward to a bodily resurrection (Romans 8:23, Philippians 3:20–21, 1 Corinthians 15:35–55). The future redemption of the believers' bodies is clearly mentioned in the Scriptures, for example, in Romans 8:23: *"Even we ourselves groan within ourselves, waiting for the adoption, to wit, the redemption of our body."*

The past, present and future of our salvation is seen in the following passage:

> *"For the grace of God that bringeth salvation hath appeared to all men,*
> *Teaching us that, denying ungodliness and worldly lusts, we should live soberly, righteously, and godly, in this present world;*
> *Looking for that blessed hope, and the glorious appearing of the great God and our Saviour Jesus Christ"* (Titus 2:11–13).

This grace already has appeared. When did it appear? It appeared at the first coming of Jesus Christ. *"For the law was given by Moses, but grace and truth came by Jesus Christ"* (John 1:17). Salvation here is referring to our saved spirit.

Teaching denotes the present and refers to the soul being taught at the present time. Taught what? *"That, denying ungodliness and worldly lusts, we should live soberly, righteously, and godly, in this present world"* (Titus 2:12). This is the process of sanctification. Although we have been sanctified once and for all by the Lord Jesus Christ by His finished work on the cross (see Hebrews 10:10–14), sanctification has to be made an experiential reality in our lives on a daily basis. Hope is always in the future. The blessed hope refers to the second coming of Christ and has two parts: (1) the rapture and (2) Jesus coming to the earth as Judge. We will receive new bodies at the rapture, as given in Philippians 3:20–21. I should emphasize again the redemptive work of Christ is perfect, complete and finished. The manifestation of His finished work in our lives is what I am discussing. God's provision for our spirit, soul and body is discussed further in chapter 4 of *God Is Calling You: Responding to the Calling of God.* Let us now see how these concepts are illustrated by the life of blind Bartimaeus.

Scripture Spotlight

The Salvation of Blind Bartimaeus

The salvation of blind Bartimaeus is described in Mark 10:46–52. It also is discussed in Luke 18:35–43 and Matthew 20:29–34. Matthew mentions two blind men, whereas Mark and Luke mention one. They do not say, however, there was no more than one. They mention one because he probably was better known. We will focus here on the account in Mark.

A verse-by-verse exposition of Mark 10:46–52 reveals blind Bartimaeus received not one but three miracles. First, he received the miracle of forgiveness, forgiveness for his spirit, by putting his faith and trust in Jesus Christ as Savior and Lord. Then he received the deliverance of his soul: deliverance from poor self-image and low self-esteem he carried as a blind beggar. Third, he received the miracle of physical sight, the healing of his body; and he was able to see. As seen in the case of Bartimaeus, salvation in Jesus Christ provides forgiveness for your spirit, deliverance for your soul and healing for your body. Please look at these verses in the Bible as you read this book.

Scripture Source: Mark 10:46–52

Verse 46

I will make ten points based on verse 46.

1. *"And they came to Jericho."* Jesus had come to Jericho with His disciples. This city was built under a curse. *"And Joshua adjured them at that time, saying, Cursed be the man before the LORD, that riseth up and buildeth this city Jericho: he shall lay the foundation thereof in his firstborn, and in his youngest son shall he set up the gates of it"* (Joshua 6:26). Yet Christ honored it with His presence, for the Gospel takes away the curse. The Bible says, *"Christ hath redeemed us from the curse of the law"* (Galatians 3:13).

2. *"He went out of Jericho with his disciples."* Jesus was leaving this place; He was passing through Jericho. In New Testament times, when Jesus visited, Jericho was a rich, flourishing town and a trade hub. It was known for its palm trees—a sort of resort town where the rich and famous stayed. Jesus could have well stayed at Jericho and enjoyed its luxuries, but He chose to go on. To fulfill your calling, you not only have to say yes to things that will propel you toward your goal but have to be willing to say no to things that will keep you from your goal, keep you from your destiny! Too many Christians do not fulfill their calling because they are ensnared by the Jerichos in their lives. These Jerichos could be their work, hobbies, conveniences, comforts, pleasures or a variety of worldly things.

3. This is the only record of Jesus visiting Jericho. Thus, this was the first time Jesus had been in Jericho; it was the last time He would be there. He was passing through it on His way to Jerusalem— on His last journey to Jerusalem, a little more than a week before the crucifixion. Thus, this was the first and last opportunity Bartimaeus had to receive from God. For some people when they hear the Gospel, it might well be the first and last opportunity—the only opportunity to receive the salvation Jesus Christ alone offers. It is so important preachers realize this truth and avail of every opportunity to proclaim the message of salvation. It is equally important for hearers to take the Gospel message

seriously and give heed as it might be their last opportunity to receive this gift from God.

4. *"Blind Bartimaeus, the son of Timaeus, sat by the highway side begging."* Bartimaeus was an insignificant blind beggar, sitting at the gate of Jericho. He did not even have a proper name. "Bartimaeus" simply means "son of Timaeus"! Bartimaeus often was ignored by people, as were all beggars. And yet Jesus, the Son of God, stopped in His walk and called out to him. Jesus had compassion for him and responded to his need. He treated Bartimaeus with dignity, respect and acceptance. Jesus granted him the desire of his heart and gave him spiritual and physical sight. Like Bartimaeus, the Lord Jesus Christ loves, respects and accepts you just as you are! Come to Him in faith, as Bartimaeus did.

5. *"And a great number of people."* This verse states a great number of people followed Jesus, but only one received miracles. So it is today. Many people are seemingly following Jesus, but very, very few are receiving miracles. Why was Bartimaeus the only one to receive miracles; why not the others? Because he sought the Miracle Worker and not the miracles. He was seeking the Lord Jesus Christ in faith. Why am I saying that emphatically? Many times, to figure out what is happening at the beginning of an account, one has to read the end. As seen in verse 52, after Bartimaeus received the miracles of forgiveness of sins, deliverance and physical sight, he followed the Lord Jesus Christ. *"And Jesus said unto him, Go thy way; thy faith hath*

made thee whole. And immediately he received his sight, and followed Jesus in the way" (Mark 10:52). After receiving his sight, Bartimaeus did not do his own thing; he did not go into the world and seek its worldly pleasures. Rather, he followed the Lord Jesus Christ. This shows he was seeking the Lord Jesus Christ. The problem with many in the Church is they are seeking miracles, not the Miracle Worker. They are off on a tangent! Nowhere in the Bible are we told to seek miracles. However, time and again, we are admonished to seek God, to give the Lord Jesus Christ the first place in our lives. The Lord Jesus Christ said, "*But seek ye first the kingdom of God, and his righteousness; and all these things shall be added unto you*" (Matthew 6:33).

6. Verse 46 states Bartimaeus was "*blind.*" He could not see. Whether he was born blind or became blind later, we do not know, for the Bible does not tell us. However, we know from Scriptures some people are born blind. For example, in John 9, Jesus healed a man who was born blind.

7. Furthermore, Bartimaeus was "*begging*"; he was a beggar. Begging for money, food and alms. Looking to man for help. "Can some man give me some money? Can some man give me some food? Can some man give me some help?" If he would have continued that way, he would have remained destitute, helpless and without hope. The Bible says, "*Vain is the help of man. Through God we shall do valiantly*" (Psalm 60:11–12). "*Thus saith the LORD; cursed [be] the man that trusteth in man,*

and maketh flesh his arm, and whose heart departeth from the LORD" (Jeremiah 17:5). Who are you trusting in today? Yourself, your money, wealth, job, position, family, friends or church? You need to take your trust off these things and focus upon the Lord Jesus Christ and trust in Him alone.

8. Bartimaeus "*sat.*" Too many people are sitting down and watching as spectators from the sidelines. They are not involved as actors in the Kingdom of God. They are not doing anything to advance the Kingdom of God. Rather, they are criticizing from the sidelines those children who are standing up for the Lord Jesus Christ and for the principles of His Word. Are you one of them?

9. Bartimaeus sat *"by the highway."* Unfortunately, he was on the wrong highway. Jesus talked about two highways in Matthew 7:13–14. He said, *"Broad is the way, that leadeth to destruction"*; and many people are on that highway. *"Narrow is the way, which leadeth unto life"*; and few people are on that way. Bartimaeus was on the broad way leading to destruction and eternal separation from God in hell. If Bartimaeus would have continued along this way, he would have remained blind and a beggar and would have died and gone to hell.

10. Bartimaeus, in this state, represents the condition of every person living her or his life apart from the Lord Jesus Christ. Every person is born spiritually blind. The cause of spiritual blindness is sin. The Bible says every person is a sinner (Romans 3:23). Spiritual blindness prevents a person from relat-

ing to God and from worshipping God. "*In whom the god of this world hath blinded the minds of them which believe not, lest the light of the glorious Gospel of Christ, who is the image of God, should shine unto them*" (2 Corinthians 4:4). Spiritually, every person apart from Christ is a beggar. Regardless of how much wealth, possessions, education, fame or resources you may have, if you do not know the Lord Jesus Christ as Savior and Lord, you are a beggar. Such people include those who belong to a church. Jesus Christ told the church at Laodicea: "*Because thou sayest, I am rich, and increased with goods, and have need of nothing; and knowest not that thou art wretched, and miserable, and poor, and blind, and naked*" (Revelation 3:17). Apart from the Lord Jesus Christ, spiritually, every person is blind and every person is a beggar. This is not meant to condemn you. The Bible is not one of condemnation but redemption, salvation and deliverance. The Gospel means good news, not bad news. The good news is the Lord Jesus Christ loves you and wants to save you and reconcile you to God the Father. He wants to give you spiritual sight, deliverance and spiritual riches.

Verse 47

1. "*And when he heard that it was Jesus of Nazareth, he began to cry out.*" When Bartimaeus heard Jesus was passing by, he made a momentous decision. He took his focus off his circumstances, his situa-

tion and his helplessness; and he focused upon the Lord Jesus Christ. He cried out to the Lord. In the Bible, whenever people cried out to the Lord, He responded. *"O Lord my God, I cried unto thee, and thou hast healed me"* (Psalm 30:2).

2. The verb *"to cry out"* in the Greek is present, active, infinitive meaning Bartimaeus kept crying over and over to Jesus. Thus, the blind man was very persistent in his faith. As Jesus taught in the parable of the unjust judge, persistent prayer is a demonstration of faith in God. While at times God may delay His answers, He always will act decisively and justly with respect to His people (Luke 18:1–8).

3. *"Thou Son of David."* The content of the cry of Bartimaeus is all important. He confessed Jesus as Lord. He believed and confessed Jesus as *"Thou Son of David,"* a title reserved for the Messiah, the Son of God. Jesus was the fulfillment of both the Abrahamic and Davidic covenants (Matthew 1:17). Thereby, Bartimaeus was believing and confessing Jesus as the Son of God, as the Messiah.

4. Bartimaeus approached God humbly; he asked for mercy. God does not owe salvation or anything else to anyone. It is all His grace and His mercy. Grace is the free, unmerited love and favor of God, the spring and source of all the benefits we receive from Him. Mercy is benevolence and tenderness of heart that leads God to treat a sinner better than she or he deserves. *"It is of the LORD'S mercies that we are not consumed, because his compassions fail*

not" (Lamentations 3:22). Like this blind beggar, we should approach God humbly when we pray.

5. "*Have mercy on me.*" He asked for mercy. Why did Bartimaeus ask for mercy? Because, in the Scriptures, mercy is closely linked to the covenant of God. Jesus Christ came "*to perform the mercy promised to our fathers, and to remember his holy covenant*" (Luke 1:72). This mercy was prophesied in the Old Testament. Isaiah 53 is all about the cross; and subsequently, Isaiah 54:10 says, "*For the mountains shall depart, and the hills be removed; but my kindness shall not depart from thee, neither shall the covenant of my peace be removed, saith the LORD that hath mercy on thee.*" Jesus Christ was crowned with thorns so we might be crowned "*with loving kindness and tender mercies*" (Psalm 103:4).

6. Bartimaeus received his first miracle, the miracle of forgiveness. His spirit was saved. It must be noted only the belief and confession Bartimaeus made, that is, believing and confessing Jesus Christ as Lord, Messiah and the Son of God will save a person. Any confession less than that is no good. Many people believe Jesus Christ was a good teacher, a prophet; and some even accept Him as a god in the multitude of gods in their polytheistic religious framework. These kinds of confessions will not lead to salvation. "*That if thou shalt confess with thy mouth the Lord Jesus, and shalt believe in thine heart that God hath raised him from the dead, thou shalt be saved. For with the heart man belie-veth unto righteousness; and with the mouth confes-*

sion is made unto salvation" (Romans 10:9–10). Bartimaeus received his first miracle, the miracle of salvation in Jesus Christ. He obtained forgiveness for his spirit.

7. The Jewish religious leaders missed the fundamental truth that Jesus is the Son of David. However, this blind man saw this truth, embraced it and was blessed by it. Although physically blind, Bartimaeus has the spiritual sight to see Jesus for Who He really is: the Son of God and the Savior of mankind! So it is even today. The wise of this world are made blind and stumble over the Gospel, but those who confess their spiritual blindness see the truth and receive Jesus Christ as their Savior and Lord. As Paul said in 1 Corinthians 1:23, "*But we preach Christ crucified, unto the Jews a stumblingblock, and unto the Greeks foolishness.*" This is what Jesus meant in John 9:39, "*And Jesus said, For judgment I am come into this world, that they which see not might see; and that they which see might be made blind.*"

Verse 48

1. "*Many charged him that he should hold his peace*" (Mark 10:48). Bartimaeus had taken a stand of faith, but the people opposed him. The people were saying, "Keep quiet, Bartimaeus. Hush!" The word "*charged*" is strong and means to "censure severely." I imagine some were even rude and admonished him by saying, "Shut up, you blind

beggar!" Whenever you take a stand of faith, expect opposition from the people around you, opposition from without the church and, sometimes, opposition from within the church. People will oppose you. Satan will try to raise his ugly head one more time before God gives His miracle. But you must stand firm in faith; otherwise, you will lose the miracle(s) God has for you.

2. *"He cried the more a great deal, Thou Son of David, have mercy on me."* Bartimaeus stood firm in his faith. He did not hold his peace, that is, he did not keep quiet. Rather, *"he cried the more a great deal"* (Mark 10:48). If this world will try to shout down your faith, you shout down the world with the Word of God. If the devil will try to shout you down, you shout down the devil with the Word of God. Be sure you are shouting and proclaiming the Word of God and not your words. Bartimaeus stuck to his Scriptural confession, calling Jesus the *"Son of David."* Our words have no power. In contrast, the Word of God has the power of God in it and behind it. We must hold fast to our confession and the profession of our faith. *"Let us hold fast the profession of our faith without wavering; (for he is faithful that promised)"* (Hebrews 10:23). When the devil whispers in your ears, "Quit trying. You are not going to make it," that is when you should try harder. Harder, not in your own strength, but in the power of the Holy Spirit.

3. *"He cried the more a great deal."* Bartimaeus had a strong desire to be healed. That is why he cried

out fervently. A strong desire will lead to fervent prayers (Mark 11:24). As we read in James 5:16, *"The effectual fervent prayer of a righteous man availeth much."* A strong desire will lead to a strong faith. Bartimaeus was undeterred by opposition but persisted in his faith.

Verse 49

1. *"And Jesus stood still, and commanded him to be called."* Jesus, Who was walking briskly, stood still and called for Bartimaeus. Joshua prayed and the sun *"stood still"* (Joshua 10:12–13). Bartimaeus cried out and the Son *"stood still"* (Mark 10:49). The power of crying out to God by faith in prayer is seen clearly. This blind beggar had succeeded in getting the attention of Almighty God. The Bartimaeus kind of faith will get God's attention. God will call us when we cry out in faith (Hebrews 11:6). The people around Bartimaeus, the very people who had tried to put him down, realized the blind man had the attention of Almighty God. They said to him Jesus was calling for him: *"Be of good comfort, rise; he calleth thee."* This raises a very penetrating question for you and me. Can the people around us, who know us well, say of you and me: "This man has God's attention? This woman has God's attention!" They certainly said that of Bartimaeus.

2. Even on the way to the cross of Calvary, Jesus had the compassion and took the time to minister to

a poor, blind beggar. He recognized Bartimaeus, accepted him and treated him with dignity and respect. Can you imagine what this encouragement did to the soul of Bartimaeus? Before, Bartimaeus must have had a very poor self-image, a very low self-esteem and a very weak self-concept. He was treated as insignificant by the society, as worse than a nobody. He carried a lot of baggage because of his past as a poor, blind beggar. However, by calling for him, Jesus delivered his soul; he delivered Bartimaeus from his past. Thus, Bartimaeus received his second miracle: the deliverance of his soul.

3. People tend to be fickle and changing. The same people who were trying to put down Bartimaeus in verse 48 encouraged him in verse 49. People change with situations and circumstances. Therefore, do not put your faith and trust in them. Put your faith and trust only in the Lord Jesus Christ. He never changes; *"Jesus Christ the same yesterday, and today, and forever"* (Hebrews 13:8).

4. *"Be of good comfort."* Lots of people are seeking comfort in this life. Comfort does not come from things or from our possessions. True comfort comes from knowing Jesus is calling you. Jesus is always calling you and calling for you. Are you aware of His call? Are you responding to His calling?

5. The people, the very ones who were trying to put him down, told Bartimaeus, *"Rise; he calleth thee."* To get a miracle from the Lord, you must arise. Too many Christians keep sitting down when God

is calling them. This is the Word of the Lord to you from Isaiah 60:1: *"Arise, shine; for thy light is come, and the glory of the LORD is risen upon thee."* Receive this Word in the Name of Jesus!

Verse 50

1. *"And he, casting away his garment, rose, and came to Jesus."* Bartimaeus had to do his part to arise and come to Jesus. Likewise, you have to do your part to come to Jesus. Your part is to believe in Jesus (John 6:28–29). The word for "rose" in the original Greek means "jumped up." Bartimaeus jumped up in excitement and anticipation. One translation says he did this *"at once"* (The Message). Another translation says he *"ran to Jesus"* (Contemporary English Version).

2. When Jesus called for him, Bartimaeus stepped out in faith. He stepped out believing he could see when he was still blind. Like him, we must step out in faith. He demonstrated that by casting off his beggarly garment. He reasoned, because Jesus called him, he was healed and could see. Because he could see, he no longer needed to beg. Because he no longer needed to beg, he no longer needed his beggarly garment. Therefore, he threw away his beggarly garment and came to Jesus. This action is significant. In those days, beggars wore a special garment given by the religious establishment identifying them as beggars. This garment was in the form of a sheet. During the day, the beggar

would spread out the garment for people to throw coins on it and would use it as a blanket at night. That garment represented Bartimaeus's livelihood; it represented all that he had and all that he had been. Bartimaeus cast it away and came to Jesus.

3. That is how every person must come to Jesus, casting away all her or his self-sufficiency. What do you trust in today? Yourself, money, power, position or a job? Cast away your trust in those things and come to Jesus. Then you will experience the miracles He has for you.

4. Here Bartimaeus demonstrates the principle of faith Jesus taught in Mark 11:24: *"Therefore I say unto you, What things soever ye desire, when ye pray, believe that ye receive them, and ye shall have them."* Bartimaeus believed he had received his sight when Jesus called him although he still could not see. You have to believe you have your prayer request, and then you will have it. Believing and receiving by faith precede having it by sight, that is, getting it in the natural realm. The complete sequence to having your prayers answered is demonstrated by the Lord Jesus Christ in John 6:11. It can be described as:

Desire ➡ Pray ➡ Believe ➡ Receive ➡ Thank God by Faith ➡ Have

5. Jesus desired to feed the five thousand men besides women and children. He took the five loaves, prayed, believed God had multiplied them, believed He had received the miracle and thanked God for it. He then distributed the loaves to the disciples and the disciples to the people. Likewise, He did of the two fish. This passage of Scripture is discussed in detail in chapter 4 of the second book in this series, *God Is Calling You: Responding to the Calling of God.*

6. Bartimaeus took off the garment of human depravity and put on the garment of righteousness of God in Christ. He was tired of his old life he had lived so far; he was walking away from that life forever. He would follow Christ and live the new life the Son of God offered him. All of us should do this after coming to Christ; we should *"put off concerning the former conversation the old man"* (Ephesians 4:22). *"And that ye put on the new man, which after God is created in righteousness and true holiness"* (Ephesians 4:24).

Verse 51

1. Jesus asked Bartimaeus, *"What wilt thou that I should do unto thee?"* Almighty God, the Creator of Heaven and earth, the Omniscient One Who knows all things, asked Bartimaeus a question. Of course, Jesus knew what Bartimaeus wanted. That is not hard to figure out—even for you and me. What else can a forgiven and delivered blind

man want except he may see? Yet Jesus asked him a question. Why? Because Jesus was testing Bartimaeus to see if he knew where he stood in his faith. Secondly, Jesus wanted Bartimaeus to be specific; earlier, he had just asked for mercy—a very general request.

2. Today that same Jesus Christ is asking each one the same question: "Tom, what do you want Me to do for you? Joan, what do you want Me to do for you? Harry, what do you want Me to do for you? Linda, what do you want Me to do for you?" What do you want Jesus to do for you? Your answer will reveal your spiritual condition.

3. *"The blind man said unto him, Lord, that I might receive my sight."* Bartimaeus asked God for a miracle. Do you have the faith to ask and receive a miracle? Most Christians do not! Let me say emphatically—most Christians do not have the faith to ask God for a miracle and receive it. Why am I so emphatic? Because how does faith come? *"Faith comes by hearing and hearing by the word of God"* (Romans 10:17). The reason why most Christians do not have faith to ask for and receive a miracle from God is because they do not have the Word of God inside of them. They do not spend time reading, studying, memorizing and meditating on the Word of God. As a result, the Word is not in their spirit; so it cannot rise up as faith in them to receive the miracle God has for them. Let me challenge all of us to give the Word of God—given in the Bible—first place in our lives. We should read,

study, memorize and meditate on the Word on a daily basis.

Verse 52

1. Notice the response of Jesus in Mark 10:52: *"And Jesus said unto him, Go thy way; thy faith hath made thee whole."* Jesus could have rightly said, "I have healed you; I have made you whole" because He had. However, Jesus chose not to say that. Rather He said your faith has made you whole or healed you. Those are the exact, same words Jesus told the woman with an issue of blood in Mark 5:34. He used similar words in other situations as well. (See, for example, Matthew 15:28, Luke 7:50, and Luke 17:19.) This illustrates a general principle. God moves in response to our faith; God does not necessarily move in response to our need. He necessarily moves in response to our faith. Let me prove my point. Two thieves were crucified on the cross with our Lord—one on either side of Him. Both needed salvation equally. Yet only the thief who looked to the Lord Jesus Christ in faith was saved: *"And Jesus said unto him, Verily I say unto thee, today shalt thou be with me in paradise"* (Luke 23:43). The other thief died and went to hell. So God does not necessarily move in response to our need. Jesus did not grant salvation to the thief who reviled Him although he needed it just as much. The apostle Paul did say, *"But my God shall supply all your need according to his riches in glory by Christ*

Jesus" (Philippians 4:19). The context of this verse assumes the Philippian Christians were walking by faith. (See Philippians 4:15–18.) Philippians 4:19 is a promise of God. This promise, like any other promise in the Bible, must be inherited by faith and patience (persistence or perseverance). *"That ye be not slothful, but followers of them who through faith and patience inherit the promises"* (Hebrews 6:12). God necessarily moves in response to only those needs that are expressed in faith, not necessarily to needs in general.

2. Jesus told Bartimaeus, *"Thy faith hath made thee whole."* The Lord gave Bartimaeus the credit for exercising his faith. Actually, the faith that Bartimaeus exercised was first given to him by Jesus. *"God hath dealt to every man the measure of faith"* (Romans 12:3). The apostle Paul exemplified this in his life as he said *"the life which I now live in the flesh I live by the faith of the Son of God, who loved me, and gave himself for me"* (Galatians 2:20). In general, the Lord Jesus Christ first imparts grace to us; and then He gives us the credit and rewards us for exercising that grace. That is how good He is. Praise His holy Name!

3. *"And immediately he received his sight."* Bartimaeus received his third miracle, the miracle of physical sight. More than that, Bartimaeus was made *"whole"*—whole in spirit, soul and body. The word for "whole" in the Greek is "*sózó*" and means saved, delivered, healed and made well. As stated earlier, the Gospel provides for the redemption of the

whole man: spirit, soul and body. It provides forgiveness for our spirit, deliverance for our soul and healing for our bodies. Bartimaeus got all three, and he got them in this order. He had forgiveness for his spirit in verse 47 when he called upon Jesus as the *"Son of David."* His soul was restored in verse 49 by the way Jesus paid attention to him and accepted him. Finally, his eyes were healed in verse 52. In Luke 17, 10 lepers were cleansed, but only one who received Christ as Savior and Lord was made whole.

4. What kind of faith made Bartimaeus whole? The faith of Bartimaeus was characterized by: (1) his ability to see Jesus for Who He really is: the Son of David, the Son of God; (2) his determination and persistence as he refused to keep quiet when asked to do so by the people; (3) his belief in God's mercy and (4) his belief he had received his request when as yet he did not see the manifestation. That is the kind of faith that will get the attention of the Lord Jesus Christ and move the hand of God.

5. Jesus told Bartimaeus, *"Go thy way"*; but Bartimaeus, instead of going his way, *"followed Jesus in the way."* When you have had a real encounter with the Lord Jesus Christ, His way becomes your way, His will becomes your will, His desires become your desires and His wishes become your wishes. In fact, His wishes become commandments for you. You will want to follow Jesus Christ and surrender your all to Him.

6. Bartimaeus's response on receiving his miracles? He *"followed Jesus in the way"* (Mark 10:52). That word means he surrendered his life totally, completely and fully to the Lord Jesus Christ. It is not enough to come to Christ for our needs; but when our needs are met, we must continue to follow Him in full surrender and honor Him with our lives. Those who have spiritual eyesight see the Lordship of Christ and will be drawn to follow Him.

Conclusion

To sum up, like Bartimaeus, we must approach Jesus in faith. We must demonstrate our faith by our works since faith without works is dead (James 2:17, 20, 26). When you really believe something, it will lead to corresponding action. Bartimaeus demonstrated his faith by his works. His faith and works consisted of the following: (1) he cried out to Jesus; (2) he believed Jesus is the Son of David, the Messiah, the Son of God; (3) he persevered and stood up to opposition by the people; (4) he cast away his beggar's garment; (5) when the Lord Jesus Christ called him, he responded in obedience, believing he could see while he was yet blind; (6) he asked Jesus for the miracle of physical sight and (7) he followed Jesus after he had received his three miracles. Bartimaeus truly shows us the way to salvation and the way to the life of faith.

Author's Account

It is a blessing to share my testimony of how I came to know Jesus Christ as my personal Savior and Lord.

My Salvation in Christ

As mentioned in chapter 1, I was born into a Hindu family; and so automatically, I became a Hindu. Here is an important Biblical truth. You can be born a Hindu, a Buddhist, a Muslim or into a variety of other religions. However, you cannot be born a Christian; you have to be born again to become a Christian (John 3:1–7). This rebirth happens when a person with understanding and the exercise of free will repents and places her or his faith in the Lord Jesus Christ and receives Him as personal Savior and Lord. Of course, growing up, I knew nothing about this truth. I grew up to be a religious, practicing Hindu. I was familiar with the Hindu scriptures and read them regularly. Moreover, I prayed the Hindu prayers regularly and dutifully bowed down to the Hindu idols in my home and in the nearby temples.

I do recall, when I was about 14 years old, I had a spiritual crisis. I was seeking God and yet felt very far and distant from Him. I shared this situation with my mother. She wisely said she would set up an appointment for me with the chief Hindu priest of the temple near our home. When I saw the priest, he explained to me what I was experiencing was normal. God is holy, and we are sinful people. Thus, there is a gap between a Holy God and sinful people that is supposed to exist and persist. He commended me on my spiritual walk and sensitivity and encouraged me to keep following the path I was on. While this talk made me feel good temporarily, the distance I felt from God remained. With this spiritual background and mindset, I came to the United States at the age of about twenty-five.

In chapter 1, I shared how I came into contact with International Students Incorporated (ISI) and moved into their housing center. The ISI minister, the Rev. Soon Hong, was Korean. He lived right next to the center. I became good friends with him, his wife and their children. At times, I would go over to his house and play with his kids and chat with him and his wife. I do remember one day at his house I watched a Billy Graham telecast, and it touched my heart. Slowly, God was tugging at my heart. However, I am a very goal-directed individual. At that time, my main goal was to do well and complete my doctoral program. I said to myself, once I completed the program, I will look more into Christianity; and I let this thought lie dormant. Meanwhile, as discussed in chapter 1, I continued to experience unselfish love from the ISI staff and volunteers, a major factor impacting my life.

One day, Steve Settle, the ISI Center director, told me one of the ladies, Mrs. Gertrude Springborn, had invited some students to the church service and afterward to her place for lunch. I was one of the students she had invited. Steve wanted me to give a definite answer as to whether I would attend. I said, "If you want the answer right now, it is no." I explained to him these things had a very low priority with me. However, if I did finish all of my work for the week by Saturday, there was a possibility I would attend on Sunday, March 19, 1978. Steve responded by saying I should not say no and he would mention to Mrs. Springborn I was unsure, but there was a possibility I would attend. We left it at that, but then I forgot about it.

On the nights of March 18 and March 19, 1978, I finished all of the work for the week by 1:30 a.m. That was wonderful as I used to work in my office on the campus until 3:30 or 4:00 a.m. routinely. Thrilled about the early completion, I went to my house, ate something, flipped through a magazine and retired to bed. At 8:30 a.m., there was a knock on my door. "Come in," I said half asleep. It was Steve. He asked me if I was coming. "Coming where?" I asked. He reminded me about the invitation from a lady to go to her church and then her house for lunch. At that moment, I decided to attend. I thought I would endure the church service and enjoy the lunch. As a student, you do not get many free, good meals; and I have always liked good food.

With this frame of mind, I walked into the Metropolitan Chapel of Buffalo on March 19, 1978. Becoming a Christian was the last thing on my mind. However, the Lord had other plans. The pastor's message penetrated my heart. The pastor, Rev. Andrew, said believing in God does not mean anything. Most people believe in God; there are few who profess to be atheists. What matters is you believe in Jesus Christ as the Son of God and receive Him as your Savior and Lord. Toward the end of the service, when the invitation was given, I felt a compulsion from within to respond. I now understand that to be the force of the Holy Spirit. Thank God I yielded. I went forward and received the Lord Jesus Christ as my personal Savior and Lord and gave my life to Him. That day was March 19, 1978. It was Palm Sunday. I have never forgotten it and never will.

I remember distinctly there was so much joy in my heart after I made my commitment to the Lord Jesus Christ. After the service, I met my professor, Dr. Arun K. Jain, for a planned research meeting. I told him I had become a Christian. Going to my house after the meeting, I went singing all the way. There was so much joy in my heart. That joy remains, and I pray it will never diminish.

When the ISI staff and committee members learned about my commitment, they were overjoyed. Many said they had been praying for me. I was able to receive their love in a new way. They encouraged me to grow in my new faith. God put a hunger for the Word in my heart. In the first year that I was a Christian, I read through the entire Bible, the Old and the New Testaments. Since then, I read the Bible on a daily basis and have read it through several times. I have never doubted my salvation.

Encouraged by the testimony of Bartimaeus, I have been learning to approach the Lord Jesus Christ by faith for everything. I know, when I take a stand of faith, I must expect opposition from within as well as from without the church. I have seen this even in the context of my ministry and specifically in sharing the Gospel in the public schools. However, I am learning to stand firm and confess the Word of God over my situations and circumstances. Moreover, I must depend only and totally upon the Lord Jesus Christ. I must trust in Him and in Him alone for my salvation and for everything else. *"Trust in the LORD with all thine heart; and lean not unto thine own understanding. In all thy ways acknowledge him, and he shall direct thy paths*" (Proverbs 3:5–6). I cannot depend on my education, training, finances, family, church, anyone or anything. I must trust in the Lord Jesus Christ alone. As best as I know my heart, I have cast away my beggar's garment and I have come to Jesus. As I will share in the next chapter, I have tried to maintain a very steady walk with my Savior and Lord. I endeavor to get the Word of God in my spirit on a daily basis. I try to develop a solid faith, so I can ask God and believe God for miracles. God has done many miracles for me in many areas of my life. God, in His grace, has blessed me in all areas of my life. I would like to share His blessing in one area—evangelism.

In 1987, I made a serious commitment to the Lord Jesus Christ to share the Gospel with those who are lost. Since then, I have seen the Lord work in a mighty way in reaching people. I have been blessed to preach the Gospel in thirty-six countries and have seen more than 1.9 million people pray to receive the Lord Jesus Christ as Savior and Lord. Truly, this is the Lord's doing; and it is marvelous in my eyes (Psalm 118:23). I praise God and give Him all of the glory. This is a fulfillment of the vision God gave me in 2006 to see more than one million people pray to receive the Lord Jesus Christ as their personal Savior and Lord. All of these miracles of salvation are documented carefully in independent reports with each report prepared and signed by multiple senior pastors of the local churches and leaders of the Christian ministries with whom I have been working. These reports can be accessed at https://www.globalevangelisticministries.net. The list of countries where I have preached the Gospel also is given on this website.

In 2008, I was ordained as a Minister of the Gospel of the Lord Jesus Christ by my pastor, Dr. Charles F. Stanley, at the First Baptist Church of Atlanta, Georgia, USA. In 2009, I formed the Global Evangelistic Ministries, Inc. as a means to fulfill this vision. This ministry is incorporated in the USA as a 501(c)(3) organization. The vision, mission and structure of Global Evangelistic Ministries are given on our website. You will read much more about my life and ministry in the subsequent chapters. In each chapter, I will share a specific aspect of my personal testimony as it relates to my calling. I give all praise and glory to my Savior and Lord Jesus Christ!

Quest Questions

Please do some soul searching and answer the following questions. You need not share your answers with anyone. However, if you so choose, share them with your accountability partner or a person you trust.

- Do I realize I am a sinner in need of salvation?
- Do I know I am a free moral agent—free to worship God or to sin against Him?
- Do I believe I am saved because God loves everyone?
- Am I trying to earn my salvation by doing good works?
- Do I know for certain I am saved, born again and a child of God?
- Do I remember the date and the circumstances when I repented and placed my faith and trust in the Lord Jesus Christ as my Savior and my Lord?

- Do I doubt my salvation?
- Do I see myself as God sees me?
- Do I know, beyond any doubt, all my sins are forgiven? On what basis?
- Am I worried about the curses of the law coming upon me?
- Do I believe salvation is available only in the Lord Jesus Christ or there are other ways to salvation?
- What do I believe is the greatest miracle anyone can receive?
- What do I think of Christ's work on the cross?
- Am I seeking miracles, or am I seeking God?
- Am I a mere spectator in the Kingdom of God, sitting down and watching from the sidelines?
- If I am a believer, am I behaving as a new creation in Christ?
- In whom or what am I trusting for my needs?
- Do I know God loves me? Do I experience His love?
- Do I stick to my stand of faith in spite of opposition from people?
- What is my attitude toward prayer? Do I pray believing prayers, or do I waiver?
- When was the last time I cried out to God in prayer?
- When God is calling me, do I keep sitting down spiritually, or do I arise and come to Him?
- Do I seek comfort from things or my possessions?
- Do I have the faith to ask God for a miracle?
- Do I have the faith to receive a miracle from God?

- Do I believe God will necessarily move in response to my faith?
- Am I giving the Word of God the first place in my life?
- Have I surrendered my life fully and completely to the Lord Jesus Christ?
- How do I demonstrate my faith in Christ?

You can evaluate your answers to these questions in light of the following principles and precepts.

Principles and Precepts

- Every person is a sinner and needs salvation. Every person, who has been born of a human father, is born with a sin nature (Romans 3:23, 5:12–19).
- Every person, who is apart from Jesus Christ, is spiritually blind and is spiritually a beggar (Revelation 3:17).
- God loves everybody; He loves the whole world. God loves you just as you are! (John 3:16).
- Man was and is free to worship God or to sin against Him (Genesis 1:26–27).
- Not all will be saved. Only those who call upon the Lord Jesus Christ in faith, confess their sins, repent and receive Him as personal Savior and Lord will be saved (Romans 10:9–10).
- Salvation cannot be earned by good works. Your only part in salvation is to come to Jesus, confessing and repenting of your sins and believing in Him in your heart (John 6:28–29).

- God will not bless you until you see yourself as God sees you. Seeing yourself as a sinner is critical to seeing your need for salvation and being saved (Genesis 32:27–28, Matthew 4:17, Acts 2:38).
- God is a righteous, Holy God. He cannot and will not condone sin. He must judge and punish sin (Exodus 34:7; Ezekiel 18:4, 20).
- Jesus Christ died on the cross to make full atonement for all of our sins—past, present and future (Isaiah 53:6, Romans 5:11, Titus 2:14).
- Jesus died on the cross to redeem us from every curse of the law. The moment you receive Jesus Christ as your Savior and Lord, every curse in your life is destroyed and all of the blessings of God will come upon you! (Galatians 3:13, 29).
- Salvation in the Lord Jesus Christ is a gift available freely to all (Romans 10:13).
- God's salvation is available only in the Lord Jesus Christ (John 14:6, Acts 4:12).
- The power and the indwelling presence of the Holy Spirit make the believer a new creation in Christ (2 Corinthians 5:17).
- The Gospel provides for the redemption of the whole man: spirit, soul and body. It provides forgiveness for our spirit, deliverance for our soul and healing for our bodies (Matthew 8:2–4, Mark 10:46–52).
- Salvation in Jesus is the first and the greatest miracle anyone can receive (Mark 10:47).

- If you do not already have it, God wants you to have the miracle of salvation now! (2 Corinthians 6:2, 1 Timothy 2:4).
- The redemptive work of Christ is perfect, complete and finished (John 19:30).
- In terms of the manifestation of Christ's finished work in our lives, there is the past, present and future tense of our salvation. Our spirits have been saved; our souls are being saved; and our bodies will be saved in the future when we receive resurrected and glorified bodies at the rapture (Titus 2:11–13).
- For some people when they hear the Gospel, it might well be the first and last opportunity—the only opportunity to receive the salvation Jesus Christ alone offers (Genesis 6:3, Mark 10:46).
- Do not seek miracles but seek the Miracle Worker—the Lord Jesus Christ (Matthew 6:33).
- Do not be a spectator sitting down and watching from the sidelines; rather be involved as an actor in the Kingdom of God (Mark 6:46).
- Narrow is the way leading to life in Jesus Christ, and few people are on that way. Broad is the way that leaves Christ out and leads to destruction; many people are on that way (Matthew 7:13–14).
- If you look to man for help, you will be disappointed. Man will fail you, but God will never fail you or forsake you (Psalm 60:11–12, Jeremiah 17:5, Hebrews 13:5).
- To fulfill your calling, you not only have to say yes to things that will propel you toward your goal but

have to be willing to say no to things that will keep you from your goal, keep you from your destiny! (Mark 10:46, Philippians 3:13–14).

- When you take a stand of faith, expect opposition from other people (2 Timothy 3:12).
- If this world and the devil try to shout down your faith, you shout them down with the Word of God (Mark 10:48, Hebrews 10:23).
- God loves to answer our prayers that are according to His will (John 14:13–14).
- Whenever you cry out to the Lord in faith, He will respond (Psalm 30:2).
- To have our prayers answered, we must believe, receive and thank God for the answer when we pray. Keep doing this until the answer is manifested (Mark 11:24).
- We must come to Jesus, casting away all our self-sufficiency (Mark 10:50, 2 Corinthians 3:5).
- God does not owe salvation or anything else to anyone. We receive everything from Him based on His grace and His mercy (Lamentations 3:22, Isaiah 54:10, Luke 1:72, Mark 10:47).
- In the Scriptures, mercy is closely linked to the covenant of God (Isaiah 54:10, Luke 1:72).
- To get a miracle from the Lord, you must arise spiritually. Do not keep sitting down when God is calling you (Isaiah 60:1).
- Comfort does not come from things or from our possessions. True comfort comes from knowing Jesus Christ loves you and is calling you (Mark 10:49).

- Jesus will often test our faith in order to strengthen it (Mark 10:51, James 1:3).
- God necessarily moves in response to our faith; God does not necessarily move in response to our need (Mark 10:52).
- All of the promises of God have to be inherited by persistent faith (Luke 8:15, Hebrews 6:12).
- We must give the Word of God, the Holy Bible, the first place in our lives (Deuteronomy 8:3, Matthew 4:4).
- God wants to give us miracles that are consistent with His will. Let us ask Him in faith for them (Mark 9:24).
- The Lord Jesus Christ first imparts grace to us and then He gives us the credit and rewards us for exercising that grace (Mark 10:52).
- When you have had a real encounter with Jesus Christ, His way becomes your way, His will becomes your will, His desires become your desires and His wishes become your wishes (Mark 10:52, Hebrews 8:10).
- We should surrender our all and follow the Lord Jesus Christ. This is the key to victory in life (Luke 9:23–24).
- We must demonstrate our faith by our works since faith without works is dead (James 2:17, 20, 26).

Life Lesson

For our lives to count in eternity, we must live knowing the Lord Jesus Christ as personal Savior and Lord and surrendering our lives to Him. We must live this life by faith for His glory. There is no other way!

Prayer Power

To obtain salvation, pray the following prayer. If you have any doubt whatsoever about your salvation, then that is a strong indication you should pray this prayer.

Dear Lord Jesus, I confess to You I am a sinner. I believe, Lord Jesus, You are the Son of God. You love me. You died on the cross for me. You paid the penalty and bore the punishment for all of my sins by Your blood and by Your death on the cross for me. Lord Jesus, You arose from the dead and now You live forever. Lord Jesus, I am sorry for my sins; I repent. I receive Your forgiveness and Your love. I receive You, Lord Jesus, as my personal Savior and Lord. Lord Jesus, I give my life to You. From now on, I will follow You.

Thank You, Father God in Heaven, now I am a child of God because I believe in the Lord Jesus Christ as my Savior and as my Lord. In Jesus's Precious Name, I pray. Amen!

Message Ministry

You can access the audio message for this chapter by using CallingYou as the password at

https://www.globalevangelisticministries.net/Calling1-Chapter2.

CHAPTER 3

The Calling to Spiritual Growth: Growing the Roots of Your Faith

"As newborn babes, desire the sincere milk of the word, that ye may grow thereby."

—1 Peter 2:2

Preamble and Preview

Once you begin to experience the love of God (chapter 1) by receiving Jesus Christ as your Savior and Lord (chapter 2), you need to grow spiritually in your faith and in your daily walk with Him. God has to do His work in you before He can do His work through you. In this chapter, I discuss the "Central Concepts" of the need for personal spiritual growth and the means to grow spiritually. "Scripture Spotlight" looks at Paul's prayer for the spiritual growth of the Colossian Christians and draws several insights to help us grow spiritually. "Author's Account" shares my spiritual growth since receiving the Lord Jesus Christ as my personal

Savior and Lord. The next section, "Quest Questions," contains several questions that I hope will cause you to reflect on your life as it relates to your spiritual growth. There are several "Principles and Precepts" you can apply to experience greater spiritual growth and deepen your walk with the Lord. "Life Lesson" contains the most important lesson you can learn with respect to spiritual growth. "Prayer Power" contains an effectual, Scriptural prayer you are encouraged to pray in order to experience continued spiritual growth. The final section, "Message Ministry," gives a link to an audio message you are exhorted to hear.

Central Concepts

Once you are saved by receiving Jesus Christ as your personal Savior and Lord, spiritually, you are a newborn baby. You need to grow spiritually. In this section, I will focus on the need for personal spiritual growth, daily surrender, prayer, Bible study, worship, fellowship, service and witness.

The Need for Personal Spiritual Growth

In chapter 2, I discussed the need for a person to be born again. Faith in the Lord Jesus Christ as personal Savior and Lord is the only way to salvation, the only way to be reconciled to God. There is no other way (John 14:6). When a person is born physically, she or he is born a physical baby. A baby looks beautiful at birth. The same baby, if she or he did not grow at all, would present an unusual sight ten years later. Likewise, when you are born again, you are born a spiritual baby. You must grow spiritually and mature in your faith. If you do not grow, you will backslide; if you do not move forward, you will move backward. *"But they hearkened not, nor inclined their ear, but walked in the counsels and in the imagination of their evil heart, and went backward, and not forward"* (Jeremiah 7:24). Spiritually, either you are going forward or backward. There is no third state. You may say, "I am just standing still." Well, in effect, you are going backward because God is moving forward and passing you by!

Spiritual growth parallels physical growth. A baby grows physically by taking physical food. Similarly, one grows spiritually by taking spiritual food consisting of a seven-course meal. These courses consist of daily surrender, daily prayer time, daily Bible study, worship, fellowship, service and witness. Each is essential for a well-balanced spiritual diet and our walk with God, and each is discussed briefly.

Daily Surrender

You surrender your will and your life to the Lord Jesus Christ when you receive Him as your Savior and Lord. This is the act of salvation. Thereafter, you have to surrender your will to Him and to God continually as a process of spiritual growth and sanctification. Salvation is a one-time act, but the manifestation of sanctification is a lifelong process. As a result of Christ's finished work on the cross, we have been sanctified by our Savior *"Jesus Christ once for all"* (Hebrews 10:10). Furthermore, *"he hath perfected for ever them that are sanctified"* (Hebrews 10:14). Yet to experience the reality of this sanctification on a daily basis, you have to grow in your walk with your Savior; you have to surrender your will to Him continually. It is possible for you as a believer to surrender your will to God because your will has been redeemed by the Lord Jesus Christ. He has restored your will power, empowering you to say no to sin and yes to God the Father. To understand this fact, let us look at two prominent gardens in the Bible.

In the Garden of Eden, man surrendered his will to Satan when Adam disobeyed God. Eve was deceived by Satan; but Adam knowingly, deliberately and willfully disobeyed God when he ate of the forbidden fruit of the "*tree of the knowledge of good and evil*" (Genesis 2:17). The entire account of Adam's sin of disobedience is found in Genesis 3. When Adam deliberately disobeyed God, he surrendered his free will to Satan. In effect, Adam told God the Father, "Not Your will but my will be done." At this point, Adam had the free will to say no to Satan and to obey God, for he was created in the image of God (Genesis 1:26). Unfortunately, Adam chose to obey Satan, disobey God and thereby surrendered his free will to Satan. "*Wherefore, as by one man sin entered into the world, and death by sin; and so death passed upon all men, for that all have sinned*" (Romans 5:12).

In another garden, the Garden of Gethsemane, Jesus redeemed our will when He said to God the Father "*nevertheless not my will, but thine, be done*" and sweat "*great drops of blood falling down to the ground*" (Luke 22:42). Jesus not only surrendered His will to the Father, but He also shed His blood. The shedding of blood was necessary because "*almost all things are by the law purged with blood; and with-*

out shedding of blood is no remission" (Hebrews 9:22). Thus, Christ has redeemed our will. The word *redeemed* means we are ransomed or brought back to the original place. The original place where we are brought back is the Garden of Eden before the sin and fall of man where we have the free will, the will power, to say no to Satan and say yes to God the Father. In sharp contrast, a lost person, who does not know Christ as Savior and Lord, does not have this will power. The will power of a lost person is still surrendered to Satan. Such is the state of every person apart from Christ—as Paul has described in Ephesians 2:1–3. We have to make this truth an experiential reality in our lives on a daily basis. We have to pray daily, "Heavenly Father, like my Savior and my Lord Jesus Christ, I too come to my own Garden of Gethsemane and cry out to You, not my will but Thy will be done in my life this day and forevermore." This is what is meant by dying to self. The apostle Paul said, "*I die daily*" (1 Corinthians 15:31). This truth has to be made an experiential reality every day on a moment-by-moment basis. Many of us have experienced moments of surrender, but God wants us to have a lifestyle of surrender. Only then can we present our "*bodies a living sacrifice, holy, acceptable unto God*" (Romans 12:1).

As children of God, we do not have to sin; when we sin (and all believers do), we choose to sin. The power of sin over us has been broken at the cross of Calvary. "*Knowing this, that our old man is crucified with him, that the body of sin might be destroyed, that henceforth we should not serve sin. For he that is dead is freed from sin*" (Romans 6:6–7). The best way to safeguard ourselves against sin and to be at the center of God's will for our lives is to come to our own Garden of Gethsemane and surrender our wills to our Heavenly Father daily. This surrender can be done as a part of our daily prayer time. However, I have singled this out and treated this topic as a separate subsection to emphasize its importance and give it due coverage.

I should point out that the Garden of Gethsemane was the first time Jesus shed His blood for us when He sweat *"great drops of blood falling down to the ground"* (Luke 22:42). Consistent with the Day of Atonement, as described in Leviticus 16, in making the perfect atonement for us, Jesus Christ shed His blood seven times. On the Day of Atonement, once a year on the tenth day of the seventh month, Aaron was to come into the holy of holies. On this day, Aaron offered two sin offerings: a bullock for himself and a goat for the people. He sprinkled the blood of the sin offerings on and before the mercy seat *"seven times"* (Leviticus 16:14). In addition, he sprinkled the blood of both the sin offerings upon the altar *"seven times"* (Leviticus 16:19). As Paul said in Colossians 2:16–17, the Jewish feasts and celebrations were a shadow of the things to come through Jesus Christ. Therefore, Jesus shed His blood seven times to make the all-sufficient, once-for-all, perfect atonement for us. The seven times Jesus shed His blood were: (1) in the Garden of Gethsemane, (2) when He was scourged, (3) when the crown of thorns was placed on His brow, (4) when His hands were pierced by the nails, (5) when His feet were nailed to the cross, (6) when the spear was thrust into His side and (7) when He was bruised, shedding His blood on the inside. While the complete power of the atonement is embodied in the death and resurrection of our Savior and Lord Jesus Christ, each time Jesus shed His blood, He initiated a specific aspect of our redemption that was completed on the cross. He shed His blood in the Garden of Gethsemane to redeem our will. I discuss the other six places Jesus shed His blood and the specific aspects of our redemption He initiated and accomplished each time in a series of messages posted on our ministry website.

Daily Prayer Time

When we study His Word, God speaks to us; it is primarily one-way communication. When we pray, we are having a two-way communication with God. The Scriptures admonish and call us to pray. *"Call unto me, and I will answer thee, and shew thee great and mighty things, which thou knowest not"* (Jeremiah 33:3). See also 2 Chronicles 7:14, Psalm 32:6, Matthew 6:5, Luke 22:40, 1 Thessalonians 5:17, and James 5:13. Furthermore, God has promised to answer our prayers, providing a great motivation for praying. Consider the following Scriptures:

> *"Blessed be God, which hath not turned away my prayer, nor his mercy from me"* (Psalm 66:20).

> *"And it shall come to pass, that before they call, I will answer; and while they are yet speaking, I will hear"* (Isaiah 65:24).

> *"And I say unto you, Ask, and it shall be given you; seek, and ye shall find; knock,*

and it shall be opened unto you. For every one that asketh receiveth; and he that seeketh findeth; and to him that knocketh it shall be opened" (Luke 11:9–10).

While there are several principles of effective prayer, the most basic and the most important is we pray to God the Father in the Name of Jesus Christ and in the power of the Holy Spirit. Jesus taught His disciples to pray to the Father. *"After this manner therefore pray ye: Our Father which art in heaven, Hallowed be thy name"* (Matthew 6:9). (See also Luke 11:2.) Why? Because the *"Father knoweth what things ye have need of, before ye ask him"* (Matthew 6:8).

We should pray in the Name of Jesus. Why? Because the Name of Jesus is above every name. *"Wherefore God also hath highly exalted him, and given him a name which is above every name: That at the name of Jesus every knee should bow, of things in heaven, and things in earth, and things under the earth; And that every tongue should confess that Jesus Christ is Lord, to the glory of God the Father"* (Philippians 2:9–11). Jesus Himself taught us to ask in His Name. *"Ye have not chosen me, but I have chosen you, and ordained you, that ye should go and bring forth fruit, and that your fruit should remain: that whatsoever ye shall ask of the Father in my name, he may give it you"* (John 15:16). *"And in that day ye shall ask me nothing. Verily, verily, I say unto you, Whatsoever ye shall ask the Father in my name, he will give it you"* (John 16:23).

When it comes to answering prayers, the Name of Jesus is the only name recognized in Heaven. Let me illustrate this truth as follows. Suppose I had 10 million dollars in my bank account, and I wrote you a check for 10 million dollars. The check is dated, and your name is on the check; but I do not sign the check; the signature line is blank. Do you think you can cash that check? Is that check any good to you? Certainly not! It does not have my signature. If you take this check to the bank, it will be returned to you uncashed. Similarly, a prayer not signed with the Name of Jesus is not honored in Heaven; it is returned to the earth uncashed!

We should pray in the power of the Holy Spirit. Why? So we can pray according to the will of God. The Spirit makes intercession for us according to the will of God. *"Likewise the Spirit also helpeth our infirmities: for we know not what we should pray for as we ought: but the Spirit itself maketh intercession for us with groanings which cannot be uttered. And he that searcheth the hearts knoweth what is the mind of the Spirit, because he maketh intercession for the saints according to the will of God"* (Romans 8:26–27). If we pray according to His will, God will hear and answer our prayers. *"And this is the confidence that we have in him, that, if we ask any thing according to his will, he heareth us"* (1 John 5:14). In order to pray in the power of the Holy Spirit, it is very important we prepare our hearts before we present our petitions to God the Father. I will share how I do this in my personal testimony in the "Author's Account" in this chapter.

Three other principles of effective prayers are given in James 5:16. *"Confess your faults one to another, and pray one for another, that ye may be healed. The effectual fervent prayer of a righteous man availeth much."* Notice, for our prayers to avail much, all three requirements have to be met. Our prayers have to be (1) effectual, (2) fervent and (3) offered by a righteous man (or woman). Our prayers are effectual when they are consistent with and based on the Word of God. We can use Scriptures in a number of ways in prayer such as to quote a promise as an assurance of an answered prayer, to quote a fulfilled promise as a reason for praising God and to apply Bible verses to a current situation. For example, we can pray Philippians 1:9–11 when praying for discernment. Praying based on Ephesians 1:15–23 will help us to gain enlightenment and to see things from God's perspective. In situations where we feel powerless, Ephesians 3:14–21 can serve as our model prayer. In the section on "Scripture Spotlight," we will see how we can pray for spiritual growth based on Colossians 1:9–14.

To be fervent, our prayers have to be led by the Holy Spirit, as already discussed. Finally, for us to be righteous, we have to be robed in the righteousness of our Savior and Lord Jesus Christ and be walking with Him. We must be saved or born again and demonstrate that by living a holy life, as Paul has admonished us in Titus 2:11–12. We must approach God, not in our righteousness, which is *"as filthy rags"* (Isaiah 64:6), but in the righteousness of the Lord Jesus Christ, the Righteous One.

Our prayers should be mingled with thanksgiving and praise. King David said, *"Enter into his gates with thanksgiving, and into his courts with praise: be thankful unto him, and bless his name"* (Psalm 100:4). David was a giant killer; he lived in victory. Why? Because his prayers were offered with praises. The Bible says, *"God inhabits the praises of His people"* (Psalm 148:14). Therefore, as a prayer principle, we must enter into the presence of the Lord with thanks and praises. Open your heart unto the Lord, and enter into His gates with thanksgiving. As a child of God, you have plenty to be grateful and thankful for. Thank God for your salvation, the greatest gift you have received. Thank God for who you are in Christ Jesus: beloved (Romans 1:7); accepted (Ephesians 1:6); the righteousness of God (2 Corinthians 5:21); redeemed (1 Peter 1:18); justified (Romans 5:1); a child of God (Romans 8:16); a glorified, joint heir (Romans 8:17); a partaker of God's divine nature (2 Peter 1:4) and a citizen in Heaven (Philippians 3:20). When you give thanks, your difficult circumstances will change for the better. Praise and thanksgiving drive out doubts, grumblings, complaints and other negative attitudes. Then you can focus on God and start hearing God speak to you in a personal way for your specific situations and circumstances.

Finally, praying is a means of serving God. The prophetess Anna *"served God with fastings and prayers night and day"* (Luke 2:37).

Daily Bible Study

The Bible is the Word of God, and we should study it daily. It is the inerrant, infallible, eternal and unchangeable Word of the living God; and it is our final authority in life. Jesus said, *"Heaven and earth shall pass away, but my words shall not pass away"* (Matthew 24:35, Mark 13:31, Luke 21:33). Both the Old Testament and the New Testament emphasize a daily study of the Scriptures.

An important Old Testament passage is Deuteronomy 6:4–9. These verses are about reading, studying, memorizing, believing and obeying God's Word. God commanded us to learn His Word and teach it to our children and grandchildren. His Word is to penetrate our hearts, minds, wills and emotions for it to become the center of our lives. We are to write it down and use it as a handbook to guide all aspects of our daily lives. Doing, that is, obeying God's Word is the key to our success. God told Joshua, "*This book of the law shall not depart out of thy mouth; but thou shalt meditate therein day and night, that thou mayest observe to do according to all that is written therein: for then thou shalt make thy way prosperous, and then thou shalt have good success*" (Joshua 1:8). Psalm 119 emphasizes the Word of God. Of the 176 verses in this Psalm, only one verse does not contain some description, reference or title of God's Word. The Word of God is stressed in every sphere of life: in youth, in private, in public, in prosperity, in adversity, at night and during the day. In short, we are to be guided by the Word at all times, seasons, circumstances and on all occasions.

In the New Testament, Jesus quoted the Old Testament to the devil at the time of His temptation. The Lord Jesus Christ, when tempted by the devil, "*answered and said, It is written, Man shall not live by bread alone, but by every word that proceedeth out of the mouth of God*" (Matthew 4:4). The Holy Bible, both the Old and the New Testaments, is the Word come out of God's mouth. Likewise, there are several admonitions in the New Testament to study the Scriptures and give the Word of God first place in our lives. The apostle Paul exhorted his disciple Timothy, "*Study to shew thyself approved unto God, a workman that needeth not to be ashamed, rightly dividing the word of truth"* (2 Timothy 2:15). Later, Paul explained the reasoning behind this admonition in 2 Timothy 3:14–17. The Holy Scriptures are able to make us wise for salvation through faith in Christ Jesus. All Scripture is God-breathed and extremely useful, even necessary, for teaching, rebuking, correcting and training in righteousness. Through the Word, we are thoroughly equipped for our calling and for every good work. The apostle Paul was a keen student of the Scriptures, as is evident from his epistles. An analysis of the Complete Jewish Bible indicates Paul quotes or paraphrases 183 Old Testament passages in his writings. In addition, he makes numerous references to people, places and events in the Old Testament. The highest number of Old Testament quotes is in Romans (with quotes or paraphrases of eighty-four Old Testament passages).[1]

Merely reading, memorizing, meditating and studying the Word are not sufficient. These activities must be followed by obedience to the Word. We should simply do the Word, that is, act in obedience to the Word of God. In the ultimate analysis, the blessings of God are experienced by obeying the Word of God (Deuteronomy 5:1, Ecclesiastes 12:13, Luke 11:28, Revelation 1:3).

Why is the Word of God so essential to our spiritual growth and development? Because this is how faith comes (Romans 10:17). Let me give you a mathematical equation. The level of your faith is directly proportional to the level of the Word of God inside you. This is the level of the Word of God residing in your spirit because of study, memorization, meditation and obedience. An intimate knowledge of

God's Word is a key to having our prayers answered. *"If ye abide in me, and my words abide in you, ye shall ask what ye will, and it shall be done unto you"* (John 15:7). His Word is the primary and surest way God speaks to us who are believers. Christians, who do not spend time in the Word of God, will find it difficult to hear God through other means (the Holy Spirit, Godly people, circumstances, etc.). If you do not study the Bible on a daily basis, let me strongly urge you right now to make a commitment to do so.

Studying God's Word and abiding in the Word assume obedience to God's Word. Obedience to God's Word is enjoined elsewhere in the Scriptures, for example, by the Lord Jesus Christ in Matthew 7:24–27 and Luke 6:47–49. He is a wise man who obeys and builds his life on the Word of God. When the storms of this life come (such as ill health, financial difficulties, relational problems, workplace issues, etc.), this person will stand strong and emerge victorious. However, a person who merely hears (hears, reads or studies) the Word and does not obey will be defeated when the storms of this life come. James issued an even more stern warning when he said, *"But be ye doers of the word, and not hearers only, deceiving your own selves"* (James 1:22). People who merely hear the Word of God, but do not obey it, are indeed deceiving themselves. In what way? They think they are doing all required of them by listening to the Word; whereas, they are neglecting the primary requirement of obeying the Word. The message of the entire Bible can be summarized in two words: obey Jesus!

Worship

Worship of the one, true God is enjoined in both the Old and New Testaments. The call to worship in the Old Testament includes 1 Chronicles 16:29, Psalm 29:2 and Psalm 95:6. Abraham worshipped God (Genesis 22:5), as indeed did Joshua (Joshua 5:14) and many others in the Old Testament. The call to worship in the New Testament is given in John 4:23 and Acts 24:14. Of course, there is worship in Heaven (Revelation 4:10). One should worship God individually, such as privately at home, and corporately with other believers, such as in a church service. Both aspects of worship are central to spiritual growth. This pattern is seen in both the Old and New Testaments (Psalm 5:7, Psalm 132:7, Hebrews 10:25).

Two principles of worship are given by our Lord in John 4:24: "*God is a Spirit: and they that worship him must worship him in spirit and in truth.*" The first principle is worshipping God in the spirit and involves at least three aspects: (1) worshipping God with a pure heart and our whole heart, (2) worshipping God with reverence and respect and (3) worshipping God out of a holy lifestyle. We must worship God out of a pure heart (Psalm 24:3–4). That means it is necessary to prepare our hearts for worship by cleansing ourselves with the blood of the Lord Jesus Christ. We must confess and repent of our sins in a Scriptural way. (See chapter 4.) Moreover, we must worship with our whole hearts. Our spirit, soul and body must be fully engaged in the worship of God. David told God, "*I will praise thee with my whole heart*" (Psalm 138:1). Worship not from the heart is insincere and unacceptable to God. Jesus said, *"This people honors Me with their lips, but their heart is far from Me"* (Mark 7:6).

Our worship should reflect reverence for God and show deep respect for Him. The psalmist said, *"God is greatly to be feared in the assembly of the saints, and to be had in reverence of all them that are about him"* (Psalm 89:7). We should never be flippant, casual or lighthearted in our worship. Never bring God down to your level in your worship. However, reverence does not mean having a long face, folded hands or a put-on look of seriousness or piety. Worship is a time of joy—a time of offering thanks, adoration and love. Worship also involves praying, praising, feeding on the Word and proclaiming Christ to the world.

Thirdly, we must worship God out of a holy lifestyle. As Peter admonished us, *"But as he which hath called you is holy, so be ye holy in all manner of conversation; Because it is written, Be ye holy; for I am holy"* (1 Peter 1:15–16). We cannot live an unholy life and expect to worship a holy God. In a true sense, our life reflects the character of our worship because our worship is what our life is.

The second principle Jesus gave in John 4:24 is to worship God in truth. Pilate asked Jesus, *"What is truth?"* (John 18:38). This question is answered by our Savior and Lord elsewhere, *"Sanctify them through thy truth: thy word is truth"* (John 17:17). Thus, our worship must be guided by and be consistent with the Word of God. There are many ways to worship God. However, not all worship is acceptable to God. We should always examine our worship under the light of God's Word by asking, "Is this way of worship Scriptural? Is this how God wants to be worshipped?" God alone has the right to determine how we should worship

Him. God has indicated clearly how He wants to be worshipped in His Word, the Holy Bible. I believe the Word of God should be central in our worship. Reading or singing psalms, hymns or songs—consistent with Scripture—are acceptable ways to worship God. Likewise, we could worship God by centering our praise on the Covenant Names of God the Father and of the Lord Jesus Christ given in the Bible.

In addition, giving financially should be an integral part of our worship. We cannot worship God truly with our hearts if we do not give our treasure to the Lord. As our Savior said, "*For where your treasure is, there will your heart be also*" (Matthew 6:21, Luke 12:34). Giving should include, but not be limited to, the first day of the week. "*Upon the first day of the week let every one of you lay by him in store, as God hath prospered him*" (1 Corinthians 16:2). Giving financially is a practical way we acknowledge the Lordship of Jesus Christ. It is also a way to demonstrate our obedience to the Word of God. Giving sets in motion the law of sowing and reaping (Galatians 6:7–8) and causes us to receive from God not only finances but also other things necessary for our spiritual growth. The topic of giving is discussed further later in this chapter in the section on *Witness* and in chapter 3 of *God Is Calling You: Responding to the Calling of God.*

Fellowship

Fellowship is a term translated from the Greek word *koinonia,* and it refers to Christians who are in communion with each other. We who are Christians, although numerous as individuals, are united together as one body in Christ. Each of us has a distinct role to play according to our special talents and opportunities (Romans 12:5). We are as committed to each other as we are to Jesus Christ. When we have fellowship with other believers, we can encourage them and, in turn, be encouraged by them. Thereby, all can grow in their spiritual walk. In the book of Acts, the early Church devoted itself to fellowship. It was one of the objectives and one of the reasons why believers met. Acts 2:42 states, *"And they continued steadfastly in the apostles' doctrine and fellowship, and in breaking of bread, and in prayers."* The four reasons the early Church met were to study doctrine (God's Word), fellowship, eat and pray; all of these should go together.

The Bible provides several guidelines for fellowship. See, for example, Romans 12:9–21, especially Romans 12:9–13. Our fellowship should be grounded in love and be without hypocrisy. We should *"Be kindly affectioned one to another with brotherly love; in honour preferring one another"* (Romans 12:10). We should be diligent when meeting, fervent in spirit, with a motivation of serving the Lord. Our fellowship should embody rejoicing in hope, being patient in tribulation, continuing steadfastly in prayer, distributing to the needs of the saints and practicing hospitality. Let us strive for Biblical fellowship, for it is important for our spiritual growth and development.

Fellowship involves relationship, companionship and sharing with other believers. Our close friends always should be believers. *"Be ye not unequally yoked together with unbelievers: for what fellowship hath righteousness with unrighteousness? and what communion hath light with dark-*

ness?" (2 Corinthians 6:14). Close friendship is certainly one form of yoking. This does not mean we should not befriend nonbelievers or develop a relationship with them; we should do this, so we can witness to them. However, we should not be influenced by the beliefs, convictions and lifestyles of unbelievers if they are inconsistent with the Bible, as indeed they are likely to be. On the positive side, the Bible says, *"Iron sharpeneth iron; so a man sharpeneth the countenance of his friend"* (Proverbs 27:17). Christians sharpen one another to know God's Word, live Godly lives, exercise God-given gifts, love, do good works and be faithful in their calling. As the writer of Hebrews, some believe he is Paul, said, *"And let us consider one another to provoke unto love and to good works: Not forsaking the assembling of ourselves together, as the manner of some is; but exhorting one another: and so much the more, as ye see the day approaching"* (Hebrews 10:24–25). Thus, Christian fellowship is essential for spiritual growth.

While personal fellowship with physical presence is certainly desirable, it is not the only way to fellowship. We can have fellowship with other believers as long as we can communicate with them. Thus, we can have fellowship via mail, telephone, internet chats, online community forums, blogs, Facebook, Twitter and a variety of other social media. By using different media, we can have fellowship with brothers and sisters in Christ all over this globe.

It is worth pointing out that we cannot have fellowship with other Christians if we are out of fellowship with God because of disobedience and sin in our lives. As I will discuss in more detail in chapter 4, when we sin, God does not break His fellowship with us; it is we who tend to break our fellowship with God. In order to have fellowship with other believers, we must continually be walking with the Lord Jesus Christ. *"But if we walk in the light, as he is in the light, we have fellowship one with another, and the blood of Jesus Christ his Son cleanseth us from all sin"* (1 John 1:7).

Service

We are created to serve God (Ephesians 2:10) and are saved to serve Him (2 Timothy 1:9). Furthermore, we are called (1 Corinthians 7:17) and commanded (Matthew 20:27–28) to live a life of service. Our Savior and Lord Jesus Christ set the standard for us in service. *"Even as the Son of man came not to be ministered unto, but to minister, and to give his life a ransom for many"* (Matthew 20:28; see also Mark 10:45). Jesus was God in Heaven. He came to earth in the form of a servant. He did not come with pomp and glory but as a humble, lowly man. He did not require or even expect others to minister to Him. Rather He ministered to them and served them. He provided for their needs—even at the cost of suffering need for their sakes. Jesus demonstrated service at every turn in His ministry.

Consider, for example, the instance of washing His disciples' feet in John 13:1–20. This act can be understood on two levels. First, it is an obvious example of practical service focused on the needs of others—even though it involves performing menial tasks. Second, it embodies a deeper type of service and personal sacrifice modeled by Jesus when the washing of feet is viewed in light of His death and resurrection. As an ultimate act of service and obedience to God the Father, the Lord Jesus Christ took upon Himself the sins of all mankind, suffered the cruel death on the cross and made the perfect, sacrificial atonement for us.

Following the Lord Jesus Christ means serving Him, and serving the Lord means following Him. "*If any man serve me, let him follow me; and where I am, there shall also my servant be: if any man serve me, him will my Father honour*" (John 12:26). Repenting and turning away from sin and to the Lord Jesus Christ mean serving Him, as the Thessalonian Christians did. The apostle Paul wrote, "*For they themselves shew of us what manner of entering in we had unto you, and how ye turned to God from idols to serve the living and true God*" (1 Thessalonians 1:9).

Our love for God should be expressed in our service to Him. There are several places where we are admonished to serve God. "*Wherefore we receiving a kingdom which cannot be moved, let us have grace, whereby we may serve God acceptably with reverence and godly fear*" (Hebrews 12:28). Service is something we will do even in Heaven (Revelation 7:15, 22:3); but God expects us to get started here and now. On earth, we should prepare and practice for the eternal service we will be rendering.

We should serve God wholeheartedly. In the Gospels, the Lord uses servanthood to describe discipleship. Indeed, a disciple may be appropriately characterized as a servant of God because of the exclusive nature of the demand the master makes on the servant. "*No man can serve two masters: for either he will hate the one, and love the other; or else he will hold to the one, and despise the other. Ye cannot serve God and mammon*" (Matthew 6:24; see also Luke 16:13). A servant cannot serve two masters because his affections and obedience would be divided, and he would fail altogether in his duty to one or the other or to both. As a law of human nature, supreme affections can be fixed on only one object. Therefore, a believer cannot serve God and mammon. A Syriac word, *mammon,* was a name given to an idol worshipped as the god of riches. Mammon represents all forms of wealth, tempting us to compromise our commitment to God. Anything less than total commitment to the Lord Jesus Christ ultimately leads to the service of mammon.

Serving God means loving and serving one another. *"For, brethren, ye have been called unto liberty; only use not liberty for an occasion to the flesh, but by love serve one another"* (Galatians 5:13). The Gospel of the Lord Jesus Christ gives us freedom and liberty—no, not to sin, but to love and serve one another. Christians are to be governed by the royal law of love. As one manifestation of love, we serve and promote one another's welfare and well-being. While the Ephesian servants were admonished to serve their masters (Ephesians 6:7), the general principle applies to serving other Christians and even nonChristians.

Service involves sacrifice. This is noted clearly by the apostle Paul: *"I beseech you therefore, brethren, by the mercies of God, that ye present your bodies a living sacrifice, holy, acceptable unto God, which is your reasonable service"* (Romans 12:1). Most Christians are convenience Christians. They are willing to serve God when it is convenient to do so, when it fits with their schedule, their pocketbook and their desires. However, they are not willing to serve God sacrificially. They are not willing to pay the cost. There is a cost to serving the Lord. It costs time, money, effort, energy and a sacrifice of personal desires and wishes to serve the Lord.

King David said, *"Neither will I offer burnt offerings unto the LORD my God of that which doth cost me nothing"* (2 Samuel 24:24). However, the attitude of many Christians is just the opposite and may be stated, "I will serve the Lord only if it costs me nothing." This is the reason why most Christians are not serving the Lord Jesus Christ in any significant way; they are not willing to pay the cost.

Finally, service to the Lord Jesus Christ is very different in nature and character compared to service in this world. Service in this world system is built on rank and status and motivated by reward and promotion. The character of Christian service is radically different from this societal norm. Consider our Lord's contrast of the two services in Mark 10:42–45. In the world system, the mark of greatness is lordship and authority over others. According to Jesus, the true mark of greatness is serving others with humility as a servant serves his master.

Witness

Why should Christians witness? Witnessing our faith in the Lord Jesus Christ is not an option. It is a commandment given by our Lord. This commandment is given clearly in a passage commonly referred to as the Great Commission (Matthew 28:18–20). The basis of our witness is that the resurrected Lord Jesus Christ embodies all power in Heaven and earth. He is the all-powerful, omnipotent, omniscient, omnipresent God. He has commissioned us to share the Gospel because God wants salvation to be universally available. Therefore, we are to go to all nations and proclaim the good news that the mercy and grace of

God the Father from the wrath of sin are available through the perfect, sacrificial atoning death and resurrection of His Son, the Lord Jesus Christ. While salvation is available universally, it will be effective in only those who receive it by faith by receiving the Lord Jesus Christ as Savior and Lord. All those who respond in faith will be saved (Romans 10:13). Moreover, they will be sanctified continually by the Holy Spirit. As a part of our witness, we are to teach others about the life, death, resurrection and all the ordinances and commandments of God contained in His Holy Word, the Bible. We are never alone in our witness as our Savior is always with us to the uttermost parts of the world and even to the end of this age. Let His saving grace be proclaimed throughout all the earth. Amen!

But you may wonder, "Where do I begin?" The answer is given in Acts 1:8, "*But ye shall receive power, after that the Holy Ghost is come upon you: and ye shall be witnesses unto me both in Jerusalem, and in all Judaea, and in Samaria, and unto the uttermost part of the earth.*" You begin in your Jerusalem. The disciples were in Jerusalem when they received this commandment and received the Holy Ghost. Most of the disciples remained in Jerusalem until persecution arose leading to the death of Stephen (Acts 8:1). The apostles remained in Jerusalem until the death of James by Herod. (See Acts 12.) Your Jerusalem denotes your home, neighborhood, workplace, community and city. That is where you begin. Get involved in the witnessing program of your local church. It is a good idea to get some formal training in evangelism, so you can know how to lead people to Christ. If your church does not have a witnessing program, consider joining the program of another church where you can participate regularly. Once you take the first steps to witness, God will give you the grace and open doors for you to witness. *"And with great power gave the apostles witness of the resurrection of the Lord Jesus: and great grace was upon them all"* (Acts 4:33). Once you are faithful in witnessing in your Jerusalem, God will open other opportunities for you to witness in other cities in your state (your Judaea), in other states in your country (your Samaria) and in other countries (the uttermost part of the earth). It is important you begin now—right where you are.

Why is witnessing so important for your spiritual growth? Witnessing will increase and strengthen your faith based on the principle of giving and receiving. *"Give, and it shall be given unto you; good measure, pressed down, and shaken together, and running over, shall men give into your bosom. For with the same measure that ye mete withal it shall be measured to you again"* (Luke 6:38). God's way of getting is to give first. While this verse is quoted generally in the context of financial giving, it embodies a general principle applicable to other areas as well. For example, if you want love, give away your love (of course, in a Biblical sense). Witnessing is essentially giving away your faith. If you give away your faith, you will get more faith. Thus, witnessing will increase and strengthen your faith. In 2 Corinthians 4:13, Paul quotes Psalm 116:10, *"I believed, therefore have I spoken."* Like him, we should speak or witness Christ as an outpouring of our faith. Since all believers have been commissioned to preach the Gospel, let us be exhorted by the words of the apostle: *"even so we speak; not as pleasing men, but God, which trieth our hearts"* (1 Thessalonians 2:4). Our main motivation always must be to glorify God by witnessing and accurately proclaiming His Word.

The characteristics of a faithful witness are given in Acts 26:22, *"Having therefore obtained help of God, I continue unto this day, witnessing both to small and great, saying none other things than those which the prophets and Moses did say should come."* First, a good witness will obtain help from God. We must depend upon God and lean on Him for help in sharing the Gospel. Second, a true witness will continue, not giving up witnessing regardless of the obstacles, difficulties and hardships. Third, we should witness to everyone—both small and great. Fourth, a true witness will proclaim the Word of God faithfully; we must remain true to His Word. Let us all endeavor to develop these four Biblical qualities so we, like Paul, may be faithful witnesses.

Scripture Spotlight

Paul's Prayer for Spiritual Growth of the Colossian Christians

In Colossians 1:9–14, Paul's prayer for the Colossian Christians about their spiritual growth reflects the elements identified as essential concepts in this chapter. Paul reflected these elements in his walk with the Lord and expected the Colossian believers to follow his example: *"Be ye followers of me, even as I also am of Christ"* (1 Corinthians 11:1). Let us look at this passage verse-by-verse. Please look at these verses in the Bible as you read this book.

Scripture Source: Colossians 1:9–14

Verse 9

1. Paul learned from Epaphras of the Colossians' love for him (Colossians 1:7–8). Here, he is returning their love by praying for them. Praying for others can be a strong expression of your love for them.

2. Sometimes we think we cannot touch people's lives without physical presence with them. Paul exemplifies through prayer, God will give to the people for whom we pray knowledge, wisdom, understanding and spiritual growth—even without our physical presence.

3. "*Since the day we heard it.*" The word "it" refers to the Colossian believers' "*love in the Spirit*" as a result of believing the Gospel (Colossians 1:8). This includes their love for the saints mentioned specifically earlier in verse 4 (Colossians 1:4). Thus, the Colossians were walking in love, implying a strong bond of fellowship.

4. Paul says we "*do not cease to pray for you.*" Paul first talked about praying for the Colossians in verse 3 of this chapter. He now mentions praying without ceasing. Thus, Paul is practicing what he preached to the Thessalonians, "*Pray without ceasing*" (1 Thessalonians 5:17). The clear implication is the Colossian Christians ought to pray in the same manner and so should all believers.

5. Paul specifically prays and had a great desire that the Colossians "*might be filled with the knowledge*

of his will." In order to be filled with the will of God, a necessary condition is that the Colossians first surrender their will to Him. Desire, meaning an intense longing, is a key to answered prayer. Jesus said so in Mark 11:24, "*Therefore I say unto you, What things soever ye desire, when ye pray, believe that ye receive them, and ye shall have them.*" By application, you should greatly desire God's will and calling to be accomplished in your life and pray accordingly. God's will is revealed in His Word; so you should study the Bible, and obey the Word. The more you do so, the greater will be your knowledge and understanding of God's will and calling.

6. He prays they might be filled with "*all wisdom.*" Wisdom is the ability to use knowledge correctly, as God would have us use it. The wisdom of God is contained in the Word of God. As Paul wrote to Timothy, "*And that from a child thou hast known the holy scriptures, which are able to make thee wise unto salvation through faith which is in Christ Jesus*" (2 Timothy 3:15). Hence, the Colossians needed to study the Scriptures in faith, so they may gain the wisdom of God.

7. The last part of verse 9 refers to "*spiritual under-standing*" and growth of the Colossians. Paul's prayer was they would grow by understanding those things taught by the Holy Spirit and those He produces in the work of salvation. We grow by understanding the ways of God—as revealed in His Holy Word. This underscores our devotion to the Word.

8. The words "wisdom" and "understanding" are used in combination fifty-three times in Scripture.[2] Wisdom and understanding have to work together for our spiritual growth. Both are gained by studying the Bible.

Verse 10

1. Paul prays the Colossians "*might walk worthy of the Lord.*" "Walk" is used to indicate a pattern of conduct or lifestyle (1 John 1:7, 2 John 6, 3 John 3–4). Paul prays the Colossians may live as becomes the followers of the Lord Jesus Christ. They could do so by pleasing God in all things, including fellowship, love and unity with the believers. While fellowship and love are implicit in verse 10, Paul explicitly has mentioned these earlier in the chapter in verse 4: "*After hearing of your faith in Christ Jesus, and of the love which you have for all the saints*" (Colossians 1:4).

2. Paul's desire was the Colossians would be "*fruitful in every good work,*" signifying a high level of service unto the Lord. The more they understand how God works through His Spirit, the more fruitful their service will be. They can bear fruit that will remain only in the power of the Holy Spirit. Good works in the New Covenant are the fruit, not the root, of our salvation (Ephesians 2:8–10, 1 John 3:10).

3. They would be "*increasing in the knowledge of God*" by a study of the Scriptures. The word *knowledge*, in the Greek, means participatory and full knowl-

edge. What you have in your head sinks deep down in your heart. That is when you begin to experience God—not just know about Him. You get to know the Lord Jesus Christ. Spiritual growth is the process of getting to know the Lord Jesus Christ and being conformed to His image. Do you know Him? Do you talk and walk with Him? Do you experience His presence and His power on a daily basis? Paul said, *"That I may know him, and the power of his resurrection, and the fellowship of his sufferings"* (Philippians 3:10). That should be your goal; it should be the goal of every believer.

4. Even Jesus had to increase in wisdom (Luke 2:52). Jesus was God in the Spirit, but His physical mind had to be renewed by the Word. If Jesus had to grow in wisdom, how could any of us think we do not have to increase *"in the knowledge of God"* and renew our minds with the Word of God?

Verse 11

1. *"Strengthened with all might, according to his glorious power."* The apostle desired they might be strengthened for the performance of service, not by any human means, but by the glorious power of God. You can do all things God has called you to do through Jesus Christ Who gives you the strength and power (Philippians 4:13).

2. The word *strengthened* in the Greek is a present, passive participle, signifying continuous action. God does not strengthen us just one time. Rather,

it is a continuous process. Therefore, we need to keep praying that God would strengthen us according to His glorious power.

3. *"Unto all patience and longsuffering with joyfulness."* In serving the Lord, they patiently would endure their trials with joyfulness. Thus, they would pay willingly and joyfully the cost of serving the Lord. *"Longsuffering"* is a fruit of the Spirit (Galatians 5:22) and is developed as one learns to walk in the Spirit. It is a key to enduring trials joyfully—even the ones humanly unendurable (James 1:2–4).

4. Tolerance of others or situations should not be mistaken as patience and long-suffering. There is a big difference: *"joyfulness."* The counterfeit patience and long-suffering offered by the world lack joy. Worldly tolerance is the best we can do in our strength to bear with situations and people. In contrast, when we are strengthened by the glorious power of God, we can experience true patience and long-suffering and be joyful in the face of our difficult circumstances.

Verse 12

1. *"Giving thanks unto the Father."* They would worship and thank God the Father Who had provided the plan of salvation and had sent His Son to redeem them. Our special worship and thanks are due to God the Father because He is the great Author of the whole plan of salvation. Note that

thanksgiving is an integral part of praise, worship and prayer.

2. The Father *"hath made us meet to be partakers of the inheritance of the saints in light."* He already has enabled us to share in the inheritance belonging to His people who live in the light. To realize the full portion of our inheritance, we have to fulfill the calling of God. This topic is discussed in detail in chapters 6 and 7 of the second book in this series, *God Is Calling You: Responding to the Calling of God.*

Verse 13

1. Here Paul is witnessing by preaching the Gospel. God the Father has *"delivered us from the power of darkness,"* that is, from the kingdom of Satan characterized by sin and death. We were in sin and doomed to keep repeating our sins. *"Who hath delivered"* us is in the Greek aorist tense. This means the action is complete, as a whole, or as a one-time action that already has taken place. God already has delivered the believers from the power of Satan.

2. Since we already have been delivered *"from the power of darkness,"* Satan does not have any real power over us. His only weapons are deception and intimidation. Based on the truth of this verse, we should have no fear of Satan.

3. Furthermore, God has *"translated"* or transferred us *"into the kingdom of his dear Son."* The verb

"*translated*" is relating the fact of the believer being totally removed from the kingdom of darkness and brought into the kingdom of God's dear Son. Thus, we have become subjects of a new Kingdom governed by love, truth, light, mercy and grace. This is the Kingdom of Jesus Christ, the Son of God!

Verse 14

1. "*In whom we have redemption through his blood.*" Paul continues his witness, talking about redemption, conclusively stating you obtain forgiveness of sins through the blood of Christ. There is no other way. At the cross, the power of sin over your life has been broken. You have been delivered from the power of darkness and are no longer under Satan's dominion (Romans 6:6). Rather, now in the Kingdom of God, you are empowered to live a life pleasing and honoring to the Lord Jesus Christ. You have to grow and keep on growing spiritually in order to actually live such a life on a daily basis.

2. The forgiveness of our sins is a part of our salvation; it is not the ultimate goal. It is a necessary step. The real goal of salvation is relationship with Father God, and sin is a barrier to that relationship. Sin had to be dealt with to establish the relationship, and it was through the perfect, atoning death of the Lord Jesus Christ on the cross. But those who stop with the forgiveness of sins and don't go on to an intimate relationship with the

Father are missing the heart of salvation. Let us forever enjoy the ultimate benefit of our salvation by developing an intimate, love relationship with our Heavenly Father.

Conclusion

In this short passage, Paul covers all of the seven essential elements of spiritual growth. In Paul's prayers for the spiritual growth of his brethren at Colossae, we see his devotion to his Savior and his love for others. This prayer marks the ideal of Christian character. What Paul desired for the Colossians is what all believers should pray for those whom they love and should endeavor to develop for themselves.

Author's Account

With great joy, I share my growing in and walking with my Savior and Lord, Jesus Christ.

My Spiritual Growth and Walk with the Lord

Since I received the Lord Jesus Christ as my personal Savior and Lord, I have been blessed with a very steady personal walk with the Lord. I do believe in giving the first part of my day to the Lord. Therefore, the first thing I do every morning is pray. When in Atlanta, I often pray for at least an hour. When on the mission field, my prayer time is reduced to twenty to thirty minutes in the morning as I generally have early morning appointments.

The most important aspect of my prayer life is praying Scriptures. I begin by thanking God for the seven times Jesus shed His blood and praying the accompanying Scriptures. As I have shared earlier in this chapter, when Jesus sweat great drops of blood in the Garden of Gethsemane, He redeemed our will—something Adam had lost in the Garden of Eden when he willfully, knowingly and deliberately disobeyed God. I, too, come to my own Garden of Gethsemane, almost daily, where I cry out to God, "Not my will but Thy perfect will be done in my life, Abba, Father." When I started praying this request, it marked another turning point in my life. In the process of thanking God for the seven times Jesus shed His blood, I pray eighty-two Scripture verses, voicing each verse.

Of course, the cross would have no significance were it not followed by the resurrection of the Lord Jesus Christ. Like the cross, the resurrection is a cornerstone of our faith. Therefore, I pray Scriptures dealing with the resurrection.

Then I approach God via the Tabernacle, thanking God for each element of the Tabernacle. I first read about the Tabernacle method of praying in Dr. David Yonggi Cho's book *How to Pray* when I visited his church in 2007 in Seoul, South Korea. The interested reader is referred to this book. In addition, you can do an internet search and find a lot of material on the Tabernacle method of praying. Actually, I have developed my own Tabernacle method that is an amalgamation of various materials I have read on this topic. This is another discovery that transformed my prayer life. Here again, I pray several Scripture verses—too many to count. I then thank God and pray about various needs, all the time praying Scripture. I estimate I pray more than three hundred Scripture verses on many mornings, clearly speaking out each verse. I quote Scriptures from the King James Version. Most of these Scriptures I have memorized. Yet I have put all of these verses in a computer file and printed them so I can look at them while praying. Now you can see why my prayer time lasts more than an hour. The power of God is in the Word of God. Thus, praying Scriptures is very powerful. I have been blessed to see the power of God manifested in many areas of my life. Praise and worship are an integral part of my prayers.

Following the Tabernacle method, when I come to the Altar of Incense, I offer my prayers of praise and worship. I focus on the Covenant Names of God in the Old Testament and the Name of Jesus Christ, my Savior and Lord. I pray a few verses from the Psalms, focusing on God's mercy (e.g., Psalm 57:9–11 and Psalm 145:8–9) and psalms of praise (Psalms 100 and 150) and other passages of worship (e.g., 1 Chronicles 29:10–14).

Then I have some tea or coffee and study the Bible. If there are days when I have not read the Bible since I got saved, I do not remember them. I am confident such days will be less than five in number. Often I read only the Bible, but sometimes I read a commentary or two as well. In studying the Bible, my practice has been to focus on the Word of God and let the Holy Spirit reveal to me the truths from God's Word. I tend not to read a lot of commentaries or use many other resources; I feel my time is better spent on studying the Word of God directly. There are many methods of Bible study such as inductive and deductive. I do not follow any particular method per se but read and study the Bible and let the Holy Spirit minister to me. I have read the entire Old and New Testaments, word for word, several times over.

I have been blessed with good Christian fellowship over the years. I had good, close Christian friends with whom I could share my heart. They certainly have encouraged me in my walk with the Lord, and I hope I likewise have encouraged them. My wife and I consistently have preferred spending time with Christian friends than in a secular setting that otherwise may be good and clean.

As stated before, the love for God and obedience to God will result in service to God. Since 1979, service to God has been an integral part of my spiritual growth and walk. I have served God in teaching Sunday school from 1983 to 2009, serving as a deacon in the First Baptist Church of Atlanta from 1982 to present, on short-term mission trips from 1987 to present and in several other ways. There is a cost to serving the Lord.

In the summer of 1994, I was conducting evangelism in Moscow, Russia. My main ministry was presenting the Gospel to tourists who were taking guided tours of the Red Square and Kremlin. I have described this work in chapter 2 of the second book in this series, *God Is Calling You: Responding to the Calling of God*; and so I will skip the details here. Since there was no place to sit in the Red Square, I had to stand on my feet all of the time and there was a good amount of walking involved. One morning I got up and was so tired that I did not have energy to go to the restaurant for breakfast. Somehow I managed to do so. I knew my interpreter would be waiting for me in the Red Square at 9:45 a.m., and I could not let her down. I conducted a full day of evangelism in the Red Square and then taught in a local church for two hours. I reached my hotel around 9:30 p.m. Tired and exhausted, I flung myself on the bed. As I looked up, God spoke to me, "Naresh, I am willing to use you mightily; but are you willing to pay the cost?" As I was wondering how to respond, the Holy Spirit brought to my mind a verse of Scripture where King David told Araunah, he would not offer "*unto the LORD my God of that which doth cost me nothing*" (2 Samuel 24:24). I told the Lord, by His grace, I am willing to pay the cost.

This was not a one-time test. Since then, I have been tested continually. We have to be willing to pay the cost if we are to serve the Lord and be used mightily for His glory. I am convinced, when it comes to service, most Christians are convenience Christians; they will serve the Lord only when it is convenient for them to do so. They are not willing to pay the cost. When Jesus spoke about the cost of following Him, "*From that time many of his disciples went back, and walked no more with him*" (John 6:66), they were not willing to pay the cost.

Witnessing should happen naturally. A Christian should not have to get into a witnessing mode in order to witness. Witnessing should be the natural outcome of our love for the Lord Jesus Christ and our compassion for the lost. "*And Jesus, when he came out, saw much people, and was moved with compassion toward them, because they were as sheep not having a shepherd: and he began to teach them many things*" (Mark 6:34). I was trained in Evangelism Explosion (EE) in the early 1980s, then attended an advanced clinic and became a certified EE Teacher. I have trained many people in EE at the First Baptist Church of Atlanta when the church was conducting this program. EE is a good way to witness because this approach makes use of Scripture. Any approach making good use of Scripture will be effective.

Personally, I make use of many different approaches to witnessing and rely on the Holy Spirit to guide me and work in the heart of the lost person. In 1987, I was led to trust the Lord to see one person every month pray to receive the Lord Jesus Christ as Savior and Lord in personal witnessing situations in Atlanta. The Lord more than granted my request; and I saw 34 people pray to receive the Lord Jesus Christ as Savior and Lord, including at least one person every month. Encouraged by what the Lord had done, in 1988 I trusted the Lord to see fifty-two people pray to receive Christ—one every week. Again, the Lord exceeded abundantly; and I was blessed to see sixty-seven people pray to receive Christ as their Savior and Lord. These were the starting points of seeing an ever-increasing number of people praying to receive the Lord Jesus every year.

While we keep track of numbers, the Lord has shown me He is very concerned with the salvation of individual souls. Thus, my focus has to be on the salvation of an individual. If I lose my burden for an individual soul, I would lose my burden for the lost. I remind myself of this truth continually. I should add, keeping track of numbers in this manner is Biblical. Acts 2:41 states, *"Then they that gladly received his word were baptized: and the same day there were added unto them about three thousand souls."* Again, we read in Acts 4:4, *"Howbeit many of them which heard the word believed; and the number of the men was about five thousand."* God is also concerned with numbers, and an entire book in the Bible is named Numbers.

All in all, I have to say it has been a glorious walk with the Lord since I got saved on March 19, 1978; and it keeps getting better. I have been blessed to experience the power of God in many areas of my life. The most gratifying aspect of my spiritual growth and walk has been fellowship with God—to experience His presence, to talk with Him and to relate to Him as a real Person. My ministry overseas requires much time away from my family in Atlanta. However, I seldom have felt lonely or alone. My Savior and Lord Jesus Christ is always with me; "*for he hath said, I will never leave thee, nor forsake thee*" (Hebrews 13:5). Experiencing God's presence and power are indeed the greatest blessings anyone can have and are the essence of our calling.

Quest Questions

Please do some soul searching and answer the following questions. You need not share your answers with anyone. However, if you so choose, share them with your accountability partner or a person you trust.

- Am I growing spiritually? How can I tell?
- Do I surrender my will and my life to the Lord Jesus Christ on a daily basis?
- What is my understanding about sanctification?
- How much time do I spend in prayer daily?
- Do I pray to God the Father in the Name of Jesus Christ in the power of the Holy Spirit?
- Do I really believe God answers prayers? Is prayer my first response to a need, or is it the last resort?

- Do I pray Scriptures? Are my prayers mingled with thanksgiving and praise?
- Do I study the Bible daily? How much time do I spend in Bible study daily?
- How well do I know the Bible? How intimate is my knowledge of God's Word?
- Can I hear God speaking to me when I read His Word?
- Do I know how to worship God? Privately? Corporately with other believers?
- Do I worship God? Do I worship Him in Spirit and in truth?
- Is my lifestyle holy? Do I have a good testimony?
- How is my fellowship with God? With other Christians?
- Do I love other Christians? How do I express this love?
- Do I love the lost? Am I burdened about their salvation?
- Do I experience God's love on a daily basis? Do I love the Lord Jesus Christ?
- Am I following the Lord Jesus Christ? In what way?
- Am I serving the Lord Jesus Christ? Is my service selfless?
- Am I serving other people? How?
- In what way is my life a sacrifice unto the Lord?
- Am I willing to pay the cost of serving the Lord?
- Am I witnessing to others the grace of the Lord Jesus Christ in my life? To whom? In what way?

You can evaluate your answers to these questions in light of the following principles and precepts.

Principles and Precepts

- God has to do His work in you before He can do His work through you (Philippians 2:13, Colossians 1:9, Hebrews 13:21).
- Once saved, we continually have to surrender our will to the Lord Jesus Christ and to God the Father as a process of spiritual growth and sanctification (1 Corinthians 15:31).
- Salvation is a one-time act, but experiencing the reality of sanctification is a lifelong process. The manifestation of our sanctification will be complete only when we see the Lord Jesus Christ face to face (1 Thessalonians 5:23, 1 Corinthians 13:10).
- As a result of Christ's finished work on the cross, we have been sanctified by our Savior *"Jesus Christ once for all"* (Hebrews 10:10). Furthermore, *"he hath perfected for ever them that are sanctified"* (Hebrews 10:14). Yet to experience the reality of this sanctification on a daily basis, you have to grow in your walk with your Savior (Hebrews 10:10–14).
- Although believers sin, they do not have to sin; the power of sin over their lives has been broken (Romans 6:6–7).
- God has promised to answer our prayers, providing a great motivation for praying (Luke 11:9–10).

- Pray to God the Father in the Name of Jesus Christ in the power of the Holy Spirit (Matthew 6:8–9; John 15:16, 16:23; Romans 8:26–27).
- Prayers should be based on the Word of God. Praying Scripture is very powerful (Psalm 103:20, Ezekiel 12:25).
- We must approach God, not in our righteousness that is *"as filthy rags,"* but in the righteousness of the Lord Jesus Christ, the Righteous One (Isaiah 64:6, Philippians 3:9).
- Prayers should be mingled with thanksgiving and praise (Psalm 100:4, 1 Thessalonians 5:18).
- The Bible is the inerrant, infallible, eternal and unchangeable Word of the living God; it is our final authority in life. Be guided by the Word at all times, seasons, circumstances and on all occasions (Psalm 119:50, 89; Matthew 24:35; Mark 13:31; Luke 21:33).
- Study the Bible daily, memorize it and meditate upon it (Joshua 1:8, Matthew 4:4).
- Obey the Word of God. The entire message of the Bible can be summarized in two words: obey Jesus! (Joshua 1:8, James 1:22–25).
- The primary and the surest way God speaks to us is through His Word (2 Timothy 3:14–17).
- An intimate knowledge of God's Word is a key to having our prayers answered (John 15:7).
- In addition to private or personal worship, we should worship God corporately with other believers (Acts 2:46, Hebrews 10:25).

- Worship of God in the spirit involves worshipping Him with a pure heart, reverently and out of a holy lifestyle (John 4:24).
- Like prayers, our worship must be based on the Word of God (Acts 24:14).
- Giving financially should be an integral part of our worship (Matthew 6:21, Luke 12:34).
- Our fellowship should be grounded in love and be without hypocrisy (Romans 12:10).
- Christians sharpen one another to know God's Word, live Godly lives, exercise God-given gifts, love, do good works and be faithful in their calling (Hebrews 10:24–25, Proverbs 27:17).
- We cannot have fellowship with other Christians if we put ourselves out of fellowship with God because of willful disobedience and deliberate sin in our lives (1 John 1:7).
- Our love for God should be expressed in our service to Him. Following the Lord Jesus Christ means serving Him, and serving the Lord means following Him (John 12:26).
- Serving God means loving and serving one another (Galatians 5:13).
- Service involves sacrifice. It costs time, money, effort, energy and a sacrifice of personal desires and wishes to serve the Lord. We must be willing to pay the cost of serving the Lord (2 Samuel 24:24, Romans 12:1).
- A servant cannot serve two masters. You cannot serve God and wealth (Matthew 6:24, Luke 16:13).

- Serving others with humility, as a servant serves his master, is a true mark of greatness (Mark 10:42–44).
- Witnessing is not an option; it is a commandment given by our Lord (Matthew 28:18–20).
- Your Jerusalem denotes your home, neighborhood, workplace, community and city. This is where you begin witnessing (Acts 1:8).
- A good witness will obtain help from God, will continue witnessing regardless of the obstacles and will witness the Word of God to everyone—both small and great (Acts 26:22).

Life Lesson

Life is a race. To run this race successfully and finish the course, you need to grow by developing spiritual disciplines and practicing them consistently. These disciplines include daily surrender, prayer, Bible study, worship, fellowship, service and witness.

Prayer Power

Abba, Father, I thank You for loving me so much that You sent Your Son, my Savior and Lord, to die on the cross for me where You made that all-sufficient, all-encompassing final atonement for me. You raised Him from the dead, and now He lives forevermore. Jesus Christ is my Savior and Lord.

Holy God, I pray, in the mighty Name of my Savior and Lord Jesus Christ, You will help me and enable me to grow spiritually on a daily basis. I want to grow up to be a tall, mighty tree for the Lord Jesus Christ like the tall oaks of Bashan, like the cedars of Lebanon and like the evergreen Cyprus tree. O Holy Spirit, teach me to pray and help me to pray according to the perfect will of my Heavenly Father. Father God, open my eyes and my heart to see and receive the truth from Your Word and apply it in my life on a daily basis. Your Word is the truth. May Your Word be a lamp unto my feet and a light unto my path, and may I walk according to Your will and Your ways. May I hide Your Word in my heart that I might not sin against You. I want Your Word to be the final authority in my life. I want to obey You and live by Your Word.

Holy Spirit, teach me to worship my Heavenly Father in spirit and in truth. Lord Jesus, may Your praise be continually in my heart and on my lips. I ask, based on Psalm 19:14, "*Let the words of my mouth, and the meditation of my heart, be acceptable in thy sight, O LORD, my strength, and my redeemer.*" Abba, Father, bless my fellowship with other brothers and sisters in Christ; so I might encourage them and they me. I ask You to bring the right people, the ones You have chosen, into my inner circle. Lord Jesus, You love me and I want to serve You. Help me to serve You with all of my heart all the days of my life. I want to use my liberty in Christ to serve others in humility and Christian love.

Father God, Your Word says in Romans 5:8, "*But God commendeth his love toward us, in that, while we were yet sinners, Christ died for us.*" Help me to witness to others of Your love for us in sending Your Son to die on the cross for us. He arose again from the dead, and He now offers forgiveness and eternal life to all who will believe in Him. Help me to share this message of salvation with others, especially my family members, friends, neighbors and colleagues.

I pray, believe, receive and thank You for all these things in the Precious Name of my Savior and Lord Jesus Christ. Amen!

Message Ministry

You can access the audio message for this chapter by using CallingYou as the password at

https://www.globalevangelisticministries.net/Calling1-Chapter3.

CHAPTER 4

The Calling to Grow in Grace: The Foundation of Your Calling

"But grow in grace, and in the knowledge of our Lord and Saviour Jesus Christ. To him be glory both now and for ever. Amen."

—2 Peter 3:18

Preamble and Preview

In chapter 3, I emphasized the importance of spiritual growth. However, you cannot grow spiritually by relying on your efforts, strengths and abilities. The ingredients for spiritual growth discussed in the last chapter should not be performed in the flesh, that is, with self-effort or in a legalistic manner. Furthermore, they should not be performed with wrong motives such as to gain the love of God or to become more righteous in His sight. As discussed at length in chapter 1, God loves you with a perfect love. If you are a believer, there is nothing you can do or not do that will cause God to love you any more or any less! You have the full and complete righteousness of God—all because of the Lord Jesus Christ and His finished work on the cross. The only righteousness you can ever have is the righteousness of Christ and righteousness in Him (2 Corinthians 5:21). You simply cannot add to that righteousness or take away from it. In this chapter, I balance the contents of chapter 3 by stressing the way to grow spiritually is to grow in grace. *"For it is a good thing that the heart be established with grace"* (Hebrews 13:9).

In "Central Concepts," I differentiate between growing in grace versus growing by self-effort. You will get a basic understanding of what grace is, grace to overcome temptation, the law and the law versus grace. "Scripture Spotlight" gives a better understanding of grace and further highlights the difference between grace and the law by looking at the healing of an impotent man. "Author's Account" shares my personal journey of growing in grace. The next section, "Quest Questions," contains several questions that I hope will lead you to reflect on your life as it relates to your growing in grace. There are several "Principles and Precepts" you can apply to grow in grace and to draw closer to the Lord Jesus Christ. "Life Lesson" contains the most important lesson you can learn with respect to growing in grace. "Prayer Power" contains an effectual, Scriptural prayer you are encouraged to pray in order to continue growing in grace. Finally, "Message Ministry" gives a link to an audio message you are exhorted to hear.

Central Concepts

To give you a better understanding of growing in grace, I will focus on growing in grace versus growing by self-effort, understanding grace, grace to overcome sin and temptation, understanding the law and law versus grace.

Growing in Grace Versus Growing by Self-Effort

In this chapter, to balance the contents of chapter 3, I stress the way to grow spiritually is to rest in the grace of God in Jesus Christ and to yield to the working of the Holy Spirit. This is important because humans naturally have a strong inclination to rely on their ability, adequacy, capability, competence and potency in accomplishing what they want to do. Instead, God wants you to realize your inability, inadequacy, incapability, incompetence, ineptitude, insufficiency, powerlessness and impotency in and of yourselves and to operate in the omnipotence of the Lord Jesus Christ by resting in His finished work on the cross of Calvary (Ephesians 6:10). God's goal for you, as a believer, is to conform you to the image of His Son, the Lord Jesus Christ (Romans 8:29). This process of transformation occurs when you behold the glory of the Lord Jesus Christ in the Scriptures and in everything you do. "*But we all, with open face beholding as in a glass the glory of the Lord, are changed into the same image from glory to glory, even as by the Spirit of the Lord*" (2 Corinthians 3:18). Thus, the key to spiritual growth is to keep your focus on the Lord Jesus Christ and ask the Holy Spirit to reveal unto you His glory in the Bible. As you see His glory in the Word, the Holy Spirit will conform you to the image of the Lord Jesus. The focus is not on what you do or not do, but it is on beholding or seeing the glory of the Lord Jesus Christ in the Scriptures and in everything you do! This principle operates in the physical, intellectual and spiritual realms that people and living things are changed by beholding. In Genesis 30:35–43, Jacob's flocks and his fortunes were changed by beholding. Jacob *set the faces of the flocks toward the ringstraked, and all the brown in the flock of Laban*" (Genesis 30:40). So by beholding them, they might be disposed in their conception to bring forth the like. The result? *"And the man increased exceedingly, and had much cattle, and maidservants, and menservants, and camels, and asses"* (Genesis 30:43).

The book of Hebrews talks about entering into God's rest (Hebrews 4:3). Resting in the finished work of the Lord Jesus Christ does not imply laziness. The apostle Paul said, *"But by the grace of God I am what I am: and his grace which was bestowed upon me was not in vain; but I laboured more abundantly than they all: yet not I, but the grace of God which was with me"* (1 Corinthians 15:10). Resting in Christ involves hard work. Paul, the apostle of grace, worked harder *"than they all"!* *"Let us labour therefore to enter into that rest"* (Hebrews 4:11). While you work hard, you do not strive according to flesh. Rather you let God do His work in you and then do His work through you. *"Whereunto I also labour, striving according to his working, which worketh in me mightily"* (Colossians 1:29). All of this becomes clearer when you understand grace, the law and the difference between the law and grace.[1]

Understanding Grace

Grace is the undeserved, unearned and unmerited favor of God. Thus, by definition, grace cannot be deserved, earned or merited. The moment you try to merit the free favor of God through your self-effort, you nullify grace. However, grace is much more; He is the Person of Jesus Christ. You cannot separate grace from truth and truth from grace as they are both embodied in the Person of Jesus Christ (John 1:17). The grace of God flows freely from the cross of Calvary. When you receive the Lord Jesus Christ as your Savior and Lord and put your faith and trust in Him (chapter 2), you become a partaker of the grace of God. You have God's grace because you have Jesus Christ! Your righteousness is a result of Jesus's work; and you can receive His righteousness only through grace, that is, through unmerited favor by receiving it as a (free) gift. His grace will transform your life into wholeness. The goodness of God, not your striving and self-effort, will lead you to live victoriously for His glory. The favor of God, because of the presence of Jesus Christ in your life, is a (free) gift from God. You cannot perform enough good works to merit His favor or righteousness.

You are righteous because of the divine exchange on the cross. God took all of your sins and punished them in the body of His Son Jesus Christ. God took all of Jesus's righteousness and put it upon you. Jesus took all of your sins; and in exchange, you took all of His righteousness (2 Corinthians 5:21). Wow! What an exchange! There are two types of righteousness mentioned in Philippians 3:8–9: (1) a righteousness coming from our obedience to God and us trying to earn it and (2) a righteousness coming from faith in Jesus Christ. The first type of righteousness is enjoined by the law. However, the law cannot justify you or make you righteous (Galatians 2:16). Under grace, God wants you to focus on your righteousness in Jesus Christ (Romans 5:17–21). Your righteousness in Christ is a gift of grace from God; it cannot be earned, deserved or merited (Romans 5:17–19). Grace is all about believing and having faith in Jesus Christ and His finished work on the cross— not about you doing good works in self-effort. You cannot improve your standing with God by depending upon your obedience to the law. *"Then said they unto him, What shall we do, that we might work the works of God? Jesus answered and said unto them, This is the work of God, that ye believe on him whom he hath sent"* (John 6:28–29).

Christ's righteousness, received by grace, grants you constant access to the presence of God the Father. At the cross, Jesus gave up the presence of God (Matthew 27:46, Mark 15:34); while you received the presence of God Jesus had. The blood of Jesus Christ grants us access to the constant presence of God the Father (Matthew 27:51, Hebrews 4:16). On the cross, Jesus, for the first time, addressed His Father as God; so believers could call Him Father. The Covenant Name of God—revealed by Jesus more than any other—is Father. Jesus referred to God as His Father more than 150 times, and He spoke of God as being our Father thirty times.[2] In fact, the Covenant Name of God in the New Testament is Abba, Father, the most intimate and loving name for a father. It appears thrice in the New Testament. It is used by Jesus once in the Garden of Gethsemane (Mark 14:36), and twice it is applied to believers (Romans 8:15, Galatians 4:6).

Grace is not a license to sin. Rather grace is a powerful force, propelling us to holiness in Jesus Christ. This holiness then will be manifested in good works done in the power of the Holy Spirit to the glory of Christ. As the apostle Paul explained, the grace of God teaches us to deny ungodliness and worldly lusts and to live soberly, righteously and Godly in this present world. It results in our zeal for good works done to express our gratefulness and thankfulness to God (Titus 2:11–14). The more conscious you are about your righteousness in Christ, the more God's grace and unmerited favor will be manifested in your life, resulting in more good works to the glory of God. When you are under God's grace and His perfect forgiveness, you will experience victory over sin.

In the New Covenant of Grace, all of the terms needed to be met for you to be blessed have been met by Jesus! You cannot add to Jesus's sacrifice nor can you deserve His favor or righteousness by depending upon your obedience to the law. God blesses you not because you are good but because He is good and that is His very nature. As a believer, you are blessed because the Lord no longer counts your sins against you (Psalm 23:6, Nahum 1:7, Romans 4:6–8, James 1:17). Because of the cross of Jesus, you never will be punished for your sins. Jesus took away your sins and gave you His righteousness; and in the process, He took upon His body the punishment for all of your sins. Because of the cross, God is for you (Romans 8:31). When you are confident God is for you and not against you, you can believe for restoration, breakthroughs, miracles and all of the good things of life to happen to you. All of the good things you receive from God, you receive by faith because of His grace. When you receive God's grace, it strengthens your faith. The more grace you receive, the stronger your faith becomes. This is all because of God's love for you demonstrated perfectly on the cross. As explained in chapter 1, faith works by love (Galatians 5:6).

The Bible says faith involves believing God *"is a rewarder of them that diligently seek him"* (Hebrews 11:6). The focus on reward is not inconsistent with grace but a manifestation of it. God gives you the grace in Jesus Christ. When you exercise that grace, God rewards you for exercising the grace He gave you in the first place. God is so good, indeed!

Grace to Overcome Sin and Temptation

To overcome sin and temptation, a believer should be conscious of the love of God in Christ, as was explained in chapter 1. As a basic principle, it is easier to stay out of temptation than to fight it successfully. As you walk with the Lord Jesus (chapters 3 and 4), God will show you the protective hedges you can place around yourself to stay out of temptation (Job 1:10, Ezekiel 22:30, Mark 12:1). These hedges are Biblical principles and convictions you can adopt to keep out of temptation. In keeping these hedges, your reliance has to be on the Lord Jesus Christ and not on your self-effort. To illustrate, one of my hedges is that no woman by herself, other than my daughter, may enter our house when my wife is not there. Another fundamental principle is that temptation is just as much an opportunity to do the right thing as it is to do the wrong thing—equally an occasion to do good as it is to do evil (Genesis 50:20). When you resist the temptation and do not do wrong or evil, it is tantamount to doing right or good. There are seven other principles—all rooted in grace. These principles are (1) covenant of grace, (2) righteousness in Christ, (3) no condemnation in Christ, (4) faithfulness of God, (5) co-crucifixion with Christ, (6) weapons of warfare and (7) testimony. These principles not only will help you to stay out of temptation but also will help you to be victorious when you are tempted. Each of these principles is discussed in this chapter.

Covenant of Grace

The New Covenant of grace was established by the shed blood of the Lord Jesus Christ and ratified by His resurrection, ascension and the outpouring of the Holy Spirit. It embodies the perfect, finished work of Jesus on the cross at Calvary. As a part of the New Covenant, believers have complete forgiveness of all sins: past, present and future. The main reason people do not love Jesus much is they do not understand how much He has forgiven them (Luke 7:44–48). A realization of this forgiveness propels you to holiness and gives you the power to overcome sin. *"For sin shall not have dominion over you: for ye are not under the law, but under grace"* (Romans 6:14). Your constant realization that you are operating under the New Covenant of grace will help you to defeat sin and temptation. Sin does not stop God's grace from reaching out to you, but God's grace will stop sin from reaching you.

In every temptation, the Lord Jesus Christ is the way of escape. In the King James Version, 1 Corinthians 10:13 reads, *"There hath no temptation taken you but such as is common to man: but God is faithful, who will not suffer you to be tempted above that ye are able; but will with the temptation also make a way to escape, that ye may be able to bear it."* In the original Greek text, it is *"the"* way of escape and not *"a"* way of escape. Several other English translations correctly translate it as such, including the American Standard Version, English Standard Version, World English Bible, Darby's English Translation, Young's Literal Translation, etc. What is the way of escape? The context of 1 Corinthians 10:13 gives us light. As stated in 1 Corinthians 10:16, *"The cup of blessing which we bless, is it not the communion of the blood of Christ? The bread which we break, is it not the communion of the body of Christ?"* The communion, of course, is observed in remembrance of the Lord Jesus Christ (Luke 22:19, 1 Corinthians 11:24). Thus, the way of escape out of every temptation is to look to the Lord Jesus Christ. Look to Him as the Son of God and to His perfect, finished work on the cross for your total redemption, salvation and as the way of escape out of every temptation. Jesus is never a way; He is the way always. He said in John 14:6, *"I am the way, the truth, and the life."* Always look to Jesus—even when you are tempted. As you do so, the Holy Spirit will show you specific actions to take that will help you to escape the temptation.

I want to clarify a great misapplication of the Word of God to situations where believers do yield to temptation and sin. I have heard many preachers and pastors misapply 1 John 1:9 to believers. *"If we confess our sins, he is faithful and just to forgive us our sins, and to cleanse us from all unrighteousness"* (1 John 1:9). However, the context of this verse, given in the previous verse (1 John 1:8), makes it clear this verse applies to unbelievers. If 1 John 1:9 applied to believers, then our forgiveness of sins would depend upon our confession: *"If we confess our sins."* All of us have unconfessed sins when we die. Thus, believers would die with some sins unforgiven, implying they could not go to Heaven. None of this makes any sense. In fact, what John said about the forgiveness of believers is clearly mentioned in the next chapter, *"I write unto you, little children, because your sins are forgiven you for his name's sake"* (1 John 2:12). "Children" in this verse refers to the believers. This interpretation is very consistent with the teachings of the New Testament. In the New Covenant of grace, God has promised, *"For I will be merciful to their unrighteousness, and their sins and their iniquities will I remember no more"* (Hebrews 8:12). Not only are all of our sins forgiven, but also God does not remember them anymore!

Nowhere does the Bible say the forgiveness of a believer's sins depends upon the confession of those sins. You cannot show me a single verse to that effect. The Bible does say very clearly that the forgiveness of our sins depends only on the shed blood of the Lord Jesus Christ on the cross. It is because of His grace. *"In whom we have redemption through his blood, the forgiveness of sins, according to the riches of his grace"* (Ephesians 1:7). You cannot earn the forgiveness of sins with your confessions after becoming a believer. Many believers pray something like this when they sin, "Dear God, I confess to You I have sinned. Please forgive me of this sin. Your Word says, if I confess my sin, You are faithful and just to forgive it. I promise not to commit it in the future." They pray these words only to repeat the sin next time when they are tempted. Why? Because this is not a Scriptural prayer. For the believers (who walk in the light), the apostle John said, "*But if we walk in the light, as he is in the light, we have fellowship one with another, and the blood of Jesus Christ his Son cleanseth us from all sin*" (1 John 1:7). The word "cleanseth" denotes present, continuous action. Thus, the blood of Jesus Christ already has cleansed and is continually cleansing the believer from all sin. I am definitely not against confessing sin. I do it myself but in a way consistent with Scripture. Toward the end of this section, I will share a Scriptural confession that believers can make when they sin.

Righteousness in Christ

The only righteousness you have or ever will have is the righteousness in Christ. It is also the righteousness of Jesus Christ. He is the Righteous One. As a result of the divine exchange on the cross, He has made you righteous (2 Corinthians 5:21). Furthermore, your righteousness in Christ is an "*everlasting righteousness*" (Daniel 9:24; see Hebrews 9:12). Once you have received the Lord Jesus Christ and given your life to Him, you never can become unrighteous again—not even when you sin. A realization of your righteousness in Christ will keep you from sin. After all, it does not behoove a righteous person to commit acts of unrighteousness. "*Awake to righteousness, and sin not; for some have not the knowledge of God: I speak this to your shame*" (1 Corinthians 15:34). Awaking to your righteousness in Christ will help you not to sin. Say this aloud,

"I am the righteousness of God in Christ." Say that each time you are tempted.

The righteousness in Paul's writings stands in contrast to the righteousness based on the fulfillment of the law by man as the covenant partner of God. It is *"righteousness which is of faith"* (Romans 10:6) and *"that which is through the faith of Christ, the righteousness which is of God by faith"* (Philippians 3:9). God, as the righteous Judge, places in a right relation with Himself those who believe on His Son, the Lord Jesus Christ. Thus, righteousness is a gift (Romans 5:17–18). We could never become righteous before God by our efforts to conform our lives to His will. However, having obtained the gift of righteousness in Christ, we are to serve Him out of gratitude and love. Since God has made us his own and given to us His righteousness, it is our duty and privilege to be righteous in conduct.

Before Aaron died on Mt. Hor, *"Moses stripped Aaron of his garments, and put them upon Eleazar his son"* (Numbers 20:28), signifying the transference of Aaron's office to Eleazar. In the taking off of the garments of Aaron and putting them on his son, we see a living illustration of the everlasting priesthood of Jesus (Hebrews 7:23–24). In the same manner, in the divine exchange on the cross, Jesus took off His robe of righteousness and put it upon us (Isaiah 61:10, 2 Corinthians 5:21), signifying we are now *"priests unto God"* (Revelation 1:6).

When you focus on your righteousness in Christ, the blessings of the Abrahamic and Davidic covenants and all of the promises God made to Abraham and David will be manifested in your life (Romans 4:1–25). The secret to Abraham's blessings is found in Romans 4:1–5. *"For what saith the scripture? Abraham believed God, and it was counted unto him for righteousness*" (Romans 4:3). Abraham believed God justifies the ungodly (Romans 4:5). This is the grace of God in Christ. God justifies you—even when you fail as a believer. This realization is what will give you victory over sin (Romans 6:14).

There is another misconception prevalent in the Church today concerning the role of the Holy Spirit in the life of believers when they sin. Many pastors and preachers use the following passage to conclude mistakenly that the Holy Spirit's primary role is to convict believers of sin when they sin.

> "*And when he is come, he will reprove the world of sin, and of righteousness, and of judgment:*
> *Of sin, because they believe not on me;*
> *Of righteousness, because I go to my Father, and ye see me no more;*
> *Of judgment, because the prince of this world is judged.*" (John 16:8–11)

After a close reading of this passage, it is clear the Holy Spirit has come to:

1. Convict unbelievers of the sin of unbelief and lack of faith in Jesus Christ as Savior and Lord.
2. Convict believers of the righteousness of Christ. A believer is robed in the righteousness of Christ, and righteous people do not commit sins and acts of unrighteousness.

3. Remind us the devil has been judged on the cross once and for all. Jesus Christ destroyed the devil on the cross. *"Forasmuch then as the children are partakers of flesh and blood, he also himself likewise took part of the same; that through death he might destroy him that had the power of death, that is, the devil"* (Hebrews 2:14).

Thus, the Holy Spirit primarily and directly convicts a believer of everlasting righteousness in Christ. He only indirectly convicts a believer of sin by pointing to our righteousness in Christ and the fact that righteous people do not sin. This distinction and emphasis are all important. God wants us to be righteousness conscious and not sin conscious. On the other hand, the devil wants you to be sin conscious. Sin consciousness will lead to an evil conscience, making you feel guilty (Hebrews 10:22). Sin consciousness will lead you into temptation and sin—as seen from the very beginning in the life of Eve. When God planted the Garden of Eden, He placed *"the tree of life also in the midst of the garden"* (Genesis 2:9). The *"tree of knowledge of good and evil"* is mentioned then but without any description of its position. "Midst" means He wanted the tree of life to be the focus of Adam and Eve's attention. The tree of life represents the Lord Jesus Christ (John 6:35, 10:10, 11:25, 14:6, 17:3, 20:31) Who is the Righteousness of God (Romans 3:22, 26; 5:17, 21; 2 Corinthians 5:21). Thus, God wanted Adam and Eve to be righteousness conscious by focusing on the tree of life. However, Eve told Satan the tree of knowledge of good and evil was in the midst of the garden (Genesis 3:3). Eve's focus was on the forbidden tree; she was sin conscious. Thereby, she fell into temptation and into sin.

The focus on righteousness consciousness, as opposed to sin consciousness, also is seen in the Levitical sacrifices. The burnt offering, as described in Leviticus 1, transferred the righteousness of the unblemished animal to the offerer. The burnt offering was both a morning and an evening sacrifice (2 Chronicles 13:11) because God wants His people to be righteousness conscious. The sin offering, described in Leviticus 4, transferred the sin of the offerer to the innocent animal. The sin offering was not a daily offering because God does not want His people to be sin conscious. As another illustration, in Proverbs 5, we are admonished that, to avoid sexual sin, a man should focus his attention on his wife (righteousness in Christ) and not on a strange woman (sin). A focus on sin consciousness and unscriptural confession of sin lead to repeated acts of sin, leading to repeated unscriptural confessions of sin, thus perpetuating the sin cycle. The power to overcome sin is found in knowing you are righteous in Christ and in focusing on that righteousness. When you fail and sin, that is when you should exercise your faith and confess (loudly if possible), "I am the righteousness of God in Christ." What stops God's grace from flowing to you is not sin but self-righteousness, the mother of all sins. Self-righteousness leads to condemnation, leading to sin. That is why the Jewish religious leaders could not put their faith in Jesus and committed the sin of unbelief.

There is another misconception rampant in the Church. Many people of God mistakenly proclaim that God breaks His fellowship with you when you sin but that your relationship remains intact. The truth is God does not break His fellowship with you if you are a believer, even when you sin, although you may break your fellowship with God. As far as God is concerned, both your fellowship and your relationship with God always remain intact. Both relationship and fellowship share the same root Greek word *Koinonia*. The word declares, *"For he hath said, I will never leave thee, nor forsake thee"* (Hebrews 13:5). "Never" includes the times when you sin. As a believer, you are righteous—not only until your next sin. You have continual, unchanging, unalterable, everlasting righteousness in Christ. When God looks at you, He sees Christ and in Him finds you perfect, holy and without blame (Ephesians 1:4). Next time when you sin, turn to God; experience His presence and power in a new way. Do not run away from Him; rather run to the Father in the Name of the Son. He is waiting with open arms to embrace you (Luke 15:20–24). Thank God for your forgiveness, your righteousness in Christ and for the Holy Spirit Who indwells you. Ask the Holy Spirit to help you to overcome that sin. You will experience victory. Remember, sin does not stop God's grace from flowing to you; but God's grace in your life will stop sin. Victory over sin comes only when you realize the *"abundance of grace and of the gift of righteousness"* (Romans 5:17).

No Condemnation in Christ

The Bible says, *"There is therefore now no condemnation to them which are in Christ Jesus"* (Romans 8:1). Although the King James Version and some other translations add "who walk not after the flesh, but after the Spirit," that phrase is NOT found in the original Greek text. Several English translations correctly leave this phrase out, including the American Standard Version, Bible in Basic English, Contemporary English Version, Darby Bible, Easy-to-Read Version, English Standard Version, Good News Bible, God's Word, International Standard Version, Lexham English Bible, Revised Version, Weymouth New Testament, etc. Why am I belaboring this point? It is crucial for you to recognize, as a believer in Christ, you are under no condemnation! This truth will help you successfully ward off feelings of guilt and condemnation from the devil. It will help you to be victorious over sin. On the other hand, people who are living under guilt and condemnation are very likely to repeat their sins. When you see yourself as free from condemnation, this fact gives you the power to resist temptation, as we see in John 8.

In John 8:1–11, the scribes and Pharisees brought to Jesus a woman caught in the very act of adultery. Jesus told them, *"He that is without sin among you, let him first cast a stone at her"* (John 8:7). They wanted to condemn her, but they could not because of sin in their lives. Jesus could have condemned her as He was without sin, but He would not. Instead He told her, *"Neither do I condemn thee: go, and sin no more"* (John 8:11). It is noteworthy Jesus first gave this woman the gift of no condemnation and then commanded her to sin no more. By giving this woman the gift of no condemnation, He empowered her to overcome sin and live to glorify God. The punishment of the law for adultery, death by stoning, did not stop this woman from committing the act. Jesus knew the gift of no condemnation would set her free. Jesus was more concerned with removing the condemnation of sin than with punishing the woman. In Christ, you are under no condemnation. This truth enables you to overcome sin and temptation and empowers you to live victoriously and glorify God.

I am sorry to say the attitude of many churches is, by and large, the opposite. These churches, in effect, say, "Go and sin no more, and then we will not condemn you." In a recent meeting with some African American pastors and church leaders, it was mentioned many teenage girls, who get pregnant, drop out of church and go for secular counseling. They do not go back to church because they are afraid the church will condemn them. Church should be a safe place where the believers feel secure when they sin; church is the place where they should seek help and freedom from the bondage of sin.

Condemnation is often the root cause of adverse behaviors and consequences, as in the Garden of Eden. When Adam and Eve sinned (Genesis 3:6), they felt condemned that they were naked (Genesis 3:6). Then they became fearful and were afraid (Genesis 3:10). Then came stress in their lives: Eve would have sorrow in conception (Genesis 3:16), while Adam would eat in sorrow and by the sweat of his face (Genesis 3:17–19). Thus, we have the following cause-and-effect sequence:

$$\text{Sin} \longrightarrow \text{Condemnation} \longrightarrow \text{Fear} \longrightarrow \text{Stress} \longrightarrow \text{Consequences}$$

The devil heaps guilt and condemnation upon you, pointing to your past sins. When, as a believer, you agree with the devil and condemn yourself, you are a hypocrite. What you are doing is not only displeasing to God, but it is an abomination to God because you are condemning the just or the righteous (yourself). *"He that justifieth the wicked, and he that condemneth the just, even they both are abomination to the LORD"* (Proverbs 17:15). You have been justified and made righteous by the blood of Jesus Christ. Do not condemn yourself.

Let me state emphatically I am not advocating sin. In fact, I am very much against sin. By its very nature, sin destroys. Like the saying goes, sin will take you farther than you want to go, keep you there longer than you want to stay and cost you more than you want to pay. That is the nature of sin. Let us all be forewarned. God does not want you to sin! But know, when you sin as a believer, there is no condemnation upon you because you are the righteousness of God in Christ. Jesus has washed away all of your sins by His blood. Far from leading you to sin, this truth is a powerful motivation for you to live in victory over sin and have a holy lifestyle.

Faithfulness of God

The faithfulness of God is one of the essential characteristics of God. *"God is faithful, by whom ye were called unto the fellowship of his Son Jesus Christ our Lord"* (1 Corinthians 1:9). God is omniscient, and He knows how much temptation you can handle. He is faithful to limit the temptation to that you can handle, as in the life of Job. Moreover, God always will make the way for you to escape the temptation, to overcome it (1 Corinthians 10:13). When you are tempted, remember, in Christ, you can handle it because God is faithful! Thank God He has shown you the way to escape He already has provided. As discussed earlier in the section on "Covenant of Grace," the way of escape, the key, is to keep your focus on the Lord Jesus Christ and His perfect, finished work on the cross and recall His faithfulness. God's faithfulness to us does not depend on our faithfulness to Him. God is faithful even when we are unbelieving and unfaithful. The faithfulness of God is extolled throughout Scriptures. Memorize some of the following verses and quote them when you are tempted.

> *"Know therefore that the LORD thy God, he is God, the faithful God, which keepeth covenant and mercy with them that love him and keep his commandments to a thousand generations"* (Deuteronomy 7:9).

> *"God is faithful, by whom ye were called unto the fellowship of his Son Jesus Christ our Lord"* (1 Corinthians 1:9).

> *"But the Lord is faithful, who shall stablish you, and keep you from evil"* (2 Thessalonians 3:3).

> *"If we believe not, yet he abideth faithful: he cannot deny himself"* (2 Timothy 2:13).

Co-Crucifixion with Christ

When you receive Jesus Christ as your personal Savior and Lord, you are translated from being in Adam to being in Christ. In Adam, you were dead in your trespasses and sins because sin had dominion over you. However, in Christ, all of your sins are forgiven and the power of sin over you is destroyed. You are made free and alive to love and serve the living God. *"For as in Adam all die, even so in Christ shall all be made alive"* (1 Corinthians 15:22). Moreover, you completely identify with the Lord Jesus Christ—past, present and future. Thus, when Christ died on the cross, you died with Him. When Christ was raised from the dead by the Father, you were raised with Him and in Him. This complete identification with the death, burial and resurrection of the Lord Jesus Christ is a key to continuous victory over sin and temptation. *"Knowing this, that our old man is crucified with him, that the body of sin might be destroyed, that henceforth we should not serve sin"* (Romans 6:6). The old you, who wanted to sin and live in a lifestyle of sin, died when Jesus died on the cross. In Jesus, you are now dead to sin. A dead person does not sin. When Christ was resurrected, you were resurrected with Him as a new person, one who wants to love God and honor Him with your life. Memorize Romans 6:6, meditate upon it and quote this verse each time you are tempted; and you will experience victory.

Weapons of Warfare

The moment you received the Lord Jesus Christ as your Savior, you were enrolled as a soldier in His army and are engaged in spiritual warfare (Ephesians 6:10–18). This topic is introduced here and is discussed in more detail in chapter 5 of *God Is Calling You: Responding to the Calling of God.* Your enemy is the devil and his fallen angels or demons. God has given you certain weapons to fight this spiritual warfare. These weapons are the Name of Jesus, the blood of Jesus, the Word of God and your standing in Jesus Christ. Jesus humbled Himself to become a man, led an obedient life and made the ultimate sacrifice on the cross for you and me. Therefore, God has exalted Him highly and given Him a Name above every name. At the Name of Jesus, the devil, his demons and all the powers of darkness have to bow and submit to His authority.

> *"Wherefore God also hath highly exalted him, and given him a name which is above every name:*
>
> *That at the name of Jesus every knee should bow, of things in heaven, and things in earth, and things under the earth;*
>
> *And that every tongue should confess that Jesus Christ is Lord, to the glory of God the Father"* (Philippians 2:9–11).

Use the Name of Jesus when you are tempted. In the Name of Jesus, resist the devil and he will flee (James 4:7).

Likewise, the blood of Jesus is all powerful. It has washed away all of your sins, made you righteous and given you the gift of no condemnation. His blood made you a child of God and has given you constant access to the very presence of God (Hebrews 10:19). His precious blood is cleansing you continually from all sin (1 John 1:7). The blood of Jesus is *"the blood of the everlasting covenant"* (Hebrews 13:20). The blood will overcome the enemy. *"And they overcame him by the blood of the Lamb…"* (Revelation 12:11). So always plead the blood of Jesus upon yourself, your situations and your circumstances.

Then you have the Word of God. Jesus defeated the devil during His temptation in the wilderness by quoting Scriptures. Each time the devil tempted Him, Jesus said, *"It is written"* (Matthew 4:4, 7, 10). Jesus quoted the Word of God, and He was victorious over the devil. The Word of God is the only offensive weapon mentioned in the armor of God given in Ephesians 6. Therefore, use the Word to fight the devil and his temptations. The Word of God is one of the Names of Jesus (John 1:1, 14; Revelation 19:13). Use the Word to attack the enemy, the devil, the tempter.

Finally, your standing in Christ gives you the victory over sin. You are robed in the righteousness of the Lord Jesus Christ. As you get established in His righteousness by faith, the weapons that the enemy, the devil, may use against you will not prosper but will be brought to naught. This is part of your heritage in Jesus Christ (Isaiah 54:14–17). It is very important for you to realize that your standing with God is not determined by anything you do or not do. It is determined only by the finished work of the Lord Jesus Christ on the cross. As far as your standing is concerned, when God looks at you, He sees Christ. Your standing is who you are in Christ; your standing is based on grace and grace alone. Thus, you do not deserve any of it nor can you ever deserve it. By God's grace, you stand perfect and complete in Christ Jesus (Romans 5:2). Your standing is perfect, and it can never improve or get better because you cannot improve upon or add to the finished work of Christ. *"For by one offering he hath perfected forever them that are sanctified"* (Hebrews 10:14).

The use of these weapons doubtlessly will lead to victory over sin and temptation.

> *"For the weapons of our warfare are not carnal, but mighty through God to the pulling down of strong holds;*
> *Casting down imaginations, and every high thing that exalteth itself against the knowledge of God, and bringing into captivity every thought to the obedience of Christ"* (2 Corinthians 10:4–5).

Testimony

To live victoriously, it is important you testify of the grace of the Lord Jesus Christ. First, you should not be ashamed, either implicitly or explicitly, of your testimony. Paul admonished Timothy, *"Be not thou therefore ashamed of the testimony of our Lord"* (2 Timothy 1:8). Second, be sure your testimony is rooted in grace and it exalts and brings glory to the Name of our Savior and Lord Jesus Christ. I have heard testimonies of Christians, including those of missionaries, that had little grace and did not exalt Jesus Christ. I was not encouraged by hearing them and labeled them as examples of how not to testify.

The importance of testimony is found throughout the Bible. In the Old Testament, books like Psalms exhort us to testify of the grace of God. *"Come and hear, all ye that fear God, and I will declare what he hath done for my soul"* (Psalm 66:16). The prophet Jeremiah said, *"The LORD hath brought forth our righteousness: come, and let us declare in Zion the work of the LORD our God"* (Jeremiah 51:10). The New Testament emphasizes our role and responsibility to testify. The Lord Jesus Christ Himself set this example before us. *"I give thee charge in the sight of God, who quickeneth all things, and before Christ Jesus, who before Pontius Pilate witnessed a good confession"* (1 Timothy 6:13). This was the life message of the apostle Paul. *"And I, brethren, when I came to you, came not with excellency of speech or of wisdom, declaring unto you the testimony of God. For I determined not to know any thing among you, save Jesus Christ, and him crucified"* (1 Corinthian 2:1–2). We find this admonition right up to the book of Revelation—nine times in eight verses in the King James Version. The power of testimony to overcome the devil also is mentioned. *"And they overcame him by the blood of the Lamb, and by the word of their testimony; and they loved not their lives unto the death"* (Revelation 12:11). As you share your testimony, you will appropriate more grace. *"And with great power gave the apostles witness of the resurrection of the Lord Jesus: and great grace was upon them all"* (Acts 4:33).

The more you get rooted in grace, the more power you will experience to overcome sin and the devil and the more powerful will be your testimony. Like your calling, your testimony is unique. Make use of every opportunity to share it! It can be a very effective way of presenting the Gospel, as exemplified many times by the apostle Paul. For example, in Acts 26:1–28, Paul shares his testimony with

King Agrippa. *"Then Agrippa said unto Paul, Almost thou persuadest me to be a Christian"* (Act 26:28).

Scriptural Confession of Sin

When you sin as a believer, make a Scriptural confession. I suggest the following: "Abba, Father, I confess I have sinned in this way (name it; be specific and direct). I thank You, in the New Covenant of grace, my sin already is covered by the blood of my Savior and Lord Jesus Christ. He has paid for it in full; actually, He made an overpayment for it. Thank You that You love me so much. Your Word declares that I am the righteousness of God in Christ. Thank You that I am under no condemnation because I am in Jesus Christ. Abba, Father, thank You for Your faithfulness in forgiving my sin and empowering me through Your Holy Spirit to overcome this temptation in the Name of Jesus. All of what You have done for me is a powerful motivation for me to live a holy life. By faith, in Jesus's Name, I thank You now for the victory in this area. In the Name of my Savior and Lord Jesus Christ, I pray. Amen!"

Understanding the Law

In the Bible, "the law" commonly refers to the decrees found in the first five books of the Bible collectively named the Torah. Obedience to this law was the awesome responsibility of the Israelites as they attempted to merit God's favor and blessing. This covenant between God and the nation of Israel is referred to as the Old Covenant. Transgression of the law resulted in the breaking of the covenant, leading to a broken relationship with God! Penalties were prescribed and sacrifices were required to restore the broken relationship.

God gave the law. It is the Word of God! The law is holy, just and good. However, it has no power to make you holy, just and good. It was designed to expose your inability to be holy, just and good. No amount of trying to keep the law can make you holy. In the entire Bible (both the Old and New Testaments), no one, not a single person, was justified by trying to keep the law. All failed to meet the perfect standards and requirements of the law! Paul states this truth clearly in Romans 9:31–32. It is humanly impossible to keep the law, which was designed to put an end to all human effort to earn God's favor and acceptance. God gave the law to expose man's sin and to point to man's need for a Savior, the Lord Jesus Christ (Galatians 3:24). Only the blood of Jesus Christ can make you holy. Only the finished work of Jesus on the cross can grant to you redemption, wholeness, completion, righteousness and acceptance with God.

Moreover, the law was given only for a specified period. Specifically, the law was given 430 years after the Abrahamic promise (Galatians 3:16–17). The law was in effect only until the promised Seed, Jesus Christ, came (Galatians 3:19). Thus, the law was in effect for a relatively short period of time; and its temporary nature needs to be recognized. Jesus Christ came to fulfill the demands of the law, and He kept the law perfectly! (Matthew 5:17). When you receive Jesus as Savior and Lord, God reckons in Christ that you have fulfilled the law. The Bible says the law was nailed to the cross of Jesus (Colossians 2:14). The law had to be fulfilled and all of its demands met. No human could do it. The good news is the Lord Jesus Christ has done it for us. This truth is so important for you to realize that I quote:

> *"For the law of the Spirit of life in Christ Jesus hath made me free from the law of sin and death.*
>
> *For what the law could not do, in that it was weak through the flesh, God sending his own Son in the likeness of sinful flesh, and for sin, condemned sin in the flesh:*
>
> *That the righteousness of the law might be fulfilled in us, who walk not after the flesh, but after the Spirit"* (Romans 8:2–4).

Do not go about, either consciously or subconsciously, trying to keep the law in order to please God. In doing so, you cannot please God. The only way to please God is by faith in the Lord Jesus. *"But without faith it is impossible to please him"* (Hebrews 11:6). In fact, the Bible says the law is the opposite of faith. *"And the law is not of faith"* (Galatians 3:12). You cannot add to the finished work of Jesus Christ on the cross by trying to deserve His favor and acceptance or by depending upon your obedience to the law. When you attempt to do so, you fall from grace into the law because grace is above the law. This is what the apostle Paul meant in Galatians 5:4, a much misunderstood verse. No, this verse does not mean you lose your salvation. You are eternally saved in Christ! However, you are denying yourself the blessings of His grace by trying to earn them through obedience to the law. If you try to earn the unmerited favor of God through your self-effort and by your performance (dependence upon the law), you are, in effect, nullifying the many blessings of His grace. You became a child of God by grace. Continue in grace. You don't begin with grace and end up with the law, which would be going backwards. You don't begin with the New Covenant and end up with the Old Covenant. That is what many Christians are doing today when they try to live the Christian life by trying to keep the law. The law cannot give you your identity and standing in Christ; only grace can do so.

You may wonder, how did people get saved before the cross? By faith! By looking forward to the cross of Jesus Christ in faith! Jesus said, "*Your father Abraham rejoiced to see my day: and he saw it, and was glad*" (John 8:56). The statement the "*just shall live by faith*" appears both in the Old Testament as well as the New Testament (Habakkuk 2:4, Romans 1:17, Galatians 3:11, Hebrews 10:38). God's way of justification always has been by faith in Jesus Christ! The Gospel has been preached since the beginning of mankind with the first reference found in Genesis 3:15. It is important to know the law never was designed to impart salvation. "*Knowing that a man is not justified by the works of the law, but by the faith of Jesus Christ, even we have believed in Jesus Christ, that we might be justified by the faith of Christ, and not by the works of the law: for by the works of the law shall no flesh be justified*" (Galatians 2:16).

The Bible says, "*But if ye be led of the Spirit, ye are not under the law*" (Galatians 5:18). We are not to live the Christian life by letter of the law but be led by the

Holy Spirit; *"for the letter killeth, but the spirit giveth life"* (2 Corinthians 3:6). Yet there are spiritual principles embedded in the law that are very consistent with walking in grace, and those we should practice in the power of the Holy Spirit in our grace walk. To give a couple of examples, the first commandment (Exodus 20:3) embodies the principle of priority. The Lord Jesus Christ always should be first in our lives (Matthew 6:33, Colossians 1:18). The fourth commandment of rest on the Sabbath day (Exodus 20:8–11) points to resting in the Lord Jesus Christ and His perfect, finished work on the cross. In the New Testament, Sabbath rest is simply a relationship with God in that we have ceased from working by our self-efforts and we are letting God do His work in us and through us (Matthew 11:28; Galatians 2:20; Hebrews 4:3, 9–11). The same is true of the other commandments in the law; they embody spiritual principles that we should apply in the power of the Holy Spirit as we walk in grace.

The Law Versus Grace

Many believers today are struggling to live the Christian life. They mean well and love the Lord. They want to do right but are trying to do so with a lot of self-effort. They are trying to perform and to measure up. They want to produce fruit but are not seeing much of it because of their self-effort. In the Bible, self-effort denotes the "flesh" and has, at its roots, the reliance on the law. They are trying to do, do and do; Christianity is done, done and done. Jesus Christ has done it all. He said on the cross, *"It is finished"* (John 19:30). The way to live the Christian life and to be fruitful is to rest in His finished work. You must be plugged into the *"true vine"* Who is the Lord Jesus Christ (John 15:1). This means you live every day, keeping your focus on the Lord Jesus, practicing His presence, being conscious of His grace and who you are in Christ. Your focus is on the Lord Jesus Christ and His Word. You are depending totally on the Holy Spirit and not on your self-efforts. You are consciously partaking of the love of your Abba, Father. This is what it means to walk in the Spirit, live by grace and abide in Christ. Then you will bear fruit effortlessly as you focus on the Son-light and are watered by the living water of God's Word ministered to you by the Holy Spirit. Believers have a natural tendency, consciously or subconsciously, to revert back to the law in living the Christian life. They know they are saved by grace through faith (Ephesians 2:8–9), but they are trying to perform in an attempt to please God and gain His approval. They are walking in the law.

Since walking in grace is so critical, I highlight a few differences between the law and grace to help you better understand grace. In these comparisons, the reference is to the letter of the law rather than to the spirit of the law.

- The Old Covenant of the law was cut between God and man, between God and the nation of Israel. God's part was to bless His people if they obeyed all of His laws. Man's part was to obey all of God's laws. If Israel did not do their part, instead of blessings, the curses would come upon them. As the Bible tells us, man could never keep his part. *"For finding fault with them, he saith,*

Behold, the days come, saith the Lord, when I will make a new covenant with the house of Israel and with the house of Judah" (Hebrews 8:8). The New Covenant of grace was cut between God the Father and Jesus the Son representing man, between two infallible parties—each more than able to keep the covenant. Man's part in the New Covenant is to believe and receive.

Under the law, it was all about what man had to do or not do. In the Ten Commandments given in Exodus 20:1–17, *"Thou shalt"* is mentioned once and *"Thou shalt not"* is mentioned ten times in the King James Version. In addition, there are other mentions of similar phrases. Now let us focus on the New Covenant of Grace as given in Hebrews 8:10–12. The focus is entirely on what God said He will do. God says, *"I will"* four times and *"will I"* once for a total of five times. Five is the number of grace in the Bible. Thus, in the New Covenant, the focus is on what God will do as a manifestation of His grace. In fact, Christ's work of redemption on the cross is perfect, all encompassing and complete. *"It is finished"* (John 19:30). As a result, the grace of God flows freely from the cross of Calvary.

- The law is a merit-based system. You are expected to earn and deserve all good things by meeting the requirements of the law (Deuteronomy 28:1). Grace, by definition, is unmerited, unearned and undeserved (Ephesians 2:8–9).

- Under the law, you are expected to perform by keeping all of God's commandments. Obedience to the law brings blessings. Under grace, you don't have to perform to get God's blessings. Jesus Christ has fulfilled all of the requirements of the law on your behalf (Romans 8:1–4). God already has blessed you with all spiritual blessings in Christ (Ephesians 1:3).
- Under the law, breaking even one commandment brings God's judgment (Deuteronomy 28:15, James 2:10). Under grace, all of your sins have been judged already on the cross of Jesus Christ (1 John 2:2, 1 Peter 2:24).
- Under the law, God will visit your sins and iniquities *"unto the third and fourth generation"* (Exodus 20:5). Under grace, God will *"remember no more"* (Hebrews 8:12) your sins and iniquities.
- The law has no power to stop sin in your life. In fact, the law makes you a sinner (1 Corinthians 15:56). Under grace, *"sin shall not have dominion over you"* (Romans 6:14).
- Under the law, God demands righteousness from you (Deuteronomy 6:25). The law has no power to make you holy or righteous. Under grace, God imparts righteousness to you through Christ (2 Corinthians 5:21). You are holy through Christ (1 Peter 2:9).
- The law represents a standard impossible for you to achieve. No one born of man has been able to keep the law (Romans 3:20). The grace of God in

Christ is available to all. Whosoever will can partake of God's grace freely (Romans 10:13).

- The law condemns (2 Corinthians 3:7); but grace justifies (Romans 3:24, 28).
- The law kills; it is *"the ministration of death"* (2 Corinthians 3:7). In the New Covenant of grace, Jesus gives life and life more abundantly (John 10:10).

Determine to live your life by grace, not by your performance or self-effort rooted in the law. Do not try to measure up; you simply cannot! Instead live by grace through the measure of faith dealt to you by God in Jesus Christ (Romans 12:3).

Scripture Spotlight

The Healing of the Impotent Man by Grace

One passage bringing out the differences between grace and the law is the healing of the impotent man described in John 5:1–16. In this passage, there is a sharp contrast between the grace of Jesus Christ to heal, deliver, set free and give life and the powerlessness of ordinances of the law, serving only to bind and leave man chained in his hopeless state. This poor man had an infirmity for thirty-eight years and could not perform. Through his self-effort, he could not be the first to step into the pool after the troubling of the water. This is typical of the law, imposing a standard impossible for man to meet. The impotent man had the desire and will to be healed but not the strength or the power to perform. The grace of our Lord Jesus Christ is embedded in His words, *"Rise, take up thy bed and walk."* His words imparted healing power and strength and made the man whole. Note this impotent man did not merit or deserve healing. Only the grace of God, through Jesus Christ, reached out to him. The man rises and carries away his bed on the Sabbath day. Instead of rejoicing, the legalistic Jews took the pretense of a violation of the Sabbath. In their narrow and mistaken focus on the law, they found fault not only with the man who was healed but also with the Lord Who had healed him. The grace of God knows no Sabbath but is manifested in our lives continuously. His grace is available to all who will call upon the Lord Jesus Christ in faith. Let us look at this passage, verse-by-verse, and draw out principles we can apply in our lives to experience a greater manifestation of His grace. Please look at these verses in the Bible as you read this book.

Scripture Source: John 5:1–16

Verse 1

1. *"After this there was a feast of the Jews; and Jesus went up to Jerusalem."* A feast is a joyous occasion. Jesus heals and ministers during happy as well as sad seasons. The presence, grace and the power of God are available to us constantly, at all times, in all seasons.

2. The religious people went to Jerusalem to engage in religious activities. The Lord Jesus Christ went there to do the work of God—to heal an impotent

man. When Jesus went to Jerusalem, He ministered grace to people in need. He did not merely go
to the temple; but He also visited the pool below
the temple where the helpless, poor and sick lay
in prolonged suffering. Jesus has a heart for people who are sick, suffering or hurting and showers
grace upon them. The legalistic Jews avoided such
places because of the potential for violation of rit-
ual purity laws.

Verse 2

1. *"A pool, which is called in the Hebrew tongue
   Bethesda."* The word "Bethesda" means "the house
   of mercy." This pool was named appropriately, for
   here the mercy of God was manifested to those
   who were sick and suffering. Our God is a God of
   mercy. God's mercy shields you from the punishment and penalty of your sins that you so richly
   deserve. Mercy is a central aspect of God's nature
   and character (Lamentations 3:21–23). God's love,
   mercy and grace sent Jesus Christ to the cross and
   established the New Covenant of grace.
2. *"Having five porches."* This pool had five porches.
   Five is a number of grace. Jesus Christ is the God
   of mercy, and He is the God of grace. Grace is
   the unmerited favor of God. Grace gives you the
   good things you do not deserve. Grace is the New
   Covenant. Grace is the Person of the Lord Jesus
   Christ (John 1:17).

3. Under the New Covenant, mercy and grace go hand-in-hand as both come *"from God our Father and Jesus Christ our Lord"* (1 Timothy 1:2) and impart to us the peace of God (2 Timothy 1:2, Titus 1:4, 2 John 1:3). Mercy, grace and peace can be appropriated only through the Lord Jesus Christ.

4. *"By the sheep market a pool..."* More accurately, sheep market should be called the Sheep Gate, as indeed it is mentioned in many other translations. See for example, the American Standard Version, Contemporary English Version, Darby Bible, English Standard Version, International Standard Version, New International Version, New American Standard Bible, New Living Translation and many others. Thus, Jesus, *"the good shepherd"* (John 10:11, 14), went by the Sheep Gate looking for lost sheep, so He could restore them.

5. You should look to Jesus and not look to the pool. Jesus is the Healer, and He is all you need. It is useless to look to things and other people and depend upon them. You should get your eyes on Jesus and on the Word of God. The man got healed when he took his eyes off the pool, looked to Jesus and obeyed His Word. Expect good things from God as a result of His grace in the Lord Jesus Christ.

Verse 3

1. *"In these lay a great multitude of impotent folk."* There were a great number of people lying in the

porches and by the pool who were weak and feeble. Only one received a miracle. So it is today! It seems many are following Jesus, but very few are receiving any miracles. Why? Because their eyes are on the pool and not on Jesus and His Word. They are operating under the law and not under grace.

2. *"Of blind, halt, withered."* Three sorts of diseased people lay at the pool: blind, halt and withered— either in one particular part, as the man with the withered hand (Matthew 12:10), or all over paralytic. These people are mentioned because they were the least able to help themselves into the water. They represent the spiritual condition of every person apart from Jesus Christ. Spiritually, we are all, by nature, impotent folks who are blind, halt and withered because of sin (2 Corinthians 4:4). We must come to Jesus to be healed. He is the only One Who can heal us of sin. The only way to get healed of our spiritual condition is to receive Jesus Christ as our personal Savior and Lord! When you receive Jesus Christ as your Savior and Lord, you are made whole spiritually. All of your sins are forgiven; you are made righteous and reconciled to God the Father. The order of these three words is significant. There were the blind who could not see, the lame (halt) who could not walk and the withered who could not work. God wants people: (1) first to get revelation from His Word (spiritual sight), (2) then to walk with Him and (3) finally to work for Him. People can do all of this by accepting the grace the Father offers

in Jesus Christ, His Son (chapters 1 and 2); then growing in grace (chapters 3 and 4) and discerning and responding to the calling of God (chapter 5 and the second book in this series, *God Is Calling You: Responding to the Calling of God*).

3. *"Waiting for the moving of the water."* These people were waiting in hope for the moving of the water. Many of them went hoping down to the grave. To receive from God, you must have faith by believing the Word of God. You have to have hope before you can have faith (Hebrews 11:1). But if all you have is hope, you are falling one step short. Hope is a good waiter but a poor receiver. You receive from God by faith. Hope looks to the future; faith is now! It is in the present. Believing prayer always ends in the glad confession that it is mine. I have it now! The difference between faith and hope is this truth. Hope believes God will heal me some day. Faith believes I am healed now! God does not necessarily move in response to our hope, but He does necessarily move in response to our faith. *"Then touched he their eyes, saying, According to your faith be it unto you"* (Matthew 9:29; see also Mark 5:34, 10:52).

Verse 4

1. *"For an angel went down at a certain season into the pool, and troubled the water."* The angel came and troubled the water. This is literally true because the Bible says so. In addition, this denotes a movement

of the Holy Spirit. As a believer, you must stir up the gift within you. When you are cold and dull spiritually, the waters settle and you are not able to grow in grace and receive miracles from God. As the apostle Paul admonished Timothy, *"Wherefore I put thee in remembrance that thou stir up the gift of God, which is in thee by the putting on of my hands"* (2 Timothy 1:6). The gift God has given you is a manifestation of His grace.

2. *"Whosoever then first after the troubling of the water stepped in was made whole of whatsoever disease he had."* The angel stirred the waters but left the diseased to themselves to get in. This required self-effort or help from others. This is a picture of the law. The law was given *"by the disposition of angels"* (Acts 7:53). Under the law, man has to perform in order to get God's blessings.

The waters of Siloam, in this pool, signified the kingdom of David and of the Son of David, Jesus Christ (Isaiah 8:6). Formerly, these waters had been used for purification; but now they were for healing. These waters, therefore, signify both the cleansing and healing power of the blood of Jesus. He is Jesus *"Who forgiveth all thine iniquities; who healeth all thy diseases"* (Psalm 103:3)—not at certain seasons but at all times. Whoever will, let him come to Jesus for cleansing from sin, for healing from sickness and disease and for meeting all needs whatever they may be. You do not deserve these blessings, but they are available to you as a result of His grace.

Verse 5

1. *"Which had an infirmity thirty and eight years."* The man had this infirmity for thirty-eight years, implying an incurable disease. It does not matter what your condition is and how long you have been in it, for Jesus can and will heal you. Come to Him!

2. In the Bible, thirty-eight years is a picture of Israel under unbelief. From the time Israel expressed unbelief at Kadeshbarnea to the time they entered the Promised Land was thirty-eight years. *"And the space in which we came from Kadeshbarnea, until we were come over the brook Zered, was thirty and eight years; until all the generation of the men of war were wasted out from among the host, as the LORD sware unto them"* (Deuteronomy 2:14). This man had been operating in unbelief for thirty-eight years. Unbelief will stifle your faith and hinder the manifestation of the grace of God. This impotent man is a type of Israel.

Verse 6

1. *"When Jesus saw him lie, and knew that he had been now a long time in that case."* Jesus knew and considered how long he had been in this condition. Sometimes when you are in a difficult situation for an extended period, you have a tendency to think God is not aware of what is happening; He has forgotten you. This verse should give you the

assurance that God is fully aware and knows what is happening to you and for how long, knowing your state.

2. Jesus asked this man a very direct and very important question, "*Wilt thou be made whole?*" The word "thou" focuses on the personal desires and involvement of the individual. Faith of the individual, who is sick, is one channel of healing. The words "be made" are in the present tense. Faith is in the now (Hebrew 11:1). Jesus was asking him, "Do you want to be made whole now?" The word "whole" focused on the man's real need. Your real need is wholeness, not simply healing, finances or any other thing. Wholeness includes wholeness of the spirit, soul and body. Salvation in Jesus Christ, the Son of God and our Savior and Lord, provides for our spirit, soul and body. It provides forgiveness for our spirit, deliverance for our soul and healing for our body. (See chapter 2.)

3. Jesus wanted to bring this man to a point of decision regarding his healing. It is important to do so—just as it is to bring people to a point of decision regarding the forgiveness of their spirit in Jesus Christ. Jesus wanted the man to examine whether he had the will to be healed. The man may have gotten so accustomed to his impotency and prolonged state of illness as to regard deliverance from his condition as a doubtful blessing. Some people enjoy the attention, sympathy and pity they receive from being sick. Some receive medical benefits through insurance and entitlements. This can

be the case spiritually as well. Many sinners are not willing to be cured of their sins because they do not want to give up their sinful lifestyle, having gotten so accustomed to it. If people are willing to be made whole, the Lord Jesus Christ is willing to make them whole, including healing them of sickness and disease (Matthew 8:3).

4. Right now, Jesus is asking you the very same question, "*Wilt thou be made whole?*" Whole in your health, finances, marriage, home, job, relationships or whatever your need might be? He wants you to locate where your faith is. Faith is a matter of the will: the real element of effective faith. Real faith acts through a firmly decided will. You have to will to believe; you have to will to receive. No one can receive much from God without a firm and decided will. "*And whosoever will, let him take the water of life freely*" (Revelation 22:17). It should be emphasized man is not whole and cannot be whole without the Lord Jesus Christ.

Verse 7

1. When people are trying to perform under the law, they rely on self-effort, look to others for help and look to the means. All of these are evident in this man's life. This man was relying on self-effort; he was not totally incapacitated. The phrase "*while I am coming, another*" implies he could move, at least to some extent, on his own. The futility of self-dependence characterizes those who are trying

to perform under the law. They are trying their best but always falling short. Don't be one of them. Instead appropriate the grace of God, flowing freely from the cross at Calvary.

2. *"Sir, I have no man."* The impotent man was looking to man. The Bible says vain is the help of man but through God we shall do valiantly (Psalm 60:11–12). It is foolish to depend upon "man," that is, look to others. Others cannot help you and, sooner or later, will disappoint you. You must depend only upon Jesus. He is the only One Who can give you a miracle, and He will help you (Isaiah 41:10–16).

3. *"To put me into the pool..."* This man was looking to the pool as the means of his healing. A focus on the means will take your focus away from God. This was probably true of the *"great multitude of impotent folk"* who were *"waiting for the moving of the water"* (John 5:3). Their focus was on the pool, and they missed the presence of Jesus Who was right there among them.

4. This man had become disappointed. His efforts to be the first in the pool, after the stirring of water, had failed time and again. We all face disappointments and setbacks. Maybe you got some bad news concerning your health, or maybe a relationship didn't work out. It was a setback. It's easy to get discouraged, lose your enthusiasm or even be tempted to just settle where you are. But if you are going to see God's best, you have to have a "bounce-back" mentality, meaning when you get knocked down, you

don't stay down. You get back up again. You have to know that every time adversity comes against you, it's a setup for a comeback! If you stay in faith and keep a good attitude, you will rise again. God will turn those stumbling blocks into building blocks, the slippery stones into stepping stones, the rejected stones into cornerstones and headstones; and you'll move forward into His victory! To quote my pastor, Dr. Charles Stanley, "Disappointment is inevitable, but discouragement is a choice."

How do you deal with disappointment? Start by changing what comes out of your mouth. Instead of speaking about your situation, speak to your situation. Every day declare, "This is the day the Lord has made. He is taking me into seasons of increase. I'm moving forward with strength through the joy of the Lord!" Remember, what happens to you is not nearly as important as what happens in you.

5. This man blamed others for his condition: "*another steppeth down before me.*" As the saying goes, if you pass the blame, you will remain the same. If you pass the buck, you will remain stuck (in your present situation) (John 5:7, 2 Corinthians 8:20).

6. This man had a poor view of God's grace, having been under the law for a long time. He seemingly had become convinced that God's grace, like the law governing the pool, operated on the basis of first come, first served; and only one served. He thought the grace of God was limited only to one person, the first who stepped into the pool. It is important that you have a Scriptural view of grace. God's grace is

unlimited, inexhaustible and always available when you call on Jesus Christ in faith.

Verse 8

1. *"Rise, take up thy bed, and walk"* was impossible for the impotent man to do; he had not been able to do so for thirty-eight years. These are, in part, the identical words Jesus addressed to the paralytic (Mark 2:9). Jesus will ask you to do something. He wants you to demonstrate your faith and obedience. In fact, often Jesus will ask you to do what is humanly unreasonable or even impossible. Of course, Jesus supplies the grace to you to do whatever He asks. He knows you cannot do it on your own (Matthew 19:26, Mark 10:27). Jesus did not touch him or use any other method. He merely spoke the Word to effect the cure. The Word of God carries the power of God!

2. Getting up and walking was totally an act of faith for this man and why Jesus told him to do it. When people approached Jesus on their own initiative, they already had taken a step of faith in coming to Jesus for healing. However, in this case, Jesus had approached this man out of sheer grace. Thus, there had been no act of faith on his part. Therefore, it was necessary that Jesus stir up some degree of faith in this man. Healing does not come without some manifestation of faith on the part of the one who is receiving it (Mark 6:5–6). That is the reason why Jesus often told people to do something when He

ministered healing to them (Matthew 12:9–13; Luke 7:11–15, 17:12–19; John 9:6–7, 11:39–44).

3. Christ did not ask the impotent man to rise and go into the waters, as the law required. He said rise and walk. Christ did for us what the law could not do and fulfilled the law on our behalf (Romans 8:3–4). *"For Christ is the end of the law for righteousness to every one that believeth"* (Romans 10:4).

4. Jesus asked the man to walk away from the pool because the pool reminded him of his helpless, hopeless past. This impotent man carried a lot of emotional baggage as a result of his despair for the past thirty-eight years. Jesus wanted to deliver him from his past; He wanted to deliver this man's soul. The Gospel provides deliverance for our soul.

5. To change your circumstance, you have to get rid of the old and do something new.

Old	New	Reason
Lying down	Arise.	You cannot shine unless you arise.
On the bed	Take up your bed.	The bed is a provision for relapse.
By the pool	Walk away from the pool.	Look to Jesus (grace) and not to the pool (law).

6. Right now, Jesus is asking you to arise out of whatever situation is confronting you. *"Arise, shine; for thy light is come, and the glory of the LORD is risen upon thee"* (Isaiah 60:1). You can arise because Jesus

Christ Himself is your light (John 8:12), and He has bestowed His glory upon you (John 17:22). He already has supplied you the grace to arise. No matter your circumstances, you can do it through Christ! (Philippians 4:13).

7. *"Take up thy bed..."* These words are identical to what the Lord said to the paralytic man in Mark 2:9, 11. Why did Jesus ask these two healed men to carry their beds? So they could testify to others how God had delivered and healed them from those beds. You get to carry that from which God has delivered and healed you. It becomes a part of your testimony of God's grace in your life, a part of your story (Mark 2:9, 11; John 5:8). Secondly, the bed was a provision for relapse. Never provide for a relapse for that from which God has delivered you. *"But put ye on the Lord Jesus Christ, and make not provision for the flesh, to fulfil the lusts thereof"* (Romans 13:14).

Verse 9

1. *"And immediately the man was made whole, and took up his bed, and walked."* As the man obeyed, he was made whole. When you obey, the miracle will take place. Faith always appropriates the power to do the impossible.

2. The proof of your spiritual growth is you rising and walking (chapters 3 and 4). Have you grown in the grace of God? Go wherever Christ sends you, and take up whatever burden He lays upon

you. Walk with Him and follow Him. Jesus said, *"And he said to them all, If any man will come after me, let him deny himself, and take up his cross daily, and follow me"* (Luke 9:23).

3. Jesus did not merely try to help the man, but He healed him. Jesus did not tell him, "I will help you get into the pool when the water is stirred." He bypassed the pool and healed the man. That is the nature of grace. Religion will try to help you; but grace will heal you, minister to your need and restore you.

4. *"And on the same day was the sabbath."* It is no coincidence the impotent man received his miracles on the Sabbath, the day of rest for the Jews. Indeed the woman oppressed with a spirit of infirmity (Luke 13:10–13) and the man with a withered hand (Luke 6:6–10) likewise received their miracles on the Sabbath. In fact, the Bible records Jesus did seven miracles on the Sabbath day. The number seven denotes perfection and completeness. The seven Sabbath miracles indicate perfection and completeness of Jesus's ministry of miracles. When you rest, as on the Sabbath, God goes to work. God's Word says, *"There remains therefore a rest for the people of God"* (Hebrews 4:9). The day you cease from your laboring and striving under the law and rest in the finished work of Christ is the day you will start receiving miracles from God.

5. You, too, may have been struggling to solve a problem or get out of a situation that has sorely weighed you down. You have tried to do your best,

but it has not worked. You feel frustrated and want to give up. When you work by striving in the flesh, God will rest. However, if you rest in Christ, God will go to work for you. My friend, the Lord Jesus Christ wants you to cease from all your struggles and receive His offer of grace to turn your situation around. Whatever you need, He has provided at the cross. So just be at rest in Him and receive your miracle! (Matthew 11:28–30).

Verse 10

1. *"It is the sabbath day: it is not lawful for thee to carry thy bed."* The Jews told the man who had been healed it was not lawful for him to carry his bed on the Sabbath. The term *"the Jews,"* as used here, denotes the religious opponents of Jesus. The Jews went by the letter of the law (Exodus 20:10, 35:3). If you go by the letter of the law, you will go wrong. *"Who also hath made us able ministers of the new testament; not of the letter, but of the spirit: for the letter killeth, but the spirit giveth life"* (2 Corinthians 3:6). The reliance by the Jewish leaders on the letter of the law was in sharp contrast to the grace of Jesus. There is a sharp contrast between the law and grace in the Bible, as I have discussed already earlier in this chapter. Jesus healed this man on the Sabbath day, thus establishing that the healing of the body was sacred enough to be done on the Sabbath day. Physical healing was an important part of the ministry of Jesus. These Jews were not

interested in the good deed done by our Lord or in the man's joy. The Jews in this story were not interested in the welfare of people but merely in their rules and traditions. All they could see was a man carrying a bedroll and breaking the Sabbath law. A rigid adherence to the law will lead you astray, and you will miss God's perspective.

Verse 11

1. The Jews ignored the healing done because of grace and mercy and brought a charge of violation of the Sabbath law. The man who was healed did not do it in contempt of the law and the Sabbath but in obedience to the One Who made him whole. By curing him, Jesus had proven He is greater than the law and the Sabbath. The man who was healed went by the Word of God—unlike the Jews who went by the letter of the law.

2. "*He that made me whole.*" The man's focus was on the One Who had healed and restored him. As yet, the man did not know He was Jesus. Even after getting His blessings, keep your focus on the Lord Jesus Christ and on His perfect, finished work on the cross!

3. Christ, by curing another paralytic (Mark 2:1–12), proved His power to forgive sin. Here He proves His power to give law. His miracles prove He had both powers.

4. When you obey people, you will get what people can do. When you obey God, you will get what

God can do. People had not been able to help this man. He made the right choice in obeying Jesus. You should do the same (Romans 6:16).

Verse 12

1. The Jews asked the healed man, "*What man is that which said unto thee, Take up thy bed, and walk?*" Note they did not ask him, "What man is that who made thee whole?" If you go by the letter of the law, you will end up making incorrect decisions. The Jews looked upon Christ as a mere man: "*What man is that?*" Moreover, they looked upon Him as a bad man in spite of the good deed done by Him in healing the impotent man. The letter of the law will cause you to have the wrong focus. Instead of focusing upon the healing and the act of mercy and grace, they focus on the carrying of the bed on the Sabbath. Thus, they totally missed God.

Verse 13

1. The man did not know Who healed him; he did not know Jesus Christ but had a desire to find out. Because God is good and gracious, Christ bestows many blessings on those who do not know Him. (See Isaiah 45:4–5, Matthew 5:45.) He hopes His goodness will lead them to repentance (Romans 2:4). The grace of God reaches out to the lost. "*For the Son of man is come to save that which was*

lost" (Matthew 18:11). Even for believers, we are blessed not so much because of our knowledge of Him but His knowledge of us. We know God or, rather, are known of Him (Galatians 4:9).

2. Jesus did not withdraw to escape danger or harm but to avoid the acclamation and praise of the crowd in the place where He had done the miracle.

Verse 14

1. It is likely the man who was impotent realized the hand of God in his healing; and he went to the Temple, the house of God, to offer his thanksgiving and praise.

2. Jesus said unto him, *"Behold, thou art made whole."* The Lord first emphasized the mercy and grace of God that the man had received. Wholeness implied he had forgiveness for his spirit, deliverance for his soul and healing for his body. Then He told him, *"Sin no more."* This also is how Jesus dealt with the woman who was caught in the act of adultery (John 8:11). Then Jesus warned him of the consequences of sin *"lest a worse thing come unto thee."* Continuing in sin, after he had experienced such a wonderful manifestation of God's grace, would have consequences worse than thirty-eight years of lameness. Apparently, this man's sickness was a result of past sin in his life.

3. Not always—but sometimes—our sickness, trials and troubles are the direct result of sin in our lives. If you are going to walk in health and wholeness,

you have to walk holy before God. All calamities are not the result of sin. However, all sin will result in calamities. That is the nature of sin (Romans 6:23).

4. When our personal sins are involved, a *"worse thing"* can come upon us. Satanic forces are freed to work in our lives because of sin (Proverbs 5:22; John 8:34, 10:10; Romans 6:16; 2 Timothy 2:26; 1 Peter 5:8; 2 Peter 2:19). Problems, diseases, difficult situations, etc., are never God blessing His children (Deuteronomy 28:1–68) or God's method of correction (John 15:3, 2 Timothy 3:16) but are works of the devil.

5. Believers will not come under this punitive judgment of God (Nahum 1:2; Romans 5:9; 1 Thessalonians 1:10, 5:9). Jesus bore that judgment on our behalf (Isaiah 53:4–6, 11; Romans 5:8–10; 1 Corinthians 15:3; Galatians3:13). The reason sin is still damaging to believers is it lets Satan loose to work in our lives (Romans 6:16).

6. Like this man who had been impotent, every believer has been empowered by Christ to sin no more. Jesus has broken the power of sin over our lives (Romans 6:14). This is another manifestation of His love and grace in our lives. He has robed us in His righteousness and given us the gift of no condemnation, empowering us to sin no more. I already have discussed these truths in detail earlier in this chapter.

7. When God gives you a new beginning, He expects you to make a new ending. This man was *"made*

whole" in his spirit, soul and body. Jesus had given him a fresh start in life. Jesus expected him to "*sin no more*" but rather to live to the glory of God.

8. "*Lest a worse thing come unto thee.*" Christ has delivered us from the power of sin and darkness. He has delivered the captives and "*set at liberty them that are bruised*" (Luke 4:18). If you abuse your liberty, you will go back into captivity (Galatians 5:1, 13; 1 Peter 2:16).

Verse 15

1. "*The man departed, and told the Jews that it was Jesus, which had made him whole.*" Note that the man did not tell the Jews it was Jesus Who told him to take up his bed and walk on the Sabbath; that was the question they asked him in John 5:12. Rather, the man testified to the Jews that it was Jesus Who had healed him and made him whole. Most likely, he did this to honor Christ and benefit the Jews. As discussed earlier in this chapter, our testimony is very powerful. His motive may have been to express his gratitude, or it may have arisen from a sense of obligation to answer the question the Jews had posed earlier in verse 12.

2. Jesus not only has your cure; He is your cure. He is all you need! (Acts 17:28, 1 Corinthians 1:30). Look to Him and live for Him (2 Corinthians 5:15).

Verse 16

1. The Jews, entangled in the stronghold of the law, were caught up in rage and enmity. Instead of rejoicing and worshipping Jesus, the Jews persecuted Him and sought to kill Him. Their envy, bitterness and anger were camouflaged under the zeal for the Sabbath and the law.

2. These religious leaders wanted to kill the Lord in the Name of the Lord. This is how blind they were. They entirely missed the message Jesus was conveying to them. By making whole this man, who is a type of Israel (see verse 5), Jesus was communicating and demonstrating He had come to offer the nation of Israel the same wholeness in terms of forgiveness for their sins, deliverance for their souls and healing for their bodies. Attempting to follow the law legalistically will blind you to the truth of God's salvation in Jesus Christ.

3. Jesus is Lord over the Sabbath (Matthew 12:8). The work of God is sacred enough to be done on the Sabbath. Jesus is the One Who gave the law; He is the One Who wrote on the tablets of stone. He is the One Who fulfilled the law. He fulfilled it for you and me!

4. In the Old Testament, the Sabbath was symbolic. In the New Testament, the Sabbath was only a shadow of things to come that was fulfilled in Christ (Colossians 2:16–17). There is a Sabbath rest available to all born-again believers but not necessarily effective in all believers (Hebrews 4:1–

11). This New Testament Sabbath rest is simply a relationship with God, in that we have ceased from working by our self-efforts and are letting God do His work in us and through us (Galatians 2:20, Hebrews 4:10). The Sabbath is not a day but rather an ongoing relationship with God through Jesus Christ. I urge you to enter into this Sabbath rest.

Conclusion

The grace of God in Jesus Christ was manifested in the forgiveness of the spirit, deliverance of the soul and healing of the body of this impotent man. The impotent man received the grace of Jesus, believed in Him and received his miracles of salvation. He was made "*whole.*" He was no more lying in despair by the pool, but Jesus sent him on his way in a body made well. He had forgiveness of sins and the power to sin no more. The Jews rejected Jesus and remained lost in their sins, in despair and without hope. What about you? Will you, like this impotent man, receive and grow in the grace of our Savior and Lord Jesus Christ?

Author's Account

My Grace Walk

I began developing a deeper understanding of growing in grace when I was exposed to the ministry of Pastor Joseph Prince. In the summer of 2013, I attended his New Creation Church while I visited Singapore. As a student of the Word and having read the Bible many times through,

I was familiar with the fundamental teachings of grace. However, I lacked a deeper appreciation of the grace walk. My spiritual walk, up to this point, was heavily characterized by "doing" (thou shalt) and "not doing" (thou shalt not) rather than resting in Christ's finished work on the cross ("it is done"). To be honest, I have to admit I was living the Christian life more by implicitly trying to keep the law than by explicitly appropriating the grace flowing freely from the cross of Calvary.

However, by listening to Pastor Prince's messages and reading his books, I obtained a much better understanding of the "*Gospel of the grace of God*" (Acts 20:24). I must acknowledge that many of the ideas expressed in these two books have been impacted by the preaching and teaching ministry of Joseph Prince of New Creation Church. While reading the Old and the New Testaments, I am now better and more easily able to behold the glory and majesty of Jesus Christ in the Scriptures, and the Holy Spirit has been conforming me to His image (2 Corinthians 3:18). I continue with all of the spiritual disciplines discussed in chapter 3 but do so now not with reliance on any degree of self-effort but by consciously appropriating the grace of God and trusting His Holy Spirit to do His work in me and through me. Oh! What a difference it has made.

I now realize, more than ever before, the Christian life is not about "doing" but about "being"—being who I am in Christ by the grace of God. Rather than relying on self-effort, I must let God do His work in me and then through me. The only way this can happen is that I look to the Lord Jesus Christ and rely totally on the Holy Spirit. I am learning to cease from my strivings and enter into His rest while working harder than ever before. Grace is opening my eyes to see how much the Father loves me and what a great sacrifice Jesus has made for me. First, this new outlook deepened my love for Jesus, then for Abba, Father and then for the Holy Spirit. As I am growing in grace, I am growing in my faith. I am living by practicing the presence of Jesus more than ever before. Praise the Name of Jesus from Whom all grace flows!

Quest Questions

Please do some soul searching and answer the following questions. You need not share your answers with anyone. However, if you so choose, share them with your accountability partner or a person you trust.

- Do I have a basic understanding of grace? Am I growing in grace? How can I tell?
- Am I trying to earn the favor and blessings of God by trying to keep the law?
- Do I have a strong inclination to rely on my ability, effort and competence to accomplish what I want to do?
- Am I being conformed to the image of the Lord Jesus Christ? How can I tell?
- Am I resting in Christ? How?
- What is my view of God's grace? His mercy?
- What is the manifestation of God's grace in my life?
- Do I view God as my Abba, Father? On what basis do I come into His presence?
- When I do good works, do I feel more righteous?

- How conscious am I about my righteousness in Christ? Do I view this righteousness as a gift of grace?
- Do I view God's grace as a license for sinning or as a motivation for holiness? Am I living holy?
- Do I believe God is for me or against me? Why?
- Am I a hard worker, a lazy bone or somewhere in between?
- Am I constantly practicing the presence of Jesus Christ in my life?
- On what do I base the forgiveness of my sins?
- Do I realize how much God has forgiven me because of the perfect atoning work of Jesus Christ on the cross?
- Do I know deep down in my heart God loves me whether or not I feel His love?
- Am I righteousness conscious or sin conscious?
- When I sin, do I feel righteous or unrighteous? What is my confession?
- Am I striving for righteousness through my good works?
- Can I discern between the conviction of the Holy Spirit and the heaping of condemnation by the devil?
- Do I condemn myself, especially when I fail? Do I no longer experience the grace of God when I fail?
- Do I break my fellowship with God when I sin? Do I run away from Him?
- Why does God bless me? Because I am good?

- Do I consciously experience the faithfulness of God on a daily basis—even when I am unfaithful to Him?
- Do I completely identify with the Lord Jesus Christ—past, present and future?
- Am I fighting the good fight of faith in the spiritual warfare going on?
- Am I proud or ashamed of my Christian testimony? Do I share my testimony?
- How do I handle temptation? Do I have a Biblical strategy for fighting temptation?
- Do I believe I am now dead to sin? On what basis and with what effect?
- Am I consciously or subconsciously trying to keep the law?
- Do I honestly find the Christian life to be a burden or a joy? Am I trying to perform or measure up through self-effort?
- Am I so preoccupied with my needs that I have no time or inclination to minister to others?
- Do I have a tendency to look to the "pool," that is, look to man, situations and human resources; or are my eyes fixed on Jesus?
- Am I aware of the gift within me? Have I stirred up this gift?
- Do I believe in the cleansing and healing power of the blood of Jesus Who forgives all my iniquities, Who heals all my diseases?
- When God tells me to *"Rise, take up thy bed, and walk,"* that is, do things that are humanly impossible, what is my response?

- Am I an optimist or a pessimist? Am I hopeful about my future and life in general?
- Beyond being hopeful, do I live by faith in the Lord Jesus Christ and by His faith?
- Do I act through a firmly decided will? Do I will to believe and will to receive from God?
- Do I assume responsibility for my actions, situations and circumstances; or do I tend to blame others?
- Am I wedded to the old ways of doing things, or am I open to doing new things as directed by the Holy Spirit?
- Am I rising and walking, going wherever Christ sends me and taking up whatever burden He lays upon me?
- Do I go by the letter of the law; do I walk in grace, or am I somewhere in between?
- Have I ceased from my laboring and striving under the law, and am I resting in the finished work of Christ?
- Am I aware of the destructive nature of sin? Are my calamities the result of some sin in my life?
- What is my response when God gives me a new beginning?
- Do I abuse the liberty I have in Christ? Am I aware that sin will take me back into captivity?
- Do I believe God is a good Father Who is for me, or do I view Him as One Who is against me?
- Do I believe Jesus is the answer to all of my problems? Do I believe He is all I need?

You can evaluate your answers to these questions in light of the following principles and precepts.

Principles and Precepts

- The way to grow spiritually is to rest in the grace of God in Jesus Christ and to yield to the working of the Holy Spirit in your life (Isaiah 59:19, John 16:13, Acts 1:4–5, Romans 8:26–27, 1 John 2:27).
- We all naturally have a strong inclination to rely on our ability, effort and competence to accomplish what we want to do. Instead God wants you to realize your inability, inadequacy and incompetence in and of yourself and to operate in the power of the Lord Jesus Christ by resting in His finished work on the cross of Calvary (1 Corinthians 15:10, Ephesians 6:10).
- God's goal for every believer is to be conformed to the image of His Son, the Lord Jesus Christ (Romans 8:29).
- We are changed by beholding. It is a principle operating in the physical, mental, emotional and spiritual realms (Genesis 30:35–43, 2 Corinthians 3:18).
- The process of transformation to the image of Christ occurs when you behold the glory of the Lord Jesus Christ in the Scriptures and in everything you do (2 Corinthians 3:18).
- Grace is the undeserved, unearned and unmerited favor of God. Grace gives you the good things you

do not deserve. Grace is the Person of the Lord Jesus Christ (John 1:17).

- Grace leads me to work hard, according to His working in my life. Resting in Christ involves hard work; it does not imply laziness (1 Corinthians 15:10).

- Faith involves believing God *"is a rewarder of them that diligently seek him"* (Hebrews 11:6).

- The New Covenant is a covenant of grace (Ephesians 2:8–9).

- Grace results in good works, glorifying the Lord Jesus Christ (Ephesians 2:10).

- Our God is a God of mercy. God's mercy shields you from the punishment and penalty of your sins that you so richly deserve. Mercy is a central aspect of God's nature and character (Lamentations 3:21–23).

- Under the New Covenant, mercy and grace go hand-in-hand as both come *"from God our Father and Jesus Christ our Lord"* and impart to us the peace of God (1 Timothy 1:2, 2 Timothy 1:2, Titus 1:4, 2 John 1:3).

- The blood of Jesus Christ has given us access to the constant presence of God as our Abba, Father (Matthew 27:51; Romans 8:15; Hebrews 4:16, 13:5).

- Grace is a powerful force, propelling us to live holy before God (Titus 2:11–12).

- You are righteous because of the divine exchange that took place on the cross. Jesus took all of your sins; and in exchange, you took all of His righteousness (2 Corinthians 5:21).

- The more conscious you are about your righteousness in Christ, the more God's grace and unmerited favor will be manifested in your life, resulting in more good works to the glory of God (Romans 5:15–21).

- When you are under God's grace and His perfect forgiveness, you will experience victory over sin (Romans 6:14).

- You have all the blessings of God in Christ (Ephesians 1:3).

- God is good; and He is for us, not against us (Romans 8:31).

- The Lord Jesus has broken the power of sin over us (Romans 6:6).

- While Biblical confession is enjoined, the forgiveness of a believer's sins does not depend upon confession; it depends only on the blood of Jesus Christ shed for the remission of our sins (Ephesians 1:7, 1 John 2:12).

- I am a beloved child of God in Christ (2 Thessalonians 2:13).

- On the cross, Jesus, for the first time, addressed His Father as God; so believers could call Him Father. In fact, the Covenant Name of God in the New Testament is Abba, Father, the most intimate and loving name for a father (Romans 8:15, Galatians 4:6).

- The only righteousness you will ever have is the righteousness of Christ and the righteousness in Christ (Philippians 3:8–9).
- A realization of your righteousness in Christ will keep you from sin (1 Corinthians 15:34).
- When you focus on your righteousness in Christ, the blessings of the Abrahamic and Davidic covenants and all of the promises God made to Abraham and David will be manifested in your life (Romans 4:1–25).
- The Holy Spirit directly convicts a believer of righteousness in Christ; He only indirectly convicts us of sin (John 16:8–11).
- A focus on sin consciousness and unscriptural confession of sin lead to repeated acts of sin, leading to repeated unscriptural confessions of sin, thus perpetuating the sin cycle (Genesis 2:9, 3:3).
- God does not break His fellowship with you—even when you sin, although you may break your fellowship with God (Hebrews 13:5).
- Next time when you sin, turn to God. Do not run away from Him; rather run to the Father in the Name of the Son. He is waiting with open arms to embrace you (Luke 15:20–24).
- God blesses you not because you are good but because He is good and that is His very nature. As a believer, you are blessed because the Lord no longer counts your sins against you (Psalm 23:6, Nahum 1:7, Romans 4:6–8, James 1:17).
- God is a rewarder of those who diligently seek Him (Hebrews 11:6).

- The main reason people do not love Jesus much is they do not understand how much He has forgiven them (Luke 7:44–48).
- Sin does not stop God's grace from flowing to us, but God's grace in our lives will stop sin from reaching us (Romans 6:14).
- It is easier to stay out of temptation than to fight it successfully. As you walk with the Lord Jesus, God will show you the protective hedges you can place around yourself to stay out of temptation (Job 1:10, Ezekiel 22:30, Mark 12:1).
- Temptation is just as much an opportunity to do the right thing as it is to do the wrong thing— equally an occasion to do good as it is to do evil. When you resist the temptation and do not do wrong or evil, it is tantamount to doing right or good (Genesis 50:20).
- In every temptation, the Lord Jesus Christ is the way of escape. Look to Him and to His perfect, finished work on the cross (1 Corinthians 10:13, 16–17).
- The blood of Jesus Christ already has cleansed and is continually cleansing the believer from all sin (1 John 1:7).
- In the New Covenant of grace, not only are all of our sins forgiven but also God does not remember them anymore! (Hebrews 8:12, 10:17).
- There is no condemnation to those who are in Christ Jesus. This is an unqualified statement (Romans 8:1).

- The gift of no condemnation in Christ will empower you to overcome sin and live to the glory of God (John 8:11).
- Condemnation is often the root cause of adverse behaviors and consequences (Genesis 3:6–19).
- When, as a believer, you agree with the devil and condemn yourself, what you are doing is an abomination to God because you are condemning the just or the righteous (yourself) (Proverbs 17:15).
- God is faithful and will not allow us to be tempted above what we are able to endure (1 Corinthians 10:13).
- God's faithfulness to us does not depend on our faithfulness to Him. God is faithful even when we are unbelieving and unfaithful (2 Timothy 2:13).
- When you receive Jesus Christ as your personal Savior and Lord, you are translated from being in Adam to being in Christ. You completely identify with the Lord Jesus Christ—past, present and future (1 Corinthians 15:22).
- The old you, who wanted to sin and live in a lifestyle of sin, died when Jesus died on the cross. In Jesus, you are now dead to sin (Romans 6:6).
- God has given us powerful weapons for spiritual warfare, including the Name of Jesus, the blood of Jesus, the Word of God and our standing in Christ (2 Corinthians 10:4–5).
- You should not be ashamed, either implicitly or explicitly, of your testimony. All those who are partakers of His grace must bear testimony (2 Timothy 1:8).

- We overcome the devil by the blood of Jesus and by our testimony of His grace in our lives (Revelation 12:11).
- The grace of God and His mercy in Christ are available to all. Whosoever will can partake of God's grace and mercy freely (Romans 10:13).
- The law is holy, just and good. However, it has no power to make you holy, just and good. It was designed to expose your inability to be holy, just and good and to bring you to Christ (Galatians 3:24).
- The law had to be fulfilled and all of its demands met, which no human could do (Romans 3:23, James 2:10).
- The perfect, atoning death of Christ on the cross has been the only way to salvation in the Old and the New Testaments (Habakkuk 2:4, Romans 1:17, Galatian 3:11, Hebrews 10:38).
- The way to live the Christian life is not to perform or measure up through self-effort but to live by grace through faith in the finished work of the Lord Jesus Christ. It is all about practicing the presence of Jesus (Galatians 2:16).
- The Old Covenant of the law was faulty as it was cut between God and man, between God and the nation of Israel. God's part was to bless His people if they obeyed all of His laws. Man's part was to obey all of God's laws. If Israel did not do their part, instead of blessings, the curses would come upon them. Man could never keep his part (Hebrews 8:7–8).

- The New Covenant of grace was cut between God the Father and God the Son representing man, between two infallible parties—each more than able to keep the covenant. Man's part, in the New Covenant, is to believe on Jesus Christ and receive (John 6:29, Hebrews 8:10–12).

- Under the law, breaking even one commandment brings God's judgment. Under grace, all of your sins already have been judged on the cross of Jesus Christ (Deuteronomy 28:15, James 2:10, 1 John 2:2, 1 Peter 2:24).

- Under the law, God will visit your sins and iniquities *"unto the third and fourth generation."* Under grace, God will *"remember no more"* your sins and iniquities (Exodus 20:5, Hebrews 8:12).

- Under the law, God demands righteousness from you. Under grace, God imparts righteousness to you through Christ. You are holy through Christ (Deuteronomy 6:25, 2 Corinthians 5:21, 1 Peter 2:9).

- The law represents a standard impossible for you to achieve. No one has been able to keep the law (Romans 3:20).

- Jesus is the One Who gave the law; He is the One Who wrote it on the tablets of stone. He is the One Who fulfilled the law. He fulfilled it for you and me! Therefore, we do not have to strive to fulfill it (Romans 8:1–4, 10:4).

- We are not to live the Christian life by the letter of the law but be led by the Holy Spirit *"for the letter killeth, but the spirit giveth life."* However, there are spiritual principles embedded in the law that are very consistent with walking in grace and those we should practice in the power of the Holy Spirit in our grace walk (Isaiah 28:10, 2 Corinthians 3:6).

- The presence, grace and the power of God are available to us constantly, at all times, in all seasons (Hebrews 4:16).

- You should look to Jesus and not look to the pool. It is useless to look to things and other people and depend upon them. Instead set your eyes on Jesus and on the Word of God (John 5:2, Hebrews 12:1–2).

- Those who do not know Jesus Christ as their personal Savior and Lord are spiritually "*blind, halt and withered*" (2 Corinthians 4:4).

- While hope is essential, we need to go beyond hope and have faith to receive from God (Hebrews 11:1).

- God does not necessarily move in response to our hope, but He does necessarily move in response to our faith (Matthew 9:29, Mark 5:34, Mark 10:52).

- Under the law, man has to perform in order to get God's blessings (Deuteronomy 28:1–2).

- As a believer, you must stir up the gift within you (2 Timothy 1:6).

- There is cleansing and healing power in the blood of Jesus. He is Jesus "*Who forgiveth all thine iniquities; who healeth all thy diseases*" (Psalm 103:3).

- It does not matter what your condition is and how long you have been in it; Jesus can and will forgive, deliver, heal and minister to you. Come to Him! (John 5:5, 2 Timothy 4:18).

- Your real need is wholeness, not simply physical, material, mental or emotional (John 5:6).

- If you look to Him, God will turn your stumbling blocks into building blocks, the slippery stones into stepping stones, the rejected stones into cornerstones and headstones; and you will move forward into His victory! (1 Corinthians 15:57, 2 Corinthians 2:14).

- Jesus will ask you to do something—often what is humanly unreasonable or even impossible. He wants you to demonstrate your faith and obedience (John 5:8).

- Jesus supplies the grace to you to do whatever He asks; He knows you cannot do it on your own (Matthew 19:26, Mark 10:27).

- Faith is a matter of the will. Real faith acts through a firmly decided will. You have to will to believe and will to receive from God (John 5:6, Revelation 22:17).

- When people are trying to perform under the law, they rely on self-effort and look to others for help but in vain (John 5:7).

- You must depend only upon Jesus. He is the only One Who can give you a miracle, and He will help you (Isaiah 41:10–16).

- If you pass the blame, you will remain the same. If you pass the buck, you will remain stuck (in your present situation) (John 5:7, 2 Corinthians 8:20).

- To change your circumstance, you have to get rid of the old and do something new (John 5:8).
- You cannot shine unless you arise out of whatever situation is confronting you. You can arise because Jesus Christ Himself is your light, and He has bestowed His glory upon you (Isaiah 60:1; John 5:8, 8:12, 17:22).
- The proof of your spiritual growth is you rising and walking. Go wherever Christ sends you, and take up whatever burden He lays upon you. Walk with Him and follow Him (Luke 9:23).
- The day you cease from your laboring and striving under the law and rest in the finished work of Christ is the day you will start receiving miracles from God (Hebrews 4:9).
- Whatever you need, Jesus has provided at the cross. So just be at rest in Him and receive your miracle (Matthew 11:28–30).
- You get to carry that from which God has delivered and healed you. That becomes a part of your testimony of God's grace, a part of your story (Mark 2:9, 11; John 5:8).
- If you go by the letter of the law, you will do the wrong thing. Walking in grace always will lead you to do what is right; be guided by the Holy Spirit and by the Word (2 Corinthians 3:6).
- Christ has the power to forgive sin, the power to deliver and heal and the power to give law (Mark 2:1–12, John 8:11).
- Christ bestows many blessings on those who do not know Him. He hopes His goodness will lead

them to repentance (Isaiah 45:4–5, Matthew 5:45, Romans 2:4).

- The grace of God reaches out to the lost (Matthew 18:11).
- Believers are blessed not so much because of our knowledge of Him but His knowledge of us. We know God or, rather, are known of Him (Galatians 4:9).
- Not always but sometimes our sickness, trials and troubles are the direct result of sin in our lives. Not all calamities are the result of sin, but all sin will result in calamities. That is the nature of sin. Let us be forewarned! (Romans 6:23).
- Continuing in sin, after we have experienced such a wonderful manifestation of God's grace, does have consequences that may be worse than before (John 5:14).
- When God gives us a new beginning, we must make a new ending (John 5:14, 8:11).
- Christ has delivered the captives and *"set at liberty them that are bruised."* If you abuse your liberty, you will go back into captivity (Luke 4:18; Galatians 5:1, 13; 1 Peter 2:16).
- Jesus not only has your cure; He is your cure. He is all you need! Look to Him and live for Him (Acts 17:28, 1 Corinthians 1:30, 2 Corinthians 5:15).

Life Lesson

You cannot live the Christian life by relying on your effort, performance or works. The only way to live the Christian life is by appropriating the grace of God in the Lord Jesus Christ on a daily basis and allowing Him to live His life through you in the power of the Holy Spirit.

Prayer Power

Abba, Father, I thank You that even right now I am engulfed by Your grace and Your perfect love because of Jesus's finished work on the cross. The Lord Jesus Christ has robed me in His righteousness and has taken away my guilt and condemnation. I believe, with all of my heart, right now, when You look at me, You see me in Christ Jesus. In Him, You find me perfect, holy and without blame. As Your child, I have Your grace, mercy, favor and blessings. Thank You for Your abundance of grace and Your gift of righteousness in my life through Jesus Christ.

Through Jesus, I will reign in this life over every situation and circumstance. Based on Your Word, I know You are faithful and will not allow me to be tempted above what I am able to endure. You have provided the way of escape for me in Jesus Christ and through Him. I will be victorious over sin and temptation because of the Name of Jesus, the blood of Jesus, the Word of God, my standing in Christ and Your power working mightily in me. The Lord Jesus Christ has fulfilled the law on my behalf. I am no more under the law but under grace.

Thank You, Abba, Father, for loving me. Right now, I receive Your complete forgiveness; and I forgive myself for all of my sins, mistakes and shortcomings. I release them all into Your loving, merciful hands. I declare, in Christ, I am completely loved, forgiven, freed, accepted, favored, righteous, blessed, delivered and healed from every sickness and disease. In the power of Your Holy Spirit, I aim to grow in grace, walk in holiness and honor You with my life. In Jesus's Holy Name, Amen!

Message Ministry

You can access the audio message for this chapter by using CallingYou as the password at

https://www.globalevangelisticministries.net/Calling1-Chapter4.

CHAPTER 5

Discerning Your Calling: The Essence of Your Calling

"God, who separated me from my mother's womb and called me through His grace."

—Galatians 1:15

Preamble and Preview

It is assumed, by now, you have received the love of God for you in Christ (chapter 1) by giving your life to Jesus as your Savior and Lord as discussed in chapter 2. If you have not done so, I urge you to go back and pray the prayer given in "Prayer Power" in chapter 2. It is a requirement, a necessary condition, that you be saved and be a child of God if you are to discern and respond to your calling. In fact, that is the first calling of God to you. The first calling of God to every person is to receive His love by receiving Jesus Christ as Savior and Lord (chapters 1 and 2). Furthermore, you should be walking with the Lord on a daily basis by practicing the spiritual disciplines discussed in chapter 3 and growing in grace as discussed in chapter 4. Otherwise, it will be difficult for you to discern the call of God. However, if you are doing so, then you are well positioned to discern the calling of God.

I explain the concept of calling and discuss its importance in "Central Concepts." You will understand how your calling relates to ministry, your natural skills, talents, abilities, spiritual gifts, your deepest desires and burdens. Responding to the calling of God requires you to pay the price. You will see the difference between your calling and career. In "Scripture Spotlight," we get a better understanding of calling by taking a close look at Peter's call to the ministry. This is followed by "Author's Account" where I detail my call to the ministry. The next section, "Quest Questions," contains several questions that I hope will lead you to reflect on your life as it relates to discerning your calling. There are several "Principles and Precepts" you can apply to discern and respond to the call of God upon your life. "Life Lesson" contains the most important lesson you can learn with respect to calling. "Prayer Power" contains an effectual, Scriptural prayer you are encouraged to pray to discern and passionately pursue your calling. Finally, "Message Ministry" gives the link to an audio message you are exhorted to hear.

Central Concepts

Your Calling and Its Importance

God has a calling for every believer. Romans 8:30, talking about believers, states, *"Moreover whom he did pre-*

destinate, them he also called: and whom he called, them he also justified: and whom he justified, them he also glorified." Jude opens his epistle by stating every believer is called, *"Jude, the servant of Jesus Christ, and brother of James, to them that are sanctified by God the Father, and preserved in Jesus Christ, and called"* (Jude 1:1). As stated in the Introduction, your calling is rooted in the call to follow Jesus Christ as your Savior and Lord and participate in his redemptive work in the world in the special way He has called you. If you have been saved by the grace of God by putting your faith and trust in the Lord Jesus Christ, then God has a special call upon your life. This calling is the way you are to live on the earth. It encompasses all your being and doing. It defines and encompasses your total lifestyle and includes your spiritual life, family life, ministry and vocation. This calling is unique to you and uniquely tailored to the gifts, talents and abilities God has given to you. It uniquely fits God's plan and purpose for your life. There are many callings on a person, for example, to be a spouse, parent, community member and citizen. Yet there is one calling that uniquely defines your mission and sets you apart to serve the Lord Jesus Christ on this earth. No one else can fulfill your calling but you as it has been designed by God just for you. Discerning, pursuing and fulfilling your calling are what will give purpose and significance to your life. God sent His Son to die on the cross for you. Jesus Christ purchased for you a blood-bought right to a fruitful, fulfilled life embedded in your calling.

Paul knew he was called to be an apostle of Jesus Christ (1 Corinthians 1:1). In fact, God had called Paul when he was in his mother's womb (Galatians 1:15). Likewise,

God told the prophet Jeremiah, "*Before I formed thee in the belly I knew thee; and before thou camest forth out of the womb I sanctified thee, and I ordained thee a prophet unto the nations*" (Jeremiah 1:5). The calling and the ministry of John the Baptist was to point to Jesus Christ as "*the Lamb of God, which taketh away the sin of the world*" (John 1:29). The angel Gabriel told Zacharias about John, "*He shall be filled with the Holy Ghost, even from his mother's womb*" (Luke 1:15). John actually began his ministry in his mother's womb. When Mary was pregnant with Jesus, she went to visit Elisabeth who, in turn, was pregnant with John the Baptist. This is what Elisabeth told Mary, "*For, lo, as soon as the voice of thy salutation sounded in mine ears, the babe leaped in my womb for joy*" (Luke 1:44). While yet in his mother's womb, John the Baptist was pointing to Jesus as the Son of God and the Lamb of God.

Like the apostle Paul, Jeremiah and John the Baptist, God has called you from your mother's womb. Therefore, this calling is not based on anything you have done or not done. In your mother's womb, you could do no right or wrong. This calling is based on the grace of God in Jesus Christ! You have a special calling and a destiny in the Lord Jesus Christ, the Son of the Living God!

It is crucial that you know what this calling is. This calling is a primary means God uses to conform you to the image of the Lord Jesus Christ and use you for His glory (Romans 8:28–30). The calling is not limited to evangelism or church service but encompasses everything necessary to make the world what God wants it to be. Your calling is a part of establishing the Kingdom of God on the earth. A woman could view herself as just a homemaker or know she is called of God to be a homemaker. Likewise, a man could view himself as just a policeman or know he is called of God to be a policeman. There is a vast difference between these two viewpoints. One view is that of a chore, and the other viewpoint is that of a calling. A chore is performed routinely—a job somehow to be done. In contrast, a calling is a mission pursued with promise, planning, purpose, passion, persistence, perseverance and praise to our Lord Jesus Christ.

Many Christians have the wrong belief that church ministers—like evangelists, missionaries and pastors—have a higher calling than nonchurch workers. This position is not Biblical. The term "calling" applies just as much to nonchurch work as to church work. Nonchurch work, when consistent with and recognized as a calling, is as much "full-time Christian service" as church work. All believers are called to do everything, round the clock, as full-time service to Christ: *"And whatsoever ye do, do it heartily, as to the Lord, and not unto men"* (Colossians 3:23).

The importance of calling is brought out in several places in the Bible, especially in the New Testament. I quote a few verses below. Note these verses refer to and apply to the believers in general—not just to ministers or those who are church workers.

> *"For the gifts and calling of God are without repentance"* (Romans 11:29).

> *"For ye see your calling, brethren, how that not many wise men after the flesh, not*

REV. NARESH K. MALHOTRA, PH.D.

many mighty, not many noble, are called" (1 Corinthians 1:26).

"Let every man abide in the same calling wherein he was called" (1 Corinthians 7:20).

"The eyes of your understanding being enlightened; that ye may know what is the hope of his calling, and what the riches of the glory of his inheritance in the saints" (Ephesians 1:18).

"There is one body, and one Spirit, even as ye are called in one hope of your calling" (Ephesians 4:4).

"I press toward the mark for the prize of the high calling of God in Christ Jesus" (Philippians 3:14).

"Wherefore also we pray always for you, that our God would count you worthy of this calling, and fulfil all the good pleasure of his goodness, and the work of faith with power" (2 Thessalonians 1:11).

"Who hath saved us, and called us with an holy calling, not according to our works, but according to his own purpose and grace,

which was given us in Christ Jesus before the world began" (2 Timothy 1:9).

"Wherefore, holy brethren, partakers of the heavenly calling, consider the Apostle and High Priest of our profession, Christ Jesus" (Hebrews 3:1).

"Wherefore the rather, brethren, give diligence to make your calling and election sure: for if ye do these things, ye shall never fall" (2 Peter 1:10).

Your Calling Is Centered Around a Ministry

A central aspect of your calling is a ministry unto the Lord. God has a ministry for every believer. While it is clear in the Bible, this idea seems foreign to Christians and churches. In the Old Testament, God promised the nation of Israel they will be priests and ministers unto the Lord.

"And ye shall be unto me a kingdom of priests, and an holy nation. These are the words which thou shalt speak unto the children of Israel" (Exodus 19:6).

"But ye shall be named the Priests of the LORD: men shall call you the Ministers of our God: ye shall eat the riches of the Gentiles, and in their glory shall ye boast yourselves" (Isaiah 61:6).

In the New Testament, the ministry of the Great Commission is given to every believer—not just to the apostles, pastors and those in full-time Christian ministry.

> *"And Jesus came and spake unto them, saying, All power is given unto me in heaven and in earth.*
>
> *Go ye therefore, and teach all nations, baptizing them in the name of the Father, and of the Son, and of the Holy Ghost:*
>
> *Teaching them to observe all things whatsoever I have commanded you: and, lo, I am with you alway, even unto the end of the world. Amen"* (Matthew 28:18–20).

The general nature of the ministry God has for you is to preach the Gospel and serve the Lord. Jesus not only calls you to come to Him but also to proclaim His Gospel. The calling to proclaim the Gospel is so significant that it is emphasized in the first five books of the New Testament (Matthew 28:19–20, Mark 16:15, Luke 24:47, John 20:21, Acts 1:8). There are different ways to preach the Gospel and different ways to serve the Lord. You could do this by directing cars in the parking lot, serving food in the church kitchen, serving as an usher, singing in the choir, teaching Sunday school or in a variety of different nonchurch jobs. I know of several Christians who view their so-called secular jobs as their primary ministries, and God is blessing them. God has a unique ministry for you and for that He has gifted you uniquely. God has a unique plan for your life, involving a unique way He wants you to minister to Him (Jeremiah 29:11).

What is the calling God has for you? Well, you have to go before the Lord and ask Him to show you. In general, growing spiritually (as discussed in chapter 3) and growing in grace (as discussed in chapter 4) will help you in discerning the calling of God. The following sections contain additional guidelines that will help you answer this critically important question.

Your Natural Skills, Talents and Abilities

The calling God has for you is something far beyond what you can do with your natural skills, talents and abilities. These are abilities, talents and skills you were born with or have acquired them through education, training or use. In the Bible, God called ordinary people to accomplish extraordinary things. He called Abram, a common person living in a heathen culture, and made him the father of many nations. He called Judah, a person with many faults and shortcomings, as the tribe through which the Messiah would come. He called Moses, a person wandering in the desert for forty years, as the prophet who would deliver the nation of Israel from the Egyptian bondage. He called David, an ordinary, common shepherd boy, to defeat the mighty Goliath and to be the king of Israel and be in the lineage of the Messiah. The list goes on. All of the twelve disciples who Jesus called were *"unlearned and ignorant men"* (Acts 4:13). This principle is given to us in clear, unmistakable terms by Paul in 1 Corinthians 1:26–29. The reason God calls ordinary people is stated clearly in that no one can glory in the presence of the Lord. Do you feel inadequate, unworthy, deficient, short, insufficient, lacking and wanting for the calling you sense God has for you? If yes, you meet one of the requirements. God loves to use such people for His glory.

You cannot perform God's calling in the natural, that is, with your natural gifts, talents, abilities, wisdom and resources (1 Corinthians 3:18–19). In fact, the Bible says, in the natural, we lack the spiritual discernment to know or receive the things of God (1 Corinthians 2:14). The work of God requires the supernatural power of God, working in you and through you, to accomplish results—fruit that remains to His glory (Zechariah 4:6, John 15:4). It is true that you cannot perform your calling by relying on your natural skills, talents and abilities. However, once you have surrendered these to the Lord, they become God's skills, talents and abilities in your life. Then the Holy Spirit can and will use these mightily for the glory of the Lord Jesus Christ, as in the account of Moses's rod:

> *"And the LORD said unto him, What is that in thine hand? And he said, A rod.*
>
> *And he said, Cast it on the ground. And he cast it on the ground, and it became a serpent; and Moses fled from before it.*
>
> *And the LORD said unto Moses, Put forth thine hand, and take it by the tail. And he put forth his hand, and caught it, and it became a rod in his hand"* (Exodus 4:2–4).

God told Moses to cast his rod on the ground before Him. When Moses did, it became a serpent. Then God told Moses to take it up again by the tail, *"and it became a rod in his hand"* (Exodus 4:4). However, there was a big difference. First, it was the rod of Moses, an ordinary rod; and with that, Moses could do no miracles. Once Moses laid it down before the Lord and then picked it up at His command, it became the rod of God in the hand of Moses. With God's rod in his hand, Moses did many mighty miracles as recorded in the Bible; he even parted the Red Sea (Exodus 14:16–30).

Note that the rod became a serpent when Moses cast it to the ground. Why? The reason is there was a serpent in his rod. In fact, there is a serpent in every rod. As a result of Adam's sin, a curse came upon nature and upon all natural things (Genesis 3:14–19). There is a curse upon your natural gifts, talents and abilities. The way to break that curse is to give your "rod"—your natural gifts, talents, and abilities—to the Lord Jesus Christ and then pick them up as He instructs you to do so. God instructed Moses to pick up the rod, which had become a serpent, by the tail. God will give you specific instructions on when and how to pick up your rod and how to use it for His glory.

So what is in your hand? What are your skills, talents and abilities? Cast them before the Lord. Lay them down. Then at the Lord's command, pick them up again. They will become God's skills, talents and abilities that the Holy Spirit will use mightily in your calling for the glory of God. Amen! Your natural skills, talents and abilities, under your control, can be stumbling blocks in your calling. Why? Because of Adam's sin, there is a "serpent," a curse on everything natural. If you operate using your natural skills, talents and abilities, you are sure to catch nothing; that is, you will labor in vain without bearing any eternal fruit. However, if you labor under the order and direction of the Lord Jesus Christ, you will not labor in vain. As the Word of God declares in 1 Corinthians 15:58, "*Therefore, my beloved brethren, be ye stedfast, unmoveable, always abounding in the work of the Lord, forasmuch as ye know that your labour is not in vain in the Lord.*" This principle will be illustrated vividly in the "Scripture Spotlight" section in the context of Peter fishing in the Lake of Gennesaret, also called the Sea of Galilee and the Sea of Tiberias. However, once you have surrendered your natural gifts, talents and abilities unto the Lord Jesus Christ, the curse will be broken and God will bless them supernaturally. The good news is "*Christ hath redeemed us from the curse of the law, being made a curse for us: for it is written, Cursed is every one that hangeth on a tree*" (Galatians 3:13).

God instructed Moses when and how to pick up the rod again. He said, "*Put forth thine hand, and take it by the tail.*" Once you surrender your skills, talents and abilities to the Lord, He will instruct you when and how to pick them up again. Jesus will show you how He wants you to use them for His glory. Then they become God's instruments in your hand. Therefore, one way to discern your calling is to see what skills, talents and abilities you have. Surrender them to the Lord, and ask God in what way He wants you to use them. This submission will help in determining your calling.

I would include your personality, experience, background and training as a part of your skills, talents and abilities. Let us say you have retired after a long career as a nurse. As you discern God's call for the next phase of your life, it is likely it will involve using your nursing background. Perhaps it may be medical missions at home or abroad. While many other nurses may be involved in medical missions—indeed you may end up working with some of them, God will use you in a unique way for His glory. Again, the key is you surrender your experience, background and training to the Lord. As I will share in my personal testimony in the "Author's Account" later in this chapter, my main calling now heavily makes use of my career and credentials as a professor.

If you refuse to yield your strength (natural talents and abilities) to God, He has to turn your strength into weakness before He can use you for His glory. When returning to Canaan, God wrestled with Jacob (Genesis 32:22–32). The Angel Who wrestled with Jacob was the Lord Jesus Christ.[1] And when the Angel saw He prevailed not over Jacob, He touched the socket of his thigh so that it was wrenched out of joint (Genesis 32:25). Why his thigh? Because the thigh is the mainstay of a man's strength, and its joint with the hip is the source of physical force for the wrestler. Only afterward, once Jacob's strength was turned into his weakness, God changed Jacob's name to Israel.

Your Spiritual Gifts

God has a unique call upon your life. This calling is specifically meant for you and is different from the calling upon any other person. No two persons have an identical calling—just as they are not identical. God has gifted you uniquely in the area of His calling. It is very important you discover these spiritual gifts and operate in them. You may think or feel you are not gifted. However, the truth is God has given you spiritual gifts. *"But the manifestation of the Spirit is given to every man to profit withal"* (1 Corinthians 12:7). God has given every believer spiritual gifts, God-empowered abilities, to be used in ministry. These gifts are a manifestation of God's grace and are given only to believers (1 Corinthians 2:14). God has gifted you according to His pleasure and His will for your life. *"But now hath God set the members every one of them in the body, as it hath pleased him"* (1 Corinthians 12:18).

Today every believer is a priest of God (1 Peter 2:5, 9; Revelation 1:5–6) and, in a real sense, is called to full-time service and ministry to represent the Lord even in secular occupations—indeed, in every area of life. As believers in Christ, we are God's representatives and called to ministry, according to the gifts God gives us. Part of this occurs in the workplace, part in the home, part in the church and part with a neighbor, etc. Every believer has a spiritual gift (or gifts), and this is a foundation of God's call on your life.

What God has gifted you to do, He has called you to do. What He has called you to do, He has gifted you to do. How do you know God's calling? By knowing your spiritual gift(s). Understanding, as a believer, you have been given a spiritual gift(s), you should seek to know your gift(s), develop them and, through God's leading, put them to work for the Kingdom of God. Knowing what your spiritual gifts are will help you determine your calling and God's will and direction for your life from the standpoint of priorities, commitments, goals and preparation.

For instance, if you do not have one of the speaking gifts (teaching, exhortation, etc.), God has not called you to preach or be a pastor. While all believers are called to do the work of evangelism and should look for opportunities to disciple and mentor others on a one-to-one basis, you should do people a favor by staying out of the pulpit or classroom as a teacher unless you are so gifted.

Your gift may be helping or showing mercy. If so, that is where God wants to use you for His glory. *"As each one has received a special gift, employ it in serving one another, as good stewards of the manifold grace of God"* (1 Peter 4:10). A good steward is one who employs his spiritual gift(s) by faithfully developing them through training and use. Always use your gifts in love. Further, we are commanded to stir up our spiritual gifts and be zealous of them (2 Timothy 1:6). Never neglect your spiritual gifts (1 Timothy 4:14).

There is a lot of help available to assist you in discovering your spiritual gifts. For instance, there are spiritual gift inventories and tests you can access on the internet.[2] Most importantly, you should pray and ask the Holy Spirit for His help in discerning your spiritual gift(s). The Holy Spirit called Barnabas and Saul to be missionaries (Acts 13:2).

Your Deepest Desires and Burdens

The Bible says your deepest desires are important to God (Psalm 37:4, Matthew 5:6, John 16:24). As a believer in Christ (chapter 2), God has written His desires and His law on your heart. *"For this is the covenant that I will make with the house of Israel after those days, saith the Lord; I will put my laws into their mind, and write them in their hearts:*

and I will be to them a God, and they shall be to me a people" (Hebrews 8:10). If you are walking with the Lord and growing in grace (chapters 3 and 4), then your desires are Godly desires. When you delight in the Lord Jesus Christ, His desires become your desires and God has promised to grant them to you (Psalm 37:4). Ask yourself, "In what way do I want to serve my Savior and Lord Jesus Christ?" As you do, the Holy Spirit will guide you to your calling.

In addition, God may lay certain burdens on your heart. He may help you to see certain needs that others do not quite see in the same way. One indicator of what God wants you to do is your burden of what needs to be done to make the world more like what God wants it to be. Following these burdens will lead you to your calling. You will know this calling by a sense of leading, purpose, passion and commitment. Your desires and your burden will intersect at your calling. As stated earlier, your spiritual gifts and your natural skills, talents and abilities—as surrendered to the Lord—also will lead to your calling. All of these factors will converge in the area of your calling. For example, a woman may experience both an intense desire and a great burden to raise up her children as mighty men and women of God. Her spiritual gift is service. She grew up in a home where her mother was a homemaker; and from her, she acquired many valuable household skills and abilities. Thus, her calling is to be a mother—at least until her children grow up and God redirects her life.

You Must Be Willing to Pay the Price

As I stated in chapter 3, there is a cost to discerning, pursuing and fulfilling your calling. It requires the sacrifice of time, money, comfort and resources. It requires the surrender of personal goals, activities and preferences to the Lord. It requires sacrificially giving of yourself to the Lord.

This principle is seen in the life and ministry of Elisha. God chose Elisha as the prophet to succeed Elijah (1 Kings 19:16). However, Elisha had to pay a big cost to pursue this calling. Elisha belonged to a wealthy, loving family. When Elijah cast his mantle upon him, Elisha *was plowing with twelve yoke of oxen before him, and he with the twelfth* (1 Kings 19:19). This speaks of wealth, for normally an individual would handle only two yoked oxen. Elisha's desire to wish his parents goodbye indicates he was from a loving family. Thus, the response to the call of God cost Elisha heavily in terms of finances and family relationships. Elisha willingly paid this cost.

In the New Testament, the apostles paid a heavy cost to fulfill their calling, as exemplified by Paul. There is a cost. If you are not willing to pay the cost, it is unlikely you will discern God's calling—let alone pursue it with a passion.

In Luke 14:26–35, Jesus talks about the cost of discipleship. Let me quote just two of these verses:

> *"And whosoever doth not bear his cross,*
> *and come after me, cannot be my disciple.*
> *For which of you, intending to build a*
> *tower, sitteth not down first, and counteth*

the cost, whether he have sufficient to finish it?" (Luke 14:27–28).

The reason most believers are not pursuing their calling is because they are not willing to pay the cost. That is why they do not bear fruit that will remain to the glory of God.

Your Calling Versus Your Career

A career is something you have chosen; whereas, a calling is what God has chosen for you to pursue. You can choose to make a career in your calling; in that case, the two will coincide. In other cases, the two may be distinct. For example, the apostle Paul had a career as a tent maker but passionately pursued and fulfilled his calling as an apostle (Galatians 1:1, Ephesians 1:1).

The difference between pursuing your calling versus pursuing your career is well illustrated by the lives of Saul and David, respectively the first and the second kings of Israel. The king of Israel was to be different than the kings of the heathen nations. The king of Israel was called to be God's servant and God's minister. Both Saul and David were handpicked and called by God to be kings. In each case, the Lord revealed His choice through the prophet Samuel who anointed them both. Although Saul started on the right note, he soon lost sight of this calling. He became rebellious and disobedient to God (1 Samuel 15:23). As a result, he lost the kingdom (1 Samuel 15:28). In sharp contrast, David understood, as a king, he was primarily God's minister. He cherished and fulfilled his calling until the end. Therefore, in spite of his sins of adultery and murder, he is known as a man after God's heart (Acts 13:22). His heart was perfect with the Lord his God (1 Kings 11:4).

Both Saul and David were unknown, insignificant men when they were called by God. They both had a divine destiny to glorify God and fulfill His plan and purpose. One fell short, and the other fulfilled his calling. Saul, in pursuing his career as king, was taking shortcuts, compromising, caring too much what people thought of him and fearing people more than God. In contrast, David had his heart set on God alone; and his life was guided by a passionate desire to fulfill his calling. God said to King Jeroboam, "*Yet thou hast not been as my servant David, who kept my commandments, and who followed me with all his heart, to do that only which was right in mine eyes*" (1 Kings 14:8).

Saul and David each had a career as the king of Israel to develop and stabilize the nation of Israel. In addition, each of them had a calling, a God-given mission, a calling not simply to rule Israel but to make it a unique nation centered on Jehovah God. Israel was to be like no other nation on the earth. Saul pursued his career and neglected his calling. He made poor choices as he listened to the wrong voices and did not listen to the voice of God. The voices to whom you listen will influence the choices you make. Israel suffered under the rule of Saul. David pursued his calling with a passion while he was mindful of his career. He had a heart for God, and the nation of Israel prospered under him.

Sometimes you may have to sacrifice your career to fulfill your calling. This truth was amply demonstrated by Jonathan, the son of King Saul. Jonathan was the crown prince and expected future king of Israel. He had been a successful and popular military leader before David arrived. He had prepared and positioned himself well to ascend to the throne after his father. Rather than perceiving David as a threat to his kingship as did his father Saul (1 Samuel 18:8), Jonathan loved David. He defended David to Saul and protected him from Saul. He knew God had anointed David to be the next king of Israel. Furthermore, he knew God had called him to support David to assume the throne. Jonathan effectively abdicated his natural right to the throne in favor of David. Jonathan said to David, *"the LORD be with thee, as he hath been with my father"* (1 Samuel 20:13). By saying this, Jonathan, in effect, transferred the kingship from Saul to David rather than to himself. Thus, Jonathan sacrificed his career as a king to pursue his calling to love, support and uphold David as the future king of Israel. Unlike his father who failed, Jonathan succeeded in fulfilling his calling.

Which king will you be? Like Saul and David, every believer has a divine calling that makes use of the person's gifts, talents and abilities to further the Kingdom of God on the earth. You, too, have a divine calling to be a great man or woman of God; and Jesus Christ died for you to fulfill it. You must think beyond your career to your calling, to the mission God has given to you as His child. Embrace your calling with conviction, commitment and passion. God is worthy of your best, and you must do your utmost to glorify the Name of Jesus. Be King David!

Responding to Your Calling

Fulfilling your calling is not optional; it is not a matter of choice. God expects you to serve Him and worship Him by performing this calling. It is your primary way of doing the good works God has called you to do. We are fond of quoting Ephesians 2:8–9 and emphasizing salvation is by grace alone, through faith alone, in Jesus Christ alone. Praise God it is so; otherwise, no one would or could be saved. But we do not give heed to the very next verse:

> *"For we are his workmanship, created in Christ Jesus unto good works, which God hath before ordained that we should walk in them"* (Ephesians 2:10).

These good works are a part of and the fruit of the calling God has given to each believer. Not only does God expect each believer to be obedient to the calling; but furthermore, He expects you to be fruitful. *"Ye have not chosen me, but I have chosen you, and ordained you, that ye should go and bring forth fruit, and that your fruit should remain: that whatsoever ye shall ask of the Father in my name, he may give it you"* (John 15:16).

Those who refuse to engage in their calling or bear fruit by doing the work, according to God's will and His way, will lose their reward but not their salvation. Jesus made this truth clear in the case of the fig tree recorded in Luke 13:6–9. In the entire Bible, there is only one instance of Jesus cursing anything (Mark 11:21). It was the fig tree Jesus approached, expecting to find fruit when

He was hungry and found none. This incidence is given in Mark 11:12–14, 20–21. To put this in proper context, I am not suggesting Jesus will curse any believer who does not bear fruit; He will NOT. He said, *"All that the Father giveth me shall come to me; and him that cometh to me I will in no wise cast out"* (John 6:37). However, when a believer stands before the Lord Jesus Christ and He looks for fruit and finds none, He will be just as disappointed as He was when He approached the fig tree. Do you want to disappoint your Savior and Lord? I discuss the loss of rewards for believers who do not fulfill their calling further in chapter 7 of the second book in this series.

Responding to the calling of God is so very important that I have written a separate book, a sequel to this one, entitled *God Is Calling You: Responding to the Calling of God.* This sequel will help you prepare for your calling, experience the transformation God has for you, get a vision from God in your calling and experience God's ministry of multiplication. It will give you principles to overcome the obstacles the devil is likely to throw at you and to gain victory in the spiritual warfare you will encounter. Furthermore, it will guide you in obtaining your inheritance and full rewards and encourage you to be faithful in pursuing your calling and enduring to the end. A brief description of each chapter was provided in the Introduction to this book.

Scripture Spotlight

The Calling of Peter

The call of Peter to the ministry in Luke 5:1–11 offers several insights into discerning and responding to the calling of God. This also is described in Matthew 4:18–22 and Mark 1:16–20. We will focus on the passage in Luke. Let us examine this passage, verse-by-verse, to draw out principles we can apply in our lives to determine the calling of God. Please look at these verses in the Bible as you read this book.

Scripture Source: Luke 5:1–11

Verse 1

1. *"And it came to pass, that, as the people pressed upon him to hear the word of God."* Jesus was preaching the Word of God. Why? Why did Jesus spend so much of His time teaching the people? For three reasons. First, this was His primary office and ministry during His first coming. The Old Testament mentions three major offices: the prophet, the priest and the king. The prophet represented God before man. The prophet said, *"Thus saith the Lord."* (This exact phrase is mentioned 415 times in the King James Version in 413 different verses.) The priest represented man before God. The king ruled for God. In a primary sense, Jesus fulfilled the office of the prophet during His first coming.

That office began when He was baptized in the river Jordan and ended at Calvary. In a primary sense, currently He is fulfilling the office of the priest (Romans 8:34, Hebrews 7:25). This office began at the cross and will end at the second coming. In a primary sense, He will fulfill the office of the King. This office will begin at His second coming and last for all eternity, and He will reign as King of kings and Lord of lords (1 Timothy 6:15, Revelation 19:16). Amen! I intentionally emphasized in a primary sense because, more generally, Jesus is operating in all three offices always at all times. Jesus Christ is the ONLY One Who has been ordained by God the Father to fulfill all three offices.

2. The second reason Jesus spent so much time teaching the people was to build up their faith (Romans 10:17). He wanted to build the faith of the people to receive the miracles God had for them. Do you have the faith to receive a miracle? Your propensity to receive a miracle from the Lord is directly proportional to the Word level inside of you. Do not seek miracles. Rather, build the Word of God inside of you. If you have the Word of God inside you, then signs, miracles and wonders will follow you (Matthew 13:57–58; Mark 6:4–6, 16:17; Hebrews 4:2).

3. The third reason Jesus taught the Word of God is because Jesus plus the Word of God equals the power of God, as in Luke 5:17. Let me give you a mathematical equation: Jesus + Word = Power

of God. Do you want to bring the power of God to bear upon a specific situation? Then speak the Word of God, and proclaim the Lordship of Jesus Christ in that situation and to that situation.

Verse 2

1. "*The fishermen were gone out of them, and were washing their nets.*" The people who received the miracle and discerned the calling of God were not those who had left their work to listen to Jesus but the fishermen who were mending their nets. If you are a fisherman, keep mending your nets. Be faithful in doing the known will of God—even though, as yet, you may not know your calling. The best way to position yourself to discern your calling and receive miracles from God is to do the known will of God for your life.

   Many great men of the Bible were called into ministry after they had demonstrated an ability and a willingness to work in a secular context and had been faithful to that calling. This hard work built character and prepared them for the ministry. It is noteworthy that Elisha was at work in the field with the rest of the field hands when Elijah placed his mantle on him. Moses and David were called as shepherds, Peter as a fisherman and Paul as a tent maker. The Lord Jesus Christ Himself was a carpenter by trade Who was trained by Joseph.

2. The fishermen were washing their nets because they had been soiled by the dirt of the sea.

Without Christ, your life is soiled and stained by sin and needs to be washed clean by the blood of Jesus. Only the blood of Jesus can wash a person as white as snow. The Bible says every person is a sinner (Romans 3:23). Thus, every person needs to repent and receive the forgiveness Jesus Christ alone offers and receive the Lord Jesus Christ as Savior and Lord. (See chapter 2.)

3. The ships were empty. Why? As we will see later in verse 5, Peter had toiled all night and caught nothing. It was a human, natural failure on the part of Peter. However, it resulted in God's supernatural success. Human failures can be stepping stones for supernatural success if we commit them to the Lord Jesus Christ.

4. Verse 2 refers to *"ships"* or boats, *"fishermen"* and *"nets."* The ships or boats refer to the structure God uses to do His work on the earth. That structure is the Church, the Body of Christ. The fishermen are those who give direction to the ship or the boat. They give direction to the Church or the Body of Christ; and they consist of apostles, prophets, evangelists, pastors and teachers—as mentioned in Ephesians 4:11. The nets represent the equipment used to catch the fish. The implication then is, to discern the calling of God, you must be plugged into the local church, be under the authority of the church leaders and be properly equipped with the Word of God.

Verse 3

1. *"And he entered into one of the ships, which was Simon's."* He used Simon Peter's ship that was lying idle (verse 2). Jesus often will use seemingly useless or weak objects and people. This principle is clearly stated by the apostle Paul in 1 Corinthians 1:26–29.

2. If the boats had been full of fish, Jesus could not have borrowed them. There would be no room for Him, as indeed was the case at His birth. Many times God has to empty a person of self to make room for Him to come in. Empty yourself of yourself if you want to discern the calling of God. So He can pour out His Holy Spirit in them, God is looking for empty vessels. The prophet Elisha told the widow in deep debt, *"Go, borrow thee vessels abroad of all thy neighbours, even empty vessels; borrow not a few"* (2 Kings 4:3). She was to *"pour out into all those vessels"* the oil she had (2 Kings 4:4). Oil is widely understood in the Bible as a symbol of the Holy Spirit. For example, in Luke 4:18 and Acts 10:38, the Holy Spirit and oil are linked directly.

3. Simon Peter let Jesus Christ into his boat. The boat represented Peter's life, symbolizing Peter inviting Jesus Christ into his life. You must invite Jesus into your life; you must be saved or born again to discern your calling. (See chapter 2.) As He did with Peter, Jesus also wants to come into your life; He is knocking at the door of your heart. Jesus said, *"Behold, I stand at the door, and knock: if any man hear my voice, and open the door, I will come*

in to him, and will sup with him, and he with me" (Revelation 3:20). Open the door of your heart to Him if you have not done so already!

4. Beyond inviting Jesus into your life, make yourself and your possessions available to God. If Simon Peter had refused to make himself and his ship available to Jesus, he would have missed a great miracle and probably would have missed discerning the calling of God—at least this time. This is one of the main reasons many Christians do not discern the calling of God because they are not willing to make themselves and their possessions available to God. In fact, you should offer the first fruits to God (Exodus 22:29). The boat is critical for fishing; you cannot fish in the deep without a boat. Thus, in lending his boat, Peter was offering the first fruits to God for the preaching of the Gospel.

5. *"And he sat down, and taught the people out of the ship."* Again, Jesus taught the people. He was sitting and teaching, implying He taught the people for a long time. Simon Peter was very much listening to the Word Jesus was expounding as he was in the boat with Jesus—indeed, so were James and John while washing their nets. Extensive and intensive instruction in the Word are needed to build up your faith to discern your calling and receive miracles from God while fulfilling it. Jesus was never in a hurry when teaching the Word. Likewise, never be in a hurry while reading, studying or meditating on the Word. Give the Holy Spirit time to minister the Word to you.

6. Jesus borrowed Peter's boat, and he was a profes-
    sional fisherman. Thus, Jesus borrowed Peter's
    profession to proclaim the Word of God. In the
    initial stage of your calling, Jesus wants to bor-
    row your profession and your job to proclaim the
    Gospel. Let me be more direct and clear. As His
    initial calling to you, Jesus wants you to proclaim
    the Gospel and witness of His grace in your pro-
    fession—whatever your profession may be! Your
    profession is your main mission field! Do you view
    it as such?

Verse 4

1. "*He Said.*" God creates by the spoken Word! When
    Jesus said it, it was as good as done! In Genesis
    1, God created the world by the spoken Word.
    "*And God said*" (Genesis 1:3, 6, 9, 11, 14, 20, 24,
    26, 29) and so it was. The New Testament con-
    firms this truth. "*Through faith we understand that
    the worlds were framed by the word of God, so that
    things which are seen were not made of things which
    do appear*" (Hebrews 11:3). God has created man
    in His image. Thus, man procreates or recreates
    by the spoken word, meaning we bring to pass the
    circumstances and situations in our lives by the
    words we speak (Proverbs 10:11; 12:14, 18; 18:21;
    Matthew 12:37; James 3:6). It is very important
    you speak and confess the Word while discerning
    and responding to your calling.

2. *"Launch out into the deep."* There are no miracles in the land or even in the shallow waters. In this case, literally, the fish were in the deep. In life, the shore or shallow waters represent areas where you can rely on yourself, your natural skills, talents and abilities. As long as you are relying on yourself, it is difficult for you to discern God's calling. The "deep" represents situations where you know that you know the Lord Jesus is your only hope. At the shore, it is calm; but in the deep, there is a storm. At the shore, you can see clearly but not so in the deep. In the deep, the Lord Jesus Christ is your ONLY hope.

3. The multitude was on the land, on the shore. They represent convenience-oriented Christians who do not want to leave their comfort zone, those who refuse to launch into the deep. They are not willing to pay the cost of serving the Lord Jesus Christ by launching out into the deep.

4. You must launch out into the deep. However, launch into the deep only: (1) based on the Word of God and (2) with the Lord Jesus Christ. Simon had the Word of the Lord, and Jesus Christ was in his ship or boat. Is Jesus in your boat? True prosperity is Jesus Christ in your boat and in your life (Genesis 39:2–3). Sad to say, too many Christians have launched into the deep on their own; and thus, they find themselves in deep trouble. However, if you launch out into the deep, based on the Word of God and with Jesus, then you will

experience wonders and miracles. God declares in Psalm 107:23–24:

"They that go down to the sea in ships,
that do business in great waters;
These see the works of the LORD, and
his wonders in the deep."

5. What kind of a Christian are you? Are you a shallow Christian or a deep Christian? Deep in the Word of God, deep in the promises of God, deep in your walk with the Lord? It is very difficult for shallow Christians to discern the calling of God—much less pursue it with a passion. There are no miracles for shallow Christians.

6. *"Let down your nets."* There is a part man has to do. Don't leave everything to God. You have to let down your nets. There comes a time when you have to act to demonstrate your faith.

7. Jesus told Peter to let down the nets—in the plural. God wants you to do big things. He wants you to dream big, to think big, to act big and to live big for His glory. Remember, God's vision for you is always bigger than what you have for yourself. He has a big vision for you in your calling. Go for it!

8. In effect, Jesus will repay Peter abundantly for the use of his boat. God will not owe man anything (Luke 18:29–30). Therefore, never hesitate to lend your possessions, time, resources and your very life unto the Lord.

Verse 5

1. *"We have toiled all the night, and have taken nothing."* We see the futility of human effort apart from
Christ. As Jesus said in John 15:5, *"For without
me ye can do nothing."* On the other hand, *"I can
do all things through Christ which strengtheneth me"*
(Philippians 4:13).

2. As discussed in the "Central Concepts," there is a
curse upon human effort due to the sin of Adam
(Genesis 3:17–19). There is a serpent in everything natural (Exodus 4:2–4). This curse is broken
when you yield your life to the Lord Jesus Christ
(Galatians 3:13).

3. Jesus often will tell you to do something that does
not make sense. Simon fished there regularly; and
he well knew fish were caught at night—not during
the day. Here was Jesus telling him to fish during
the day. Thus, what Jesus was telling him did not
make any sense to Simon. Many of the teachings
of Jesus are just the opposite of this world and do
not make sense to our natural minds. For example,
in the Sermon on the Mount, Jesus instructs us
to turn the other cheek, walk the extra mile, love
our enemies and bless those who curse us. (See
Matthew 5, 6 and 7.) These do not make sense
to our natural minds; but nevertheless, these are
God's ways.

4. *"Nevertheless at thy word I will."* This is the key
to discerning the calling of God. Unquestioned
obedience. Total obedience. Complete obedience.

Whether we understand or not, whether it makes sense to us or not, we must obey. If all would as readily obey Jesus, they would, like Peter, be blessed beyond measure. If we act on our authority and do our will, we are sure to catch nothing; but if we labor under the order and will of the Lord Jesus Christ, we will not labor in vain (1 Corinthians 15:58).

Verse 6

1. *"And when they had this done."* When you act on the Word of God in faith, you will receive your miracle. Obey fully and completely. It is not enough to tell God you will obey. You must follow through with complete obedience. In the follow through, the miracle takes place. Always remember partial obedience is disobedience. Partial obedience in the life of Saul cost him the kingdom. (See 1 Samuel 15:10–29.) This also is seen clearly in the story of the two sons in Matthew 21:28–31. Obedience matters always but especially when you are in deep waters. When facing difficult situations, you are in danger of making poor choices and most susceptible to the attacks of Satan. In such situations, you have to be determined to obey God.

2. *"They inclosed a great multitude of fishes: and their net brake."* God will more than supply our need. Our cup will be full and overflowing; our nets will be full and breaking (Proverbs 10:22). This is a characteristic of a miracle. There is abundance

of God's supply. The work of God will result in a net-breaking, boat-sinking load of fish! As we saw in chapter 2 when discussing the miracles of blind Bartimaeus, God moves in response to our faith. As Jesus said in Mark 9:23, "*If thou canst believe. All things are possible to him that believeth.*" Peter responded in faith. He demonstrated his faith by corresponding action.

3. The reason Peter's net was breaking was because he let down only one net when Jesus said to let down the nets. In verse 4, the Greek word for "net" is in the plural; whereas in verse 5, it is in the singular. This is also true in the King James Version. Thus, we must obey God fully, totally and completely.

4. After the resurrection of Jesus, a similar incident took place but with a very different outcome (John 21:1–11). The disciples had gone fishing on the Sea of Galilee, also called the Sea of Tiberias (John 21:1) or Lake of Gennesaret (Luke 5:1). They had fished all night and caught nothing. Jesus appeared to them in the morning and said, "*Cast the net on the right side of the ship, and ye shall find*" (John 21:6). They did and caught a "*multitude of fishes,*" numbering 153, that they dragged to the shore. "*Yet was not the net broken*" (John 21:11). It should be noted in Luke 5:6, the net was breaking. In John 21:11, it was not! Something supernatural happened to their net after the resurrection of Jesus! That same resurrection power is available to you today. Tap into it!

Verse 7

1. Peter and Andrew had to call upon their partners, James and John. We all need partners. Do you have partners you can call upon in times of need?

2. *"And they came, and filled both the ships, so that they began to sink."* God will more than supply your need. Your cup will be full and overflowing. The work of God always will result in abundance. Jesus said, *"The thief cometh not, but for to steal, and to kill, and to destroy: I am come that they might have life, and that they might have it more abundantly"* (John 10:10). When you discern and pursue God's calling in the power of the Holy Spirit, you will experience an abundance of fruit. Not one but both the boats—those belonging to Peter, James and John—were full of fish. All of those who discern and respond to the calling of God will be blessed.

3. Be sure nothing is lost. None of the fish were lost. After feeding five thousand men, besides women and children, Jesus told His disciples to *"gather up the fragments that remain, that nothing be lost"* (John 6:12). God wants us to be good stewards of His blessings and resources.

4. Christ here demonstrates He has the same power over the fish of the sea as He has over the frogs, lice and the locusts of Egypt. He created them— indeed the entire universe (John 1:3, Ephesians 3:9, Hebrews 11:3, Revelation 4:11).

Verse 8

1. Peter fell down at Jesus's knees and said, "*Depart from me; for I am a sinful man, O Lord.*" To discern the calling of God, you must do at least three things Peter did: (1) see your sinfulness. The Bible says all are sinners (Romans 3:23). Our righteousness is as filthy rags (Isaiah 64:6); (2) see the Lordship of Jesus Christ. He is the King of kings and Lord of lords (1 Timothy 6:15; Revelation 17:14, 19:16) and (3) respond in humility (Proverbs 22:4, Acts 20:19, 1 Peter 5:5).

2. Jesus did not say a word about Peter's sinfulness. Under the New Covenant, "*the goodness of God leadeth thee to repentance*" (Romans 2:4). Peter saw the goodness of God in the miraculous catch of the fish and repented.

3. This was one of the early encounters of Peter with Jesus; as yet, he did not know the Lord. Yet he was struck with the holiness of Jesus. The Message translation reads, "*Master, leave. I am a sinner and can't handle this holiness.*" Jesus is holy, holy, holy! People who recognize their sinfulness will recognize the holiness of Jesus instinctively. However, it takes spiritual growth and maturity to walk in the love of Jesus for you. About three-and-a-half years later, a similar incident is recorded in John 21:1–11. This occurrence was described in point number 4 under verse 6. After the miraculous catch, when Peter realized Jesus was standing on the shore, he swam toward Jesus.

It was not the holiness but the love of Jesus that drew Peter to Him.

4. Peter recognized Jesus as his Lord. He became a disciple. Are you simply a believer, or are you a disciple of Jesus Christ? There is a difference between a mere believer and a disciple. A mere believer has received the Lord Jesus Christ as Savior but not made Him the Lord of her or his life. The disciple has made the Son of God her or his Savior and Lord (John 8:31). A mere believer will serve God on her or his terms when it is convenient, when it fits her or his schedule and when no sacrifice is involved. The disciple will serve God on God's terms and is willing to sacrifice and willing to pay the cost of serving the Lord. The mere believer will make it to Heaven upon death. Yet *"he shall suffer loss: but he himself shall be saved; yet so as by fire"* (1 Corinthians 3:15). The disciple not only will make it to Heaven; but also *"he shall receive a reward"* (1 Corinthians 3:14); *"a crown of righteousness"* (2 Timothy 4:8); *"crown of rejoicing"* (1 Thessalonians 2:19); *"crown of life"* (James 1:12, Revelation 2:10) and a *"crown of glory that fadeth not away"* (1 Peter 5:4).

5. As you do these three things (see your sinfulness, see the Lordship of Jesus Christ and respond in humility) and become a disciple, the Holy Spirit will minister to you. He will help you to discern the calling of God (Acts 13:2).

Verse 9

1. *"For he was astonished, and all that were with him."* Peter was astonished. In fact, you will be astonished and overwhelmed by the grace of God when you see the power of God manifested in your situation as you respond to the calling of God. There will be no human explanation for the mighty working of God in your life.

2. We not only should be astonished, awestruck and amazed about our salvation in Jesus Christ but also continue in the same state because of God's continual work in our lives through the Holy Spirit. That is an important element of the Christian life.

Verse 10

1. *"And Jesus said unto Simon, Fear not; from henceforth thou shalt catch men."* This statement constituted Peter's calling as a disciple and as an apostle. Jesus called Simon Peter in clear, unmistakable terms. As you walk in the Spirit, according to the principles outlined in verses 1 through 9, you will hear clearly the calling of God.

2. Peter got his calling directly from the Lord Jesus Christ—not through a pastor, family member, friend or any other source. It is very important that you get your calling directly from God and from His Word. Only then you will have the faith, passion, determination and persistence to fulfill it. We see this principle clearly in the lives of Peter,

Paul and some of the other apostles. Toward the end of his life, Paul could say with a clear conscience, "*I have fought a good fight, I have finished my course, I have kept the faith*" (2 Timothy 4:7). See also the discussion of why Satan tempted Eve and not Adam in chapter 1.

3. God will call you to service in the area of your calling. Jesus said he would make Simon catch men. From a fisherman, he would be transformed to become a fisher of men. He would catch people and bring them into the Kingdom of God by leading them to the saving grace of the Lord Jesus. Jesus revealed His calling to Simon in a way he could discern, as Jesus framed it in terms of his gifts, talents and abilities. Since Peter was a fisherman, Jesus framed His calling to him in those terms.

4. Becoming fishers of men is the first stage of the calling. The next stage is to become hunters of men. The fishermen cast a wide net to catch fish. The hunters, on the other hand, have a very targeted approach and focus very sharply on their prey. You begin as a fisherman, having a very general approach. Then you become a hunter with a very targeted approach to evangelism. I have seen this process in my ministry.

"Behold, I will send for many fishers, saith the LORD, and they shall fish them; and after will I send for many hunters, and they shall hunt them from every mountain,

and from every hill, and out of the holes of the rocks" (Jeremiah 16:16).

However, there is one major difference between Jeremiah 16:16 and Luke 5:10. In Jeremiah 16:16, God would send fishermen and hunters to catch people so they could be brought to judgment. In Luke 5:10, He would send fishers of men to catch people; so they could be saved from judgment as they were brought into the saving grace of our Lord Jesus Christ. That is the difference between law and grace (chapter 4).

5. *"Henceforth thou shalt catch men."* As you respond to the call of God, you will be drawn into a greater love for God that will be expressed in service for God. In fact, you will have an intense desire to serve the Lord in your calling—not to gain His favor or become more righteous—but as an expression of your love, gratefulness and thanksgiving. Are you serving the Lord out of your love for Him?

6. Jesus said, *"Fear not."* This is the first recorded instance of Christ using the words *"fear not"* with His disciples. Fear will stifle and paralyze your faith. How do you "fear not"? The answer is found in 1 John 4:18, *"There is no fear in love; but perfect love casteth out fear: because fear hath torment. He that feareth is not made perfect in love."* Thus, in order to get rid of fear, you should focus on the perfect love of God for you as has been demonstrated perfectly on the cross of Calvary. Many Christians make the mistake of focusing on their love for God, which is

never perfect and always falls short. This topic was discussed in detail in chapter 1.

7. You have to go beyond being simply a believer to becoming a disciple to discern the calling of God. The New Testament emphasizes the Lordship of Jesus Christ. Christ is portrayed as Lord and not merely as Savior. In the New Testament, Saviour appears twenty-three times in twenty-three verses in the King James Version but Lord appears 681 times in 631 verses. Immediately after his encounter with Jesus Christ as Savior on the road to Damascus, Saul asked, *"Lord, what wilt thou have me to do?"* (Acts 9:6). Thus, Saul submitted to Jesus Christ as Lord, setting an example for us. See also the discussion in point 4 under verse 8.

8. More often than not, God will call you in the ministry out of abundance—not out of poverty or lack. Simon Peter left a boat full of fish to serve in the ministry.

Verse 11

1. *"And when they had brought their ships to land."* God will lead you into the deep, but He will not leave you in the deep. After He has accomplished His deep work of grace in you, He will bring you to the land, to your place of rest. The Christian life is not about striving in self-effort; rather it is resting in Jesus Christ and in His perfect, finished work on the cross (Matthew 11:28–30, Hebrews 4:1–11).

2. *"They forsook all, and followed him."* The correct response to the calling of God is total commitment. The parallel passage in Matthew 4:18–22, especially verse 20, states their response to the calling of Jesus was immediate, at once, straightaway, demonstrating unquestioned obedience.

3. God confirmed His call on Simon Peter through his partners. Not only did Peter forsake all and follow Jesus; but James and John, the sons of Zebedee, did the same. God will confirm His call to you through other Christians and through His Church, the Body of Christ. Peter, James and John made a commitment to pursue their calling as fishers of men rather than their careers as fishermen. They were willing to pay the cost of serving the Lord. Are you willing to do so? God wants you to make the same commitment.

4. Some people say, "I don't believe in tithing as that is an Old Testament concept. I am under the New Covenant of grace." In a way, they are right. Under the New Covenant, we are to give God all, give Him 100 percent—not just 10 percent. Give God a tithe, and He will open the windows of Heaven to bless you (Malachi 3:10). Give God 100 percent; and you will see the Heavens, in the plural, opened unto you. This truth is seen in the life of our Lord Jesus.

"And Jesus, when he was baptized, went up straightway out of the water: and, lo, the heavens were opened unto him, and he saw

the Spirit of God descending like a dove, and lighting upon him" (Matthew 3:16).

We also see this principle vividly in the life of Stephen just before he was martyred.

"But he, being full of the Holy Ghost, looked up stedfastly into heaven, and saw the glory of God, and Jesus standing on the right hand of God,
And said, Behold, I see the heavens opened, and the Son of man standing on the right hand of God" (Acts 7:55–56).

Are you willing to forsake all and follow Jesus?

Conclusion

The Bible says God *"is a rewarder of them that diligently seek him"* (Hebrews 11:6). When Jesus comes into your life, you will be rewarded amply—as was Peter. His fishing boat, representing his life, caught nothing the whole night. But when he lent his boat to Jesus and it was returned to him, it was no longer Peter's boat. It was the boat of Jesus given to Peter. It became an instrument of God's miraculous power in the life of Peter. In fact, he received a net-breaking, boat-sinking load of fish! Much more, Peter received his high calling in life that he embraced. Are you willing to allow Jesus Christ to come into your boat and follow His calling with passion and obedience?

Author's Account

As I began developing the spiritual disciplines of chapter 3 and growing in grace (chapter 4), the calling of God became clearer and clearer.

My Call to the Ministry

I obtained my doctorate from the State University of New York, Buffalo, in May 1979 and moved to Atlanta in June 1979 to take up a position as Assistant Professor in the Georgia Institute of Technology (Georgia Tech). God led me to join the First Baptist Church of Atlanta; and for that, I am very grateful. In December 1979, we had our first World Missions Conference at First Baptist Church of Atlanta. During the conference, I went forward and told the Lord I was available to give up my academic career and serve Him full-time in the ministry. I prayed—and should add—struggled with this issue for about a year. During this time, I was faithful in my personal spiritual life, church service and my academic responsibilities. Then the Lord spoke to me clearly. He said, "You are right where I have placed you. I have called you as a professor, and I am going to use you as a professor. Always be sensitive to My leading." The verse the Lord gave me was: "*Let every man abide in the same calling wherein he was called*" (1 Corinthians 7:20).

While I continued at Georgia Tech, I lent my boat, my profession, to the Lord. As a professor, I had many opportunities to travel abroad by way of lecturing in professional conferences and I received many invitations to visit foreign universities. In addition to meeting all of my professional obligations, I intentionally used these opportunities to preach the Gospel in other lands. I shared the message of salvation in universities, churches and public places such as street corners and parks. Often I would extend my stay beyond the professional duration, at my time and expense; so I could focus exclusively on the ministry. On the Georgia Tech campus, I served as a faculty advisor to two Christian organizations.

God had blessed me with certain natural gifts and abilities. As a professional researcher and teacher, I could understand complex subject matters and then present them simply so that others, especially students, could understand them clearly. I had a great desire not only to use these talents in my profession but also use them for understanding, preaching and teaching God's Word. God gave me the grace to realize these natural talents would be stumbling blocks in my profession and ministry unless I surrendered them to the Lord. That is exactly what I did. I prayed, "Abba, Father, I surrender my natural talents, especially the ability to understand complex subjects and then explain them in simple terms, to You. I ask You to use them to glorify the Name of the Lord Jesus Christ in whatever way You please." Thereafter, I was confident the Holy Spirit would use these talents mightily in my life for the glory of the Lord Jesus Christ.

In 1987, I had to make a very important decision involving a change of job and move to another university in another state. I had been at Georgia Tech for eight years, then as a tenured Associate Professor. Another university had offered me a double promotion, a prestigious Chair and a considerably higher salary. It looked very attractive from the human standpoint. However, I knew better and wanted to hear from the Lord rather than go by the human standpoint. To be able to hear clearly from the Lord, I took a spiritual inventory and the Holy Spirit brought up several issues I had to confess and repent. One of them was I did not have a burden for the lost. I asked the Lord to give me that burden; and in His grace, He responded. He put in my heart a great desire to share the Gospel with the lost in Atlanta as well as in foreign nations. God instructed me to remain at Georgia Tech. Although it did not make sense from the human standpoint, thankfully I obeyed. This decision would greatly impact my ability to discern and fulfill my calling. Later that same year, God said He formally was calling me to an international ministry of evangelism. The ministry to which God has called me and gifted me is that of an evangelist (Ephesians 4:11–12). This calling is at the intersection of my desire and my burden to preach the Gospel to the lost all over the world.

In 1987, I went on my first proper mission trip to preach the Gospel with no university commitments—although I had been doing so all along since I got saved, especially when I went overseas for professional conferences or on holiday. On this first mission trip to Bogota, Colombia, God confirmed His call upon my life. Since then, I have been going on mission trips every year. As I have stepped out in faith and obedience, God has blessed me to preach the Gospel in thirty-six countries. I praise God and give Him ALL the glory. Truly, this is the Lord's doing; and it is marvelous in our eyes (Psalm 118:23).

Until 2009, I was a professor at Georgia Tech. During this time, I asked the Lord several times if He wanted me to give up my academic career and go into full-time ministry. The answer was always: "No, I have called you as a professor; and I am going to use you as a professor." Indeed, God opened tremendous opportunities for me to share the Gospel, using my academic credentials and platforms. I would not have been able to avail of these opportunities if I was not a professor. I received invitations to speak at many international conferences and from many universities abroad. These invitations took care of most of my expenses, and I could do evangelism at a marginal monetary expense. If you give God first place, He will take you places! He will bless you in all areas (Matthew 6:33). God blessed me tremendously in my academic career as well. I rose to the top of my field and garnered several top research rankings (see my academic profile at https://scheller.gatech.edu/malhotra). I never circumvented my professional obligations to serve God in proclaiming the Gospel. In fact, I viewed my professional obligations as an integral part of my calling.

However, in 2009, after completing thirty years of service, God led me to take early retirement from Georgia Tech to focus on my Christian ministry overseas. Since I retired in September 2009, God has blessed me to see more than 1.9 million people pray to receive the Lord Jesus Christ as their Savior and Lord. All of these professions have been documented carefully in independent reports prepared by the local churches and ministries with which I have worked, and each report is signed by multiple local leaders who were involved closely with our ministry. All of these reports are posted on our website at https://www.

globalevangelisticministries.net. As can be seen from these reports, a central focus in our ministry is preaching the Gospel in public schools and universities in those countries where it is possible to do so. We gain access to these schools and universities, using my academic credentials. Indeed, I have been blessed to see the faithfulness, provision, grace and miracle-working power of God manifested on my mission trips and in our ministry time and again. As the psalmist said,

> *"The LORD is gracious, and full of compassion; slow to anger, and of great mercy.*
> *The LORD is good to all: and his tender mercies are over all his works"* (Psalm 145:8–9).

I have never doubted my salvation or the calling of God. I have tried to pursue my calling with a passion. I have had to pay the price—a small cost compared to what my Savior and Lord Jesus Christ has done for me. I took virtually all of our vacation time and money and spent them on foreign missions. My children did have some hurt that I was gone so much as they were growing up. However, the Lord has addressed these situations. My wife and children have a strong relationship with the Lord Jesus Christ, and all of us are very involved with world missions. As I look back, I am amazed at what the Lord has done. I am overwhelmed by the grace of God. I praise the Lord Jesus Christ and give Him all the glory!

Quest Questions

Please do some soul searching and answer the following questions. You need not share your answers with anyone. However, if you so choose, share them with your accountability partner or a person you trust.

- Do I know, beyond a shadow of a doubt, that I am a child of God?
- Am I walking with the Lord daily? Am I growing in grace?
- Am I aware God has a unique calling for me?
- Do I know what the calling of God is upon my life? What is my primary mission in this life?
- Do I know God has a ministry for me defined by my calling? Am I pursuing that ministry with a passion?
- Am I willing to proclaim the Gospel and witness about Jesus in my profession and in my job?
- Is God using me to accomplish extraordinary things?
- What are my natural skills, talents and abilities? Have I surrendered these to the Lord? Have I discerned how God wants to use them in my life for His glory?
- Have I surrendered my experience, background and training to the Lord?
- Have I discovered my spiritual gifts? Am I operating in them in my calling?
- What are my deep desires and burdens? How do they intersect with my calling?

- Am I pursuing my career or my calling?
- Am I pursuing my calling with a passion? Am I fruitful in my calling?
- Am I serving and worshipping God in my calling?
- Am I giving myself sacrificially to the Lord in my calling? Am I willing to pay the cost?
- Am I faithful in doing the will of God for my life as best as I know it?
- Do I commit my failures unto the Lord Jesus Christ? Do I see my failures as stepping stones to supernatural success?
- Am I too full of myself? Is there room enough in my heart for the Lord Jesus Christ?
- Am I plugged into a local church? Am I under the authority of the church leaders? Am I continually equipping myself with the Word of God?
- Am I depending totally upon the Lord Jesus Christ and upon Him alone?
- Am I willing to leave my comfort zone and launch out into the deep when asked to do so by the Lord Jesus Christ?
- Am I a deep or a shallow Christian? How deep is my walk with the Lord Jesus Christ?
- Am I willing to obey God even when what He is asking me to do does not make sense to me? Do I act on the Word of God in faith?
- To what extent is my faith demonstrated by corresponding actions?
- Do I realize how powerful my words are? Do I speak the Word of God?

- Am I conscious of my sinfulness apart from Christ? The Lordship of Jesus Christ? Do I respond in humility?
- Am I a mere believer or a disciple? Do I know the difference between the two?
- Am I still amazed about my salvation in Jesus, or has that become stale in my life?
- Am I fearful in my calling, or am I operating in the love of God?
- Am I operating in my calling in a general way (as a fisherman), or have I become more focused and targeted (as a hunter)?
- Is my love for God expressed in greater service for God?
- Have I found my place of rest in Christ?
- Am I totally committed to my calling? Am I ready to forsake all and follow the Lord Jesus Christ?

You can evaluate your answers to these questions in light of the following principles and precepts.

Principles and Precepts

- God has a unique calling for every believer (Jeremiah 1:5, 1 Corinthians 1:1, Galatians 1:15).
- It is a necessary condition that you must be saved and be a child of God if you are to discern and respond to your calling. Furthermore, you should be walking with the Lord on a daily basis and growing in grace (Romans 8:28–30, 2 Timothy 1:9).

- God's calling encompasses all of your being and doing. It defines and encompasses your total lifestyle and includes your spiritual life, family life, ministry and vocation (Ephesians 4:4).
- While there are many callings on you as a person, there is one calling uniquely defining your mission and setting you apart to serve the Lord Jesus Christ on this earth (Romans 11:29, Philippians 3:14).
- God has called you from your mother's womb. Therefore, this calling is not based on anything you have done or not done. This calling is based on the grace of God in Jesus Christ (Jeremiah 1:5, Galatians 1:15).
- This calling is a primary means God uses to conform you to the image of the Lord Jesus Christ and use you for His glory (Romans 8:29).
- Nonchurch workers have the same high level of calling as church workers. There is no distinction between "a secular job" and "a Christian job" (Colossians 3:23).
- A central aspect of your calling is a ministry unto the Lord. God has a ministry for you and for every believer (Isaiah 61:6; Matthew 28:18–20; 1 Peter 2:5, 9).
- As His initial calling, Jesus wants you to proclaim the Gospel and witness of His grace in your job and in your profession (Luke 5:3, 1 Corinthians 7:20).
- God calls ordinary people to accomplish extraordinary things, so no one can glory in the presence of the Lord (1 Corinthians 1:26–29).

- You cannot perform your calling by relying on your natural skills, talents and abilities. They are stumbling blocks. There is a serpent in every rod. As a result of Adam's sin, a curse came upon nature and upon all natural things (Genesis 3:14–19).
- Once you have surrendered your skills, talents and abilities to the Lord, they become God's rod in your hand. The curse is broken, and the Holy Spirit can and will use these mightily for the glory of the Lord Jesus Christ (Exodus 4:2–3, 1 Corinthians 3:18–19).
- Once you surrender your skills, talents and abilities to the Lord, He will instruct you on how to pick them up again. God will show you when and how He wants to use them in your life for His glory (Exodus 4:4).
- Your experience, background and training are a part of your skills, talents and abilities that you must surrender to the Lord (Exodus 4:10–12).
- If you refuse to yield your strength (natural talents and abilities) to God, He has to turn your strength into weakness before He can use you for His glory (Genesis 32:25).
- God has gifted you uniquely and spiritually in the area of His calling. It is very important you discover these spiritual gifts and operate in them (Romans 12:4–8; 1 Corinthians 12:7, 18).
- What God has gifted you to do, He has called you to do. What He has called you to do, He has gifted you to do. One way to know God's calling is by knowing your spiritual gift(s) (1 Corinthians 12:17–18).

- Your desires and burden will intersect at your calling (Psalm 37:4, Matthew 5:6, John 16:24, Hebrews 8:10).
- If you are walking with the Lord and growing in grace, then your desires are Godly desires. Pursuing your desires in a Godly way will help you determine your calling (Hebrews 8:10).
- Fulfilling your calling is not optional. God expects you to serve Him and worship Him by performing this calling. Furthermore, He expects you to be fruitful in your calling (John 15:8, Acts 9:6).
- Fulfilling your calling requires sacrificially giving of yourself and all you have to the Lord. You must be willing to pay the cost (Luke 14:27–28, Philippians 3:7).
- A career is something you have chosen; whereas, a calling is what God has chosen for you to pursue. You can choose to make a career in your calling; in that case, the two will coincide. In other cases, the two may be distinct (1 Corinthians 1:26, 7:20; Ephesians 1:18).
- You must pursue your calling rather than pursue your career (1 Samuel 15:28).
- Sometimes you may have to sacrifice your career to fulfill your calling (1 Samuel 20:13).
- Do not seek miracles. Rather, build the Word of God inside of you. If you have the Word of God inside you, then signs, miracles and wonders will follow you (Matthew 13:57–58; Mark 6:4–6, 16:17; Hebrews 4:2).

- Jesus + Word = Power of God. To bring the power of God to bear upon a specific situation, speak the Word of God and proclaim the Lordship of Jesus Christ (Luke 5:17).
- The best way to position yourself to discern your calling from God is to do faithfully the known will of God for your life (Exodus 3:1–2, 1 Kings 19:19, Luke 5:2).
- Many great men of the Bible were called into ministry after they had demonstrated an ability and a willingness to work in a secular context and had been faithful to that calling (1 Kings 19:19, Acts 18:3).
- Human failures can be stepping stones for supernatural success if we commit them to the Lord Jesus Christ (Luke 5:2).
- To discern the calling of God, you must be plugged into the local church, be under the authority of the church leaders and be properly equipped with the Word of God (Luke 5:2, Romans 13:1–5, Ephesians 3:21, 2 Timothy 2:15).
- Many times God has to empty a person of self to make room for Him to come in. God is looking for empty vessels, so He can pour out His Holy Spirit in them (2 Kings 4:1–7; Luke 2:7, 5:3).
- To discern and respond to your calling, you must have Jesus Christ in your boat and in your life. You must depend upon Him alone (1 Corinthians 1:23, 2:2; Galatians 2:20).
- To discern and respond to your calling, you must make yourself and your possessions available to God (Luke 5:3, Philippians 3:7–8).

- As His initial calling to you, Jesus wants you to proclaim the Gospel and witness of His grace in your job and profession—whatever your profession may be! (Luke 5:3).
- We bring to pass the circumstances and situations in our lives by the words we speak (Proverbs 10:11; 12:14, 18; 18:21; Matthew 12:37; James 3:6).
- You must be a deep Christian—deep in your walk with the Lord—to discern the calling of God and then pursue it with a passion (Acts 6:8, Hebrews 6:1).
- A key to discerning the calling of God is unquestioned obedience. Total obedience. Whether you understand or not, whether it makes sense to you or not, you must obey God and act on His Word in faith (Luke 5:5; John 14:21, 15:10).
- You must launch out into the deep based on the Word of God and with the Lord Jesus Christ in your boat (Psalm 107:23–24, Luke 5:4).
- You have to let down your nets. There comes a time when you have to act to demonstrate your faith. There is a part you have to do (Luke 5:4, James 2:17–26).
- Human effort, apart from Christ, is futile as it will not result in anything of eternal significance (John 15:5).
- When you discern and pursue God's calling in the power of the Holy Spirit, you will experience an abundance of fruit. Your boats will be full and your nets breaking (Luke 5:6–7, John 15:16).

- The resurrection power that raised Jesus from the dead is available to you today. Tap into it! (Romans 8:11).
- To discern the calling of God, you must do at least three things: (1) see your sinfulness; (2) see the Lordship of Jesus Christ and (3) respond in humility (Micah 6:8, Luke 5:8).
- A mere believer has received the Lord Jesus Christ as Savior but not made Him the Lord of her or his life. The disciple has made the Son of God her or his Savior and Lord. You have to become a disciple to discern the calling of God (John 8:31).
- We not only should be amazed about our salvation in Jesus Christ but also continue in that state because of God's continual work in our lives through the Holy Spirit (Luke 5:9, 1 John 2:27).
- Jesus will call you in clear, unmistakable terms. As you walk with Him, you will hear clearly the calling of God (Luke 5:10).
- God will call you to service in the area of your calling. Jesus will reveal His calling to you in a way you can discern, as Jesus will frame it in terms of your gifts, talents and abilities (Luke 5:10).
- Your calling will start in a general way (as fishermen) and then become more clearly defined and targeted (as hunters) (Jeremiah 16:16).
- As you respond to the calling of God, you will be drawn into a greater love for God that will be expressed in service for God (Luke 5:10, Philippians 3:14).

- Fear not to pursue your calling. Fear will stifle and paralyze your faith. To get rid of fear, you should focus on the perfect love of God for you that has been demonstrated perfectly on the cross of Calvary (1 John 4:18).
- God will confirm His calling to you through other Christians and through His Church, the Body of Christ (Matthew 18:16, 2 Corinthians 13:1).
- God will lead you into the deep, but He will not leave you in the deep. After He has accomplished His deep work of grace in you, He will bring you to the land, to your place of rest in Christ (Matthew 11:28–30, Hebrews 4:1–11).
- To successfully fulfill your calling, you must respond with a total commitment, forsake all and follow the Lord Jesus Christ (Luke 5:11, 14:33).
- The voices to whom you listen will influence the choices you make. Listen to the voice of God in His Word, the Holy Bible (1 Samuel 15:23, 28; Acts 13:22).

Life Lesson

The real key to living this life to the maximum of your potential and experiencing fruit and fulfillment is to discern the call of God upon your life. Then pursue that calling with total commitment, forsaking all and following the Lord Jesus Christ.

Prayer Power

Abba, Father, I thank You that You have saved me through the blood of Your Son, my Savior and Lord Jesus Christ. Help me to grow spiritually and to grow in grace and in the knowledge of the Lord Jesus. I thank You that You have a special calling and a destiny for my life. This call is based on Your grace in Jesus Christ. Abba, Father, I thank You I cannot perform Your calling by relying on my natural skills, talents and abilities. In the natural, they are stumbling blocks. Therefore, I surrender these to You and lay them down before You. Please show me when and how I should pick them up, so the Holy Spirit can and will use them mightily for the glory of the Lord Jesus Christ.

Thank You, Father God that You have gifted me uniquely and spiritually in my calling. Help me to discover fully my spiritual gifts and to operate in them in the power of the Holy Spirit. Dear Lord, reveal to me my deep desires and burdens and align them with Your perfect will for my life. Help me, through Your Holy Spirit, to discern clearly and unmistakably Your calling on my life. I want to serve You and worship You by pursuing my calling with promise, purpose and passion. Father, I sacrificially give myself to You. With the help of the Holy Spirit, I will obey You totally and completely. I will act on the Word of God in faith. I want to serve You in the area of my calling and so glorify the Name of my Savior and Lord Jesus Christ. In the mighty Name of the Lord Jesus Christ, I pray. Amen!

Message Ministry

You can access the audio message for this chapter by using CallingYou as the password at

https://www.globalevangelisticministries.net/Calling1-Chapter5.

CONTINUING YOUR JOURNEY

Discovering your calling is only the beginning of a long and exciting journey with the Lord Jesus Christ. God wants you to pursue your calling wholeheartedly with promise, planning, purpose, passion, persistence and perseverance. You must look to the Lord Jesus Christ, and to Him alone, to do His mighty work of grace in you and then do His work through you. Only then you will fulfill your calling to the praise of our Lord Jesus Christ and obtain the full reward of your inheritance. You will find the necessary help to successfully complete this journey in the second book in this series, the sequel *God Is Calling You: Responding to the Calling of God*. God bless you!

ACKNOWLEDGMENTS

First and foremost, I acknowledge and thank my Savior and Lord Jesus Christ for His grace that has been manifested in my life. In His grace, He saved me and has been working in my life in miraculous and powerful ways—some of which are documented in these books in the "Author's Account" sections. I praise Him and give to Him all the glory. As shared in chapter 6 of *God Is Calling You: Responding to the Calling of God*, God spoke to me and asked me to write these books. His Holy Spirit has helped me tremendously in writing these books; I never could have undertaken and completed this project apart from Him.

I thank my family: my wife Veena and my children Ruth and Paul for their love and support. The way they are pursuing their own callings is a big encouragement to me. I recognize with gratitude the deep impact of Dr. Charles Stanley, my pastor since 1979, and his spiritual input into my life. I also acknowledge the impact of Pastor Joseph Prince of New Creation Church, Singapore. Many of his teachings on the Gospel of Grace are reflected through-out both the books in this series.[1] I want to thank Michael S. Warren and R. Wayne Jones, respectively, the chairman and vice chairman of the Board of Global Evangelistic Ministries, Inc., for their great leadership and support.

Several people were helpful in bringing these books to print. Among them, I thank Mrs. Carolyn Cunningham for her fine copyediting work. Barbara Kingsley, Publication Specialist, and Valerie Furia, Literary Agent, both of Christian Faith Publishing, were very helpful.

My prayer is that people who read these books will be blessed by discerning the calling of God and then pursuing it with passion and obedience. May the Name of the Lord Jesus Christ be exalted and glorified through our lives and through these books. Amen!

Rev. Naresh K. Malhotra, Ph.D.

ENDNOTES

Introduction

1 William Messenger and Gordon Preece, *Calling: A Biblical Perspective*, Theology of Work Project, Inc., 2013.

2 See any standard Consumer Behavior textbook, for example, Leon G. Schiffman and Joseph L. Wisenblit, *Consumer Behavior*, 12th Edition, Pearson, New York: NY, 2019.

Chapter 1

1 https://www.biblestudytools.com/lexicons/greek/nas/agape.html, accessed July 29, 2018.

2 *The Hebrew-Greek Key Study Bible*, Spiros Zodhiates editor, AMG Publishers, Chattanooga, TN, 1984.

3 David Guzik, *Enduring Word Commentary*, online at https://enduring word.com/, accessed July 10, 2018.

4 My understanding of God's love and several of the concepts discussed in this chapter have been influenced by the writings and the messages of Pastor Joseph Prince of Singapore as mentioned and footnoted in the Acknowledgments.

5 Based on a Bible search of KJV using the e-Sword software. See also http://christianshepherd.org/meditations/doctrinal_meditations/the_ lamb_of_god_in_revelation.pdf, accessed August 6, 2018.

6 https://www.quora.com/What-books-of-the-Bible-did-Paul-write, accessed November 23, 2018.

7 See Albert Barnes' *Notes on the Bible*; John Gill's *Exposition of the Entire Bible*.

Chapter 2

1 Bill Gillham, "The Power of Sin," online at http://krowtracts.com/articles/ gillham.html, accessed July 30, 2018.

2   Albert Barnes' *Notes on the Bible*; Joseph Prince, as mentioned and foot-
    noted in the Acknowledgements.
3   Adam Clarke's *Commentary on the Bible*; John Gill's *Exposition of the
    Entire Bible*

Chapter 3
1   "Paul Regularly Used the Old Testament as the Authority for His
    Teaching" online at https://www.ucg.org/bible-study-tools/booklets/the-
    new-covenant-does-it-abolish-gods-law/paul-regularly-used-the-old
    /%2C, accessed September 17, 2017.
2   Andrew Womack, "Online Bible Commentary" at https://www.awmi.
    net, accessed June 8, 2018.

Chapter 4
1   My understanding of grace and several of the concepts discussed in
    this chapter have been influenced by the writings and the messages of
    Pastor Joseph Prince of Singapore as mentioned and footnoted in the
    Acknowledgments.
2   "How many times in Scripture God is referred as Father in the New
    Testament?" Online at http://www.answers.com/Q/How_many_times_
    in_scripture_God_is_referred_as_Father_in_the_New_testament,
    accessed November 30, 2018.

Chapter 5
1   Adam Clarke's *Commentary on the Bible*; John Gill's *Exposition of the
    Entire Bible*.
2   See, for example, https://spiritualgiftstest.com/, accessed February 24,
    2018.

Acknowledgements
1   Several of the teachings of Pastor Joseph Prince in his books and mes-
    sages are reflected throughout both the books in this series, especially
    in Chapters 1, 4 of this book. Among his books, I mention *Destined
    to Reign: The Secret to Effortless Success, Wholeness and Victorious Living*;
    *The Power of Right Believing: 7 Keys to Freedom from Fear, Guilt, and
    Addiction*; and *Live the Let-Go Life: Breaking Free from Stress, Worry, and
    Anxiety*. I also want to mention his *Daily Grace Inspiration* messages.

ABOUT THE AUTHOR

Rev. Naresh K. Malhotra, Ph.D. is an ordained minister of the Gospel and President of Global Evangelistic Ministries, Inc. that he founded in 2009. God has blessed this ministry tremendously. Dr. Malhotra has preached the Gospel in thirty-six countries and has documented, in independent reports, 1.93 million people praying to receive Jesus Christ as personal Savior and Lord. Each report is signed by multiple local pastors and Christian leaders and is posted on his ministry website at https://www.globalevangelisticministries.net. His weekly radio broadcast is aired on several radio stations in the United States and a few other countries. These reports and more information about his ministry may be accessed at his ministry website.

Previously, he was Regents' Professor (the highest academic rank in the University System of Georgia), Scheller College of Business, Georgia Institute of Technology, Atlanta. He served at Georgia Tech for thirty years prior to his retirement in 2009. Dr. Malhotra is listed in Marquis *Who's Who in America, Who's Who in the World* and has a lifetime listing in *Marquis Biographies Online*. In 2017, he received the Albert Nelson Marquis *Lifetime Achievement Award* from Marquis *Who's Who*. In 2010, he was selected as a *Marketing Legend*; and his refereed journal articles were published in nine volumes by Sage with tributes by other leading scholars in the field. In 2011, he received the Best Professor in Marketing Management, Asia Best B-School Award. He received the prestigious Academy of Marketing Science CUTCO/Vector Distinguished Marketing Educator Award in 2005. Dr. Malhotra is a highly cited author with several *best-selling* books on Marketing Research that are *global leaders*.

He was chairman, Academy of Marketing Science Foundation, 1996–1998; president, Academy of Marketing Science, 1994–1996; and Chairman, Board of Governors, 1990–1992. He is a Distinguished Fellow of the Academy and Fellow, Decision Sciences Institute. The Founding Editor of *Review of Marketing Research*, he has served as an Associate Editor of *Decision Sciences* for eighteen years. He also has served as Section Editor, Health Care Marketing Abstracts, *Journal of Health Care Marketing*, and is on the Editorial Board of several journals.

Dr. Malhotra has several *top (number one) published research rankings* based on publications in leading journals. He has consulted for business, nonprofit and government organizations in the USA and abroad and has served as an expert witness in legal and regulatory proceedings. He has special expertise in survey design, data analysis and statistical methods. He is the winner of numerous awards and honors for research, teaching and service to the profession, including the Academy of Marketing Science, Outstanding Marketing Teaching Excellence Award, 2003. More information about his academic credentials can be accessed at Georgia Tech's website at https://www.scheller.gatech.edu/malhotra. He may be contacted through his ministry website.

Dr. Malhotra is a member and deacon of the First Baptist Church of Atlanta. He has been married to Veena since 1980; and they have two grown children, Ruth and Paul.

CPSIA information can be obtained
at www.ICGtesting.com
Printed in the USA
LVHW011521200122
709000LV00004B/105